The Presentation of Self in Contemporary Social Life

To my families from blood, marriage, and work

The Presentation of Self in Contemporary Social Life

David Shulman
Lafayette College

Los Angeles | London | New Delhi
Singapore | Washington DC | Melbourne

FOR INFORMATION:

SAGE Publications, Inc.
2455 Teller Road
Thousand Oaks, California 91320
E-mail: order@sagepub.com

SAGE Publications Ltd.
1 Oliver's Yard
55 City Road
London, EC1Y 1SP
United Kingdom

SAGE Publications India Pvt. Ltd.
B 1/I 1 Mohan Cooperative Industrial Area
Mathura Road, New Delhi 110 044
India

SAGE Publications Asia-Pacific Pte. Ltd.
3 Church Street
#10-04 Samsung Hub
Singapore 049483

Copyright © 2017 by SAGE Publications, Inc.

Printed in the United States of America

Library of Congress Cataloging-in-Publication Data

Names: Shulman, David, author.

Title: The presentation of self in contemporary social life / by David Shulman, Lafayette College.

Description: Los Angeles : SAGE, [2017] | Includes bibliographical references and index.

Identifiers: LCCN 2015046005 | ISBN 9781483319438 (pbk. : alk. paper)

Subjects: LCSH: Social interaction. | Self-presentation. | Symbolic interactionism.

Classification: LCC HM1111 .S487 2017 | DDC 302—dc23
LC record available at http://lccn.loc.gov/2015046005

This book is printed on acid-free paper.

Acquisitions Editor: Jeff Lasser
Editorial Assistant: Alexandra Croell
Production Editor: Libby Larson
Copy Editor: Beth Hammond
Typesetter: Hurix Systems Pvt. Ltd.
Proofreader: Sarah J. Duffy
Indexer: Joan Shapiro
Cover Designer: Candice Harman
Marketing Manager: Jenna Retana

16 17 18 19 20 10 9 8 7 6 5 4 3 2 1

Brief Contents

Detailed Contents

Author's Note

Some readers may pick up this book interested in coverage of specific dramaturgical concepts. If so, I want to clarify up front that I do not cover Erving Goffman's concepts in the chronological or sequential order of his publications. Instead, the book begins with a broad overview of the dramaturgical approach where I cover introductory ideas such as front and backstage and spoiled identity. In subsequent chapters, I then address ideas across the dramaturgical canon, from both Goffman and other scholars. I also define ideas in the book's glossary. For reference, here is a sense of the dramaturgical and related concepts addressed in the later chapters:

Chapter Four: *Workplaces as Stages*
Interaction Order, Definition of the Situation, Deep and Surface Acting, Discrediting, Discreditable, Dramaturgical Circumspection, Discipline and Loyalty, Emotional Labor, Line, Organizational Underlife, Performance Teams and Team Collusion, Secondary Adjustments, Social Establishments, Own and the Wise, Total Institutions, Working Consensus

Chapter Five: *Modern Life as Show Business*
Communicating Out of Character, Chainscape, Celebrities, Dramaturgical Legibility, Extravagant Expectations, Image, Front and Backstage, Gender Advertisements, Marketing of Images, Mystification, Positive Idealization, Servicescape

Chapter Six: *Dramaturgical Involvements in Popular Culture*
Encounters, Engrossment, Face-to-Face Interaction, Footing, Frame Analysis, Framings, Interaction Ritual Chains, Keyings, Role Distance, Role Embracement, Situational Harness, Social Phoropter, Supportive and Remedial Interchanges

Acknowledgments

Thank you to Jeff Lasser for shepherding this book from proposal to completion. Thank you also to the excellent professionals at SAGE who worked on this book: Alexandra Croell, Beth Hammond, and Libby Larson. Thank you to anonymous reviewers. Sheldon Blackman, Kent Grayson, Rebecca Kissane, Andrea Smith, and Ira Silver all read parts of this manuscript, and I thank you all for your useful insights. Thank you also to Lafayette students who heard some of these ideas in classes and shared their reactions to them. Thank you also to Lafayette College and the Anthropology and Sociology Department for your support of this project. I have read and been inspired by many excellent scholars who write on Goffman's ideas. I want to acknowledge the debt you are owed for all the exciting works you produce that unpack these ideas and explore them empirically. Finally, I thank my wife Susan, and son Alex, for bearing with me through the writing and for discussing the book's ideas.

⑤SAGE | **50** YEARS

SAGE was founded in 1965 by Sara Miller McCune to support the dissemination of usable knowledge by publishing innovative and high-quality research and teaching content. Today, we publish more than 850 journals, including those of more than 300 learned societies, more than 800 new books per year, and a growing range of library products including archives, data, case studies, reports, and video. SAGE remains majority-owned by our founder, and after Sara's lifetime will become owned by a charitable trust that secures our continued independence.

Los Angeles | London | New Delhi | Singapore | Washington DC

The Show Must Go On

Exploring Presentation of Self in Contemporary Society

Introduction: Goffman's Ideas in the 21st Century

In 1959, Erving Goffman published *The Presentation of Self in Everyday Life* and popularized the dramaturgical perspective, which uses a theatrical analogy to analyze people's social interactions. Goffman scrutinized people's activities as if they were actors performing personas. As a result, he inspired research efforts to explore how people express themselves in order to influence the impressions that observers form about them. Goffman coined concepts to describe aspects and consequences of managing impressions, such as *face, front and backstage, stigma, frame analysis, total institutions, interaction order,* and the *presentation of self*. His analytic terms endure in the sociological lexicon and are firmly established as social science canon. This field of study is also referred to as impression management, although many sociologists refer to this perspective in an interchangeable sense as dramaturgical sociology.

Goffman's scholarship advanced beyond applying the dramaturgical analogy. He went on to develop additional analogies of frames, games, and rituals for analyzing social life (Lemert & Branaman, 1997). His applications of these analogies also continue to inspire research into impression management. For example, researchers have focused on how people understand the different "frames" that organize the experiences that they have and how "normals" and stigmatized people relate to each other (for additional examples see Chriss, 1995; Lemert & Branaman, 1997; Manning, 1992).

Fast-forward to 2016: The world has changed since 1959, producing new situations of impression management for people to engage in and experience. Monumental technological changes have taken place, such as the advent of the Internet and cyber culture, which offer new and powerful means for individuals to present images of themselves to audiences. Contemporary marketing initiatives and advertising campaigns now use cutting-edge research to design persuasive appeals, performances, and staging to beguile and entice consumers. An immersive popular culture has emerged that enraptures fans in literary fantasies, video games, and adoration of celebrities. Body modification efforts have grown and multiple changes in physical self-presentation are now technologically possible. New values, social norms, and laws have also redefined some behaviors previously considered wholly deviant and stigmatized, and those changes impact how affected individuals present themselves. Would anyone have predicted in 1959 that same-sex marriage would be legally possible today and stigmas against homosexuality lessened? Given all of these changes, the time is right to inventory some contemporary applications of dramaturgical concepts. This book aims to advance that effort.

The general questions this book addresses are as follows: What is the dramaturgical approach? How can I use this approach, in general, to think fruitfully about society? How does a dramaturgical approach shed light on specific modern social institutions like the workplace, the Internet, and popular culture? What insights do scholars currently provide? Many social scientists use the dramaturgical approach to study modern life, and scholarly journals publish articles that apply dramaturgical analyses to modern society. This book hopes to convey some key points from those works, in order to update dramaturgical concepts as they might indicate, and to sum up some "state of the art" dramaturgical and impression management ideas.

The priority in this book is to focus on how dramaturgical ideas are applied to examine contemporary organizations, events, activities, and behaviors. My goal is that this book's readers will gain a familiarity with impression management ideas and appreciate how they help make useful sense out of everything from how people act in meetings to how marketers take advantage of people's desire to put their best face forward. This authorial perspective is also informed by the tendency of scholarly writings on Goffman's ideas to exhaustively analyze and reanalyze his articles and books in sophisticated terms for audiences composed mainly of other academics and specialist scholars. I believe that theorists and researchers of dramaturgy should also be publishing more analyses aimed at interested non-specialists.

It is normal academic operating procedure for scholars of Goffman's theories to write high-end analyses for other theorists and for empirical social scientists to publish dramaturgically based research analyses of different field sites. Nothing is out of sorts in that arrangement, which is how scholarship is organized professionally. Yet something is also missing here that seems to exist additionally in other subfields. For whatever reasons, there are few straightforward texts on contemporary dramaturgical sociology written for non-specialists in mind, which is at odds with how high the interest level is in Goffman's work. So the time is right to take stock and summarize some insights that have been derived from applying Goffman's ideas to today's world. This book articulates dramaturgical sociology at a more approachable level, reports on some recent dramaturgical research, and illustrates why this approach is helpful in analyzing important aspects of modern life.

The Content of the Book

The book's organization is straightforward. I introduce and review the dramaturgical and impression management perspective. I present this perspective as a powerful theoretical approach. The main body of the book presents some applications of dramaturgical ideas to analyze different aspects of modern life. In each chapter, I reflect on individual research findings and emphasize conclusions about dramaturgical theory's relevance. I respect the scholarly works that appraise Goffman's ideas and how researchers apply impression management approaches empirically. I hope to bring more of their insights to readers by identifying an overarching range of these works.

Impression management research is also interdisciplinary. Many scholars advance variants of the dramaturgical approach in other disciplines, so exposing more of their work to a sociological audience that may not have encountered that research is important. Interdisciplinary scholars of Goffman need to keep in better touch with one another; this book comprises an effort to get us reacquainted. Scholars in marketing, for example, have long adopted Goffman's ideas for thinking about service interactions between customers and companies, such as considering how storefronts should be staged for maximum selling and service effectiveness. Management scholars have focused on impression management in leadership studies and evaluated the dramaturgical metaphor as one lens for understanding organizational behavior. Science, technology, and society scholars analyze interactions on the Internet. Psychologists also study impression management and stigma. Sample applications across fields should be considered to get a better sense of contemporary dramaturgy's applicability and relevance. This book presents an interdisciplinary treatment of dramaturgical scholarship and recognizes scholars within and outside sociology who do innovative work in studying impression management.

Of course there are limits to how much topical coverage is possible here. Scholars produce dramaturgical works on many subjects. The subjects included here are consumer research, deviance, dramaturgical theories, emotional labor, the Internet, marketing, popular culture, and workplaces. Along the way, I reference some important sociological ideas addressing inequality, gender, race, and power.

Some Analytic Directions

To foreshadow some different aspects of contemporary society that I cover, the book includes the following topics:

- Explorations of how businesses and marketers construct front stage images and apply theatrical techniques to appeal to and persuade consumers to buy
- Consideration of how Internet technologies are revolutionizing people's communications and interactions with each other, such as in catfishing, using filters, online dating, and trolling
- Examining people's dramaturgical involvements in media and popular culture, such as the increasing place of games and role-playing activities in modern life, from people playing characters in fantasy RPGs, to jobs in work-places that require displaying characters and emotions as part of one's job

In his 1962 book, *The Image*, Daniel Boorstin predicted that businesses would saturate American life with spectacles and illusions to lure, entrance, and satisfy consumers. Businesses were using techniques of impression management and theatricality to command attention and interest in their wares. Cultural critics like Neil Postman (1985) questioned whether people today are "amusing themselves to death," and Stuart Ewen (1988) examined "all consuming images." Neal Gabler (2000) argues that there is now a "deliberate application of techniques of the theater to politics, religion, education. . . . Commerce has converted them all to branches of show business where the goal is getting and pleasing an audience" (p. 5). If these arguments are true, what better approach to study contemporary life than a sociological perspective that specializes in applying dramaturgical concepts to analyze human behavior? This book reviews how the dramaturgical approach applies to studying contemporary institutions that are so centered on presenting selective images and information to audiences. Further, if contemporary life is becoming more "enchanted" and lived through "cathedrals of consumption" (Ritzer, 2005), with people engrossed in cyber cultures, and living vicariously through celebrities, I unapologetically assert that sociologists should go where that action is.

Good sociologists also advance beyond offering handwringing cultural critiques. Anyone can launch diatribes that everything is going to hell in a handbasket because people watch *Keeping Up With the Kardashians* rather than download highbrow books and listen to opera. It is not a novel insight to proclaim that an individual or commercial actor can entertain and distract people with one hand while emptying their pockets or dulling their minds with another. What is more useful is investigating how a world focused on presenting images across so many social institutions works according to dramaturgical concepts. Sociologists must address how businesses that seek to persuade and enchant people operate. How do these actors create their shows and disseminate them to diverse audiences in different markets?

Business enterprises use themes to promote products. Theming a business is a fundamental dramatic activity, whether in designing the commercial haunted houses that spring up every Halloween or as evident in Mexican chain restaurants that hang sombreros on their walls. Sociologists should study how people within these workplaces give their illusions life, what rules govern good themes and shows, and the impressions that audiences form that motivate purchasing activity. Those tasks all involve active dramaturgical considerations.

Marketers study how businesses develop what are called "servicescapes" comprised of alluring front stages and atmospherics that offer customers great service and, not coincidentally, also inspire audiences to part with their cash (Bitner, 1992). A labor market exists of occupations that specialize in different aspects of presenting images. Celebrities, advertisers, marketers, public relations experts, theme park designers, self-help professionals, cosmetic plastic surgeons—there are many professionals whose paid work is tied to impression management activities involving various objects and people. These professional illusionists comprise only the upper tier level of these practitioners. People working in service industries are on the frontline in staging retail and other storefront locations for customers. Someone has to be the prop master, give the admissions tour at colleges, wear a costume at the theme park, and showcase the results of plastic surgeries. If workplaces operate increasingly like theaters, the dramaturgical approach helps us understand them.

Consider a different example: How do people put together impressions in a virtual world? *Facebook* and cell phones are instrumental means that make today's generation of "selfie" takers the most thorough self-documentarians in history. Online dating creates more liars by the second, and *Tinder* argu- ably helps replace romance with superficiality. People cyberbully and stig- matize others online in unprecedented ways. Neo-Luddites, and even some lovers of technology, worry that too much screen time and texting interac- tions are reducing people's competence at face-to-face interaction. Theories of impression management shed light on these activities. In addition to these phenomena, changes in deviant behavior, popular culture, and workplaces are also realms where dramaturgical insights apply.

Conclusion

Sociologists argue that human behaviors are the product of individual agency and social forces operating in specific times and contexts. Impres- sion management is no exception as the kinds of performances that people and groups seek to give are mediated by what personas are in favor at a given time and the sorts of stages that exist where people perform. The 21st century context is different from the 20th century context, so applications of Goffman's dramaturgy should be updated continually to reflect the social forces in today's world.

The dramaturgical perspective teaches people the important lesson that the appearances that people create and sustain for audiences have a mutu- ally reinforcing relationship with their individual enactors. People create appearances as actors, but those appearances also affect people in terms of how others identify, judge, and treat them. Individuals confront having their impression management efforts be increasingly routinized and imposed on them by external organizations. The power to determine what appear- ances matter and how they ought to be performed has significant stakes for determining individual autonomy and mobility in the 21st century. Social categories of ethnicity, gender, and race also affect the capacity to employ and be impacted by impression management techniques.

The dramaturgical perspective is part of a sociological tradition called symbolic interactionism. Symbolic interactionism examines how people use social symbols to interpret and communicate meanings. Language is a social symbol, clothing is another, and so are gestures and different acts like handshakes, using props, and performances. Some social scientists have criticized the symbolic interaction focus as being too microscopic in nature and too distant from traditional sociological concerns with the doings of large-scale social institutions and the powers that they have over people's lives. In today's world, I argue that this criticism should not apply as forcefully.

Important institutions today, such as commercial, cultural, technological, and workplace enterprises, use heightened means of symbolic communication to attract, persuade, and determine individual activities. Culture motivates people's actions and puts them into fantasy worlds that people increasingly inhabit or attempt to make real. Commercial organizations use idealized versions of possible identities to encourage consumption and to interact with consumers. Technological advancements also increase the capacity to communicate images for good and bad effect. Workplaces in an entertainment and experience economy need workers to manifest images as a form of labor. Requirements for how people perform in the workplace can become increasingly restrictive. Some employers now even use advanced technology tracking in combination with old techniques of scientific management to insist upon rigid performative adherence on the job (Head, 2014).

The importance of images and performing in both leisure and work reflect that dramaturgy and symbols have a growing contemporary power over people. Sociologists use dramaturgical concepts to analyze how people communicate using meaningful symbols. However, we need to expand Goffman's dramaturgical lexicon to address the now large-scale use of symbolic communication and image that exists today thanks to technological advancement and institutional growth in use of persuasive imagery. If people and organizations interact through a language of appearances, then we must examine how appearances are created and enacted, for whom, why, and with what consequences. They impact people's well-being in the 21st century.

ONE

Self-Presentation and the Dramaturgical Perspective

Report: Today the Day They Find Out You're a Fraud

WASHINGTON—While experts agree you've been remarkably successful so far at keeping up the ruse that you're a capable, worthwhile individual, a new report out this week indicates that today is the day they finally figure out you're a complete and utter fraud. The report, compiled by the Pew Research Center, states that sometime within the next 24 hours, people will find out that you have no idea what you're doing, that you've been faking it for years, and that, through continuous lying and shameless posturing, you've actually managed to dupe virtually everyone around you into thinking you're something other than a weak and ineffectual person. They've had their suspicions all along, sources said, but today their suspicions will be confirmed. (The Onion, 2014)

Social relations are . . . organized more around the appearance than the content of things.

—Erving Goffman

Introduction: "Being Yourself" Is a Performance Too

There is a popular quote: "Fake people have an image to maintain. Real people don't care." Is that so? In this book, I ask you to reconsider some taken-for-granted beliefs. One belief is that people act genuinely most of the time and do not work consciously to manipulate what other individuals think about them. Our judgments of people are based on what we observe of people's naturally occurring and unthinking actions. An alternate approach is to consider people as self-reflective and strategizing actors who work consciously to cultivate a desirable impression. Erving Goffman (1959, p. 70) wrote that people mistakenly interpret individual acts as "something not purposely put together at all . . . an unintentional product of the individual's unselfconscious response to the facts of the situation." That mistaken interpretation overlooks the value of examining how people work systematically to influence how audiences respond to them.

As an example, think about what the phrase "just act naturally" means. That phrase instructs someone to act more effectively to keep an audience from discerning that anything is off and disrupting the social situation. Ironically, the phrase acknowledges that people act by stressing that they should not appear to be acting. Many everyday social interactions involve pressure to do this kind of "acting naturally." A person encounters someone that she dislikes, but she interacts pleasantly with her as if she harbors her no ill will and is pleased to see her. Her physical appearance, demeanor, and words reveal nothing untoward and offer up no indications that expose her true feelings. A man likes a woman he has known for a while and wants to ask her out on a date. He seeks to express his positive feelings but is a nervous wreck. His friends urge him to suppress his fear, be confident, and "act natural" when he speaks to her. He wants to share how he feels in an honest way but has to figure out what to do to express himself effectively.

In a nutshell, when we tell someone to act naturally, we tell him or her to do a better job managing the impressions that they are giving. Yet identifying "acting" as something that people do is conflated with the perception that people who act are insincere, deceptive, or fake. That conclusion throws the baby out with the bathwater because impression management can communicate more than just deceptions. That perception leads people to fear admitting when they put on a show or exercise strategic care to choose the right setting, appearance, or demeanor for an interaction.

This book examines the work people do to influence the impressions that others form about them. I examine steps involved in how people craft and enact the personas that they exhibit. A *persona* is a character, mask, or social role that people display in the theater to play a part, and in social life, as part of everyday activities. Readers know that people put forth images and work to fit into social roles, but how sociologists analyze those efforts may be less familiar. This book will introduce you to the concepts and ideas that sociologists refer to as dramaturgical work or impression management.

As a prelude to that explanation, pause and consider the priority people place on what others think of them and the stakes involved in influencing those impressions. Picture the intense introspective anxiety and self-conscious moments people have when they feel alone and isolated, burdened by a secret that they can't reveal for fear of embarrassment and being shamed. Consider the website *Postsecret*. Thousands of people mail in their deepest secrets, anonymously, on postcards they designed themselves to share with readers on this site. A common feature of these secrets, such as having hidden sexual desires, having strange preoccupations, or being victims or perpetrators of crimes, is that they constitute information that people must hide and not associate with their real names or they risk anger, condemnation, and disgrace.

These worries reflect people's investment in their social attachments. They are so concerned with how other people might react to them. How can we view these moments as so private, when other people's potential views keep us company in our minds? People fixate on their secret and run through internal monologues that simulate what other people might say and think if they knew and acknowledged that secret. These self-absorbed worries represent a victory of social bonds in causing people to obsess on their own time about their "fit" with the social groups that matter to them. The upshot is this: If individuals spend so much time thinking about the impressions they give, or could give to other people, we must acknowledge the serious mental exertions we put into viewing ourselves as impression managers, even when alone. People appraise themselves in the harsh light of whatever social expectations matter to them, and we are rarely off the clock.

When people fail to meet interpretations of how they ought to be, that shortfall embarrasses them. The ideals that people look to meet or surpass can be big or small, but the result of having them is that we may alter our behaviors and thoughts in front of people. Maybe someone who is sensitive about having gained weight sucks in their stomach or never tucks in clothes. You have probably observed someone present a patently fake version of herself or himself, as opposed to a real one that doesn't serve her or him well in a given moment. For example, maybe a person talked about a girlfriend or boyfriend back home that doesn't exist or said that the one that exists doesn't. Hair gets bleached, resumes get embellished, false smiles appear on faces, and silent curses and insults are muttered out of a target's earshot. Maybe an online dating profile is only "sort of" accurate. Whatever we are in those moments, we are not just being "ourselves." We know the difference between what we really think and feel versus putting on a front for others.

Think about your self-consciousness analytically, especially readers who just graduated from high school or who have that time emblazoned in their memories. You had occasion to observe how hard teenagers work to receive social approval, and high school is far from the only place where people make those efforts. So how do people act to gain the favor of others—and not in terms of "being fake"—tactically? What actions do people take? How would you study them?

Please note again that such questions go against the popular idea that a person should "just be yourself," "not worry about what other people think," and "not let anyone change who you are." According to this mainstay cliché in movies, TV productions, and after-school specials, when protagonists stay true to themselves, significant others love them more (after some tribulations that wise them up), and mean conformists all get their comeuppances. While supportive and well intentioned, this suggestion overlooks a real issue: just how pragmatic telling someone to "be yourself" really is.

For example, some social situations require trading a degree of independence for a reward. Can you really tell irritating coworkers where they can go, let professors know that you'd rather binge watch something on Netflix than do the scintillating reading on historical taxation schemes, or inform mom and dad that they should just hand over the money and forget the advice? You can be yourself and say all those things, but you are unlikely to benefit from the experience. If this assessment of "being yourself" seems too cynical and harsh, think of the converse—how often do you really want other people to "just be themselves"? Are there at least a few people where the last thing you want is for them to act like themselves? Do you really not know anyone that you wish would stop expressing his or her political opinions, whatever they are? We teach children to resist the urge to always be themselves, such as telling them not to ask strangers questions like "Why do you look like that?" We urge people in general to practice a behavior called "self-restraint." Further, many people aspire to not "just" be themselves because they set their sights on becoming a "better" version of themselves—healthier, wealthier, or in a different relationship. Do people portray themselves as thinner, richer, more attractive, and successfully employed in online profiles than they are in their off-line lives?

If we are not being ourselves, then what kind of "selves" are we being? Erving Goffman, whose ideas I address in this book, argues that people perceive themselves as representing esteemed social attributes, roles, and values (Goffman, 1952). Goffman analyzed how people demonstrate having these attributes by examining people's actions as if they were actors performing onstage for audiences. That analytic approach is referred to as the *dramaturgical perspective*, in reference to the term "dramaturgy." Dramaturgy is a theatrical term that refers to how theatrical professionals called dramaturgs adapt and stage artistic and literary works to best communicate a work's meanings to an audience. The dramaturgical perspective encourages adherents to investigate how people "stage" performances in real life. Sociologists who use a dramaturgical approach analyze *nonfiction performances*. Whereas fictional literature or performance is made up and uses imaginary characters in make-believe situations, works of nonfiction focus on actions that real people take. Nonfiction performance involves actions, communications, and intentions that audiences should interpret as "real," that happen in real life and in real time.

People are expected to embody valued attributes when in front of people, or "onstage," and they experience powerful social pressures to do so that impact their self-consciousness and affect how they interact with others. Parents tell children to be good boys and girls, and employers tell workers to act deferentially to clients. People want others to define them as possessing desirable traits, such as being "good" people, loving spouses, athletes giving 110%, or as being clean and sober. They want others to treat them as actually representing those statuses.

The idea of performing enters the picture in that people need to communicate that they demonstrate valued attributes. They must make them "easy to see," decipherable, and legible to audiences. You "knowing" for yourself that you embody some characteristic alone does not mean that other people agree or know right away what impression you mean to give. People may not automatically get credit and consequent rewards for representing a value, status, or trait without some demonstration before-hand to warrant that response. The social attributes that someone thinks he personifies must connect to the expectations that other people have for how someone with those traits appears. The person then must perform to those expectations adequately enough to demonstrate them convincingly. People need others to recognize their claims of identity—of who they are in the world—in order to be held to represent esteemed attributes.

To receive credit for being whatever "kind of" person first requires that the people around you have the competency and desire to interpret your behaviors correctly. Individuals should know and be able to perform some actions that characterize a trait that they want others to perceive them as representing. Second, the target audience should be able to inter-pret and respond to those actions accurately. For example, you can think of yourself as having a great sense of humor, but sustaining that belief is hard if no one ever laughs. Funny is not an objective fact but an interpre-tation that an audience decides subjectively. You view yourself as a leader, but do others follow your lead?

You can identify yourself in many ways, but external recognition of those labels as credible is vital. How many of us have seen episodes of *American Idol* type shows where a person who cannot sing labels him-self or herself as a star in the making, with entertainment value built on audiences enjoying rejecting such ludicrous claims? Credibility comes from others accrediting labels as accurate through evaluating actions or because the actor has the power to compel people to agree. Processes of appraisal occur between performers and their audiences, and people can become upset when either side judges wrongly.

For example, people get angry when they feel that others do not "see through" individuals who receive credit for having a social status that they view as undeserved. "Why does everyone think he is so nice when he isn't?", "Why won't she see that he is a cheater?", or "Everyone thinks she is so smart, but she just gets other people to do all the work for her." Sometimes the stakes are higher. Bernard Madoff was labeled a genius investor, a pillar of the community, and an esteemed member of the New York City investment world until he was exposed as an exploitative fraud that used a Ponzi scheme to steal people's investments. The compli-cated question is why didn't people see him for what he was?

That audiences must know how to interpret performances does not mean that audiences must agree with an actor's hoped-for interpretations but rather that audiences must have the *basic interpretive competence* to understand what an actor is doing in context. That competence involves a capacity to judge and the right background knowledge to make judgments accurately. I don't know how to appreciate the cultural messages of hipster clothing choices to know that someone hit the irony jackpot—I'm not a hipster. A person who knows the culture and slang of massive open online games will have a tough time having a detailed conversation about game strategy with someone who knows nothing about that culture. Similarly there is an expression, *know your audience*. Some audiences are not predisposed to react to your actions as you wish. Enacting the workplace fantasy of telling irritating people their flaws is not typically a good long-term career strategy.

The judgments that people make affect us. We dread negative social judgments, seek social approval, or wish to muddle through some interactions and situations without bother. Underlying how these varying judgments take place, and how people act, are social systems that organize all of that interactional traffic. Erving Goffman's dramaturgical framework provides conceptual tools to help us understand the encounters, face-to-face interactions, and nature of performances that people offer in all their diversity and patterns. Sociologists also investigate the agency that individuals and groups have to affect their circumstances and to fit into the social groups around them.

So Why Study Dramaturgy?

Familiarizing yourself with dramaturgical ideas offers you a greater purchase on and understanding of the nature and impacts of impression management in everyday life. First, whether people like it or not, *surface appearances matter in life*. People judge books by their covers, and the judgments that other people might make about you have some power over your thoughts and actions. The dramaturgical perspective provides insight into how surface appearances work and also how they may deceive. People create appearances, and people also are taken in by appearances. Examining self-presentation addresses the information that people communicate and should also remind people to think about whether some pertinent information is hidden. As we all know from various interactions, meaning comes not just from what people say but also from what people do not say. Further, individuals respond cognitively to the appearances of things, so when situations appear to connect authentically to the expectations and frames that people have for them, people often accept them, rather than go through a lot of complex exploration of whether everything is as appears. Taking the opportunity to reawaken the possibilities that appearances can deceive can make someone a more astute analyst. Good analysts understand yet go beyond the surface appearances to avoid taking things for granted.

A second reason to learn the dramaturgical approach is because *impression management tactics are attempts to exercise influence and power* in everyday life. Analyzing self-presentation makes you more insightful about how people persuade others, and those techniques can be noted, documented, and considered. As an example, marketers and commercial organizations use techniques of persuasion in advertisements and in presenting their products. Understanding more about how such performances work is useful to consumers and also to readers with interests in those areas.

A third reason is that *individuals become more self-aware* by thinking through the lens this perspective offers. The term "self" is a cognitive structure that allows people to think about themselves in "the third person." The self is reflective (Mead, 1934), meaning that people can think about themselves when they act and also reflect on who they seem to be in the eyes of other people. We have beliefs about others; we also have beliefs about ourselves called a self-concept (Leary, 1995, p. 159). The self communicates to others and to itself with presentational techniques. Thinking about impression management enables people to learn more about how their senses of self arise and stand out in interactions.

A fourth reason is to *learn more about the many social influences on how you and other people act.* People do not perform aimlessly. We all face going onto stages as rites of passage to accessing rewards in life, and we must perform well there, be they job interviews, dates, marriages, relations with coworkers, athletic fields, or in front of authority figures. We cast other people into roles as we walk down the street, and we recognize that many places comprise routine stages where we must act in certain ways, whether we feel like it or not. Society systematizes dramaturgical performances, a point discussed later as the *rationalization of dramaturgy.* People feel all kinds of pressure and obligations to perform in life; understanding why these pressures exist, what their purposes are, and what consequence they may have is worthwhile.

A fifth reason is that knowing more about the dramaturgical perspective *will add a new interdisciplinary approach to your skill set.* Anyone with interests in social psychology should familiarize themselves with this perspective. Ongoing research using this approach sheds insight into the subjects of crime and punishment, marketing and organizations, popular culture, working life, and issues of race, gender, and upward mobility. This book will introduce some examples of approaching those research topics through a dramaturgical lens.

A sixth reason is that *dramaturgical theory is interesting and makes you a more reflective and thoughtful people-watcher*. If you have an iota of curiosity about what makes people tick and how they try to construct images for themselves and social groups that they belong to, then this book offers great food for thought.

Getting Down to Business

The phrase sociologists use to describe the work involved in manufacturing personas is called *impression management*. Impression management describes the actions actors take to encourage an audience to form a particular impression. To manufacture an effective social persona is the aim of the actor's impression management.

A sociological perspective requires examining how larger social forces, at the level of organizations, groups, and social institutions, influence what impressions people want to make. All kinds of prevailing social norms, roles, and structural arrangements can affect what content audiences expect to observe in a person's impression management. Agency and autonomy can exist in how people perform their roles, but social conventions already preexist that shape how people are instructed and judged to perform roles appropriately. These social conventions, in the factory of human conformity called socialization, are akin to how default settings organize the standard operations of machines. Just as machines are built to meet particular performance specifications, people's actions and personas are aimed at meeting preexisting basic, established social conventions in a culture. When people can predict what personas and impression management techniques are expected, and on what stages they should be performed, "factory specs" (or social defaults) for everyday situations are revealed and a baseline social order comes into being.

These "factory specs" illustrate some of the underlying structure that governs interactions and social situations. For example, people know how to use knives and forks or chopsticks to eat as appropriate in a given culture or whether they should drive on the right or left side of the road. The decision to use one kind of utensil or another or to drive on one side of the road or another is not mandated by biology but by cultural expectations. People emerge from the conformity lessons of their childhoods ready to perform in accord to many basic factory specs in use within their cultures.

After providing background on dramaturgical ideas, attention will shift to exploring contemporary applications of impression management ideas. Subjects covered include examples from popular culture such as the adoration of celebrities, cosplay, reality TV, and professional wrestling; demeanor and emotional displays in workplaces and in getting a job; how dramaturgical ideas apply to contemporary commerce, such as in advertising and marketing; and how dramaturgical ideas help interpret Internet phenomena such as online dating, "catfishing," revenge porn, cell phone use, and stigma.

The remainder of this chapter will cover the provenance and some basic aspects of the dramaturgical perspective. Chapters 2 and 3 provide an overview of impression management in action and of how social contexts influence impression management. People base performances in preexisting social norms for behavior, for example, to meet required decorum and etiquette that people learn during socialization. Sometimes analysts apply a dramaturgical analysis in a superficial way to just dissect what individuals do without considering the contextual constraints and influences that are implicit in helping to determine how people act. Good analyses scrutinize what people do and consider how relevant social contexts and rules animate and motivate those behaviors. Analyzing everyday life in dramaturgical terms enhances the ability to analyze social rituals, exercises of social control, and other aspects of social life.

Acts that people perform repeatedly have cumulative implications beyond the sole individual instance in which someone does something. The next chapter considers the product of dramaturgical behaviors in not just responding to norms but helping to create and negotiate responses to norms. When sociologists can examine repeated sets of the same dramaturgical activities, they can reach some larger conclusions about how that behavior affects groups of people. For example, say that a person performs at a job interview as an interviewer or interviewee. You can identify what each person in the interaction does (studying performance techniques) and identify the context, stage, and expectations for the interview (say, social norms or arrangements around hiring or the social class of the participants). Additionally, a product of job interviews, when examined across many cases, is that interviews constitute *auditions for opportunity* in which dramaturgical activities end up impacting social stratification in terms of getting or not getting a job. Conceived from a cumulative standpoint, new research questions emerge.

For example, how are people judged to interview well by various occupational standards? Are there advantages or disadvantages involving who people know, nepotism, money, or other resources that impact access to opportunity and people's likelihoods of auditioning successfully? Are interviews a good means to allocate opportunity in social life based on the skills that are required to succeed in them? A dramaturgical framework helps to structure such questions for analysis.

The analytic approach to dramaturgy in this chapter and the subsequent one addresses how to conceptualize people's impression management, understand the social contexts that affect those actions, and identify the cumulative products that result from repeated dramaturgical actions. These chapters provide a background for examining the contemporary applications of the dramaturgical approach presented later in the book. For handy reference, an appendix contains a glossary of the dramaturgical concepts discussed in this book.

The Scholarly Provenance of Dramaturgical Ideas

Nicolas Evreinov, a noted Russian playwright and polymath, was a key early thinker in examining theatricality in everyday life. His book *The Theater in Life* (1927) argued that a *theatrical instinct* of creativity, expression, and release exists as a comprehensive force in individual and social life. This impulse is manifest in how individuals transform images and

Figure 1.1   Important Forebears in Analyzing Dramaturgy

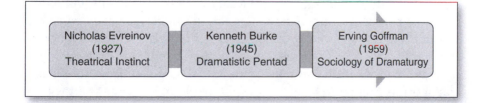

sensations from outside them, through an internal creative process, into newer images that actors express outward. Evreinov illustrates this instinct using examples that range from rites in primitive societies to children's play, arguing that theatricality is important in providing means to make people's lives more fulfilling. In his words, "Without the zest of theatricality life would be to him like tasteless food. . . . As soon, however, as he begins to theatricalize, it acquires a new meaning, it becomes *his* life, something that *he* has created" (Evreinov, 1927, p. 27). Theatricality helps people to create and invigorate life anew through creating images.

Evreinov asserts that being human involves a deep, fulfilling impulse to interpret, express, and perform. This idea is vital to orient people to think about what performances might mean to people. The theatrical instinct and performances that result from them comprise a form of empowerment. The theatrical instinct offers a "gift of *imagining* things, of imitating reality with imagination, of beautifying his miserable life with his fantasy, that is to say, of theatricalizing" (Evreinov, 1927, p. 30). We will see this point reemerge in examining popular culture and commerce.

An example where Evreinov (1927, p. 34) shows the theatrical instinct in action is in the imaginative play of children. Children transform small objects into magical play objects all the time. The smallest object easily becomes something else during play. A pencil becomes a gun or a wand, a car becomes the Batmobile, a doll becomes a child, teddy bears on the bed become protectors. Consider also how prevalent fantasy is in children's lives. A child dreams of being a sports hero in moments of great drama or of casting spells as Harry Potter; all of which redirect individuals away from the mundane banality of everyday existence.

Modern versions of such play are intrinsic in adult activities like fantasy camps, LARPing, cosplay, and video games. A theatrical impulse to empower through using one's imagination is also an adult pursuit, and many adults are enticed to pursue this fulfillment by the siren call of the marketplace. Commercial organizations advantage themselves of the theatrical instinct in how they organize marketing and develop products for consumers. Many entertainment options today immerse people in imagination-engaging products that they consume through enactment. People are mostly all equals biologically before the screen showing them an entertainment product. Whatever their incomes, their eyes all can take in the visual escapist fare before them, transporting them into Hogwarts, or the world of Westeros and the Iron

Throne, or to observe a former high school chemistry teacher who deals methamphetamines, a young woman competing in hunger games, or the remnants of civilization surviving a world full of zombies. Later, I describe one dark interpretation of that immersion; the idea that today, consumption of popular entertainment is associated with decreasing opportunity to succeed in economic life and increased consumerism. Greater immersion in fantasy may connect to an increasing distance of people from real economic opportunity, which is a depressing argument to make, but one that some theorists advance. Evreinov's point is that reality fetters us, but our imagination can free us from shackles for brief interludes. In contemporary terms, if I can choose between battling alien soldiers using superpowers and weapons on an Xbox or confront less enthralling realities like my ennui, failings, duties, or dim prospects, then I will check out from disappointment as much as possible and, as some fear, perhaps not expend that energy to challenge my economic and social circumstances.

Evreinov encouraged people to think about the meaning the theatrical impulse has for people's inner lives. Consider how drunken people engage in impression management. Excess alcohol consumption can remove restraints on people who otherwise might shrink from acting as forcefully in social situations. As the quote about drinking goes, what is "on the sober person's mind comes out of the drunk's mouth." Too much alcohol makes some people reveal themselves in dramatic fashion as some individuals drink just for that release, to get a liquid license to act out a persona that is otherwise unavailable to them in sober life. Drink to excess, and one can become an avenger, a ladies man, unrepressed, a raconteur, everybody's friend, a daredevil, or a comedian.

There are also imagined lives that preoccupy people in dramas that run themselves in loops in their heads. Many people dream of taking on a finer female or male shape with bulging muscles or curves or a lack of them that suits their ambitions. They imagine what they would do if they only looked like a particular celebrity. They fantasize about being young again or rich or having a time machine to go back and not make some mistakes in an "If only I had . . ." kind of way. Or they seethe in repressed fury at some target while hatching fantasy plots in which they wreak a righteous vengeance upon their enemies, whomever or whatever these are. People with anxiety, for example, spend time imagining the worst-case scenario that could happen to them, a tendency Albert Ellis called "awfulizing," or alternatively "catastrophizing." As an example, just let a hypochondriac diagnose their symptoms on the Internet! Other people lose themselves in thoughts of their deepest wish that someone in their life changes, becoming nicer or more successful or more attentive to them. How many dads or moms just know that their kid can be a professional athlete or performer before the child hits 10? People can spend a lot of time thinking about what they will do when the genie arrives to grant their wishes or when they win the lottery. What they do while they wait is occupy themselves in a theater in their minds.

This speaks to another sense Evreinov addressed, which is the idea of "theater of oneself," in an impression management sense. There are those who view all things around them as just being part of an overall show that revolves around them. Everyone is fixated on talking, thinking about, and judging you. Of course, people are busy living their own lives and are perhaps less interested than narcissists think, about minute events in the narcissist's life. For people who are "drama queens or kings," they act as if all actions in the world are about them personally and that everyone around them should be held as a captive audience to their thralldom.

People also playact for pleasure and escapism, by acting in the world just to amuse themselves. Sometimes people lie to strangers, fake an identity or a biographical detail, for example, to a taxi driver in a conversation or when online. Paul Ekman (1985) coined the term *duping delight* to describe the pleasure people receive from manipulating others through deception. Practical jokes, for example, involve some minor escapist theatrical pleasure when people create an innocent appearing social scene in order to take victims off their guard.

The term *sign vehicle* describes aspects of setting, manner, and appearance that people use in performances. Some types of sign vehicles that Evreinov mentions are fashion and speech. Fashion illustrates people treating clothes akin to theatrical costuming. As Evreinov (1927, p. 58) points out, people fit on their clothes like they are costumes, making efforts to stretch, pull, cut, clean, embellish, match, accessorize, lengthen, shorten, contrast, adjust to fit them, and they also contort their bodies into strange positions before mirrors to appraise all angles and vantage points of perceiving how they appear in their costumes. Clothes must "make a statement."

The theatricality of speech is also clear in how people put performances into their speech through word choice, intonation, accent, pronunciation, and pitch. "I'm f**king serious," "I love you so much," "That is sooo unbelievable," "You are amazingly beautiful!" In speech, there is emphasis, metaphor, hyperbole, and condemnation. I have heard numerous women describe something a man thinks or says, for example, by suddenly lowering their voice to a suitable caveman imitation and grunting out statements in an insulting depiction of men. People put on Southern accents in mocking ways. Kids make requests sweeter by using a "pretty please with sugar on top." People pepper their speech with adverbs to add drama to their words.

Certainly this tendency exists in writing as performance medium. As an example, consider snarky reviews on websites like *TripAdvisor* or *Yelp*. In many comments, otherwise minor events become affronts condemned as outrages that produce vindictive written responses. I looked at some reviews for a hotel I like on *TripAdvisor* and found some illustrative gems. "There are coupons available for breakfast, but good luck at getting those. When I asked for one, they acted like I was asking for a blood transfusion on the spot!" "The carpet looks old and tired, and the towels are SHAMEFUL. . . . Not like the Clarion or the Marriott, the Hampton, or Hilton, with nice big soft plushy towels. I would advise bringing your own unless you like drying off with gray sandpaper." Horrible is a descriptive word that often appears in such reviews, as in the service was "horrible." Horrible is a strong word—maybe irritating or frustrating is better. Horrible is a word people use to describe serious negative events, like major economic downturns or even kinds of movies with monsters in them, but not minor travel inconveniences. Yet many reviews suggest that no inconvenience is minor and to suffer any is horrible.

Evreinov also thought theatricality was enacted on a more societal-level scale. He used the term *stage manager* to reference the more abstract idea that societies require regular performance management to create an orderly and organized societal life. He referred to processions of street sweeping, clean storefronts, and monuments, both public and private, landscaped mansions, and decorative front porches as examples, as well as social norms and values that govern performances. The stage manager concept is a placeholder idea or shorthand to describe a sense of public stage management, of organizations and institutions being in charge of directing the performances around us. People have even invoked theater as a means of government, with the term *theatrocracy* referring to the idea that governing bodies rule through using theatrical techniques to subdue a populace (Lyman & Scott, 1975). Evreinov offers useful ideas to think about what theatricality means in analyzing dramaturgy.

Analyzing Dramaturgy

Evreinov's ideas also can partner with a proposed method for analyzing dramaturgical actions. Kenneth Burke (1945) developed the *dramatistic pentad* as an instrument for analyzing dramatic action. Narratives or stories, accounts, and talk, in fictional and nonfictional forms, are prominent vehicles for communicating dramatic action. In Burke's view, all of the above, as rhetoric, have five key elements to scrutinize. These elements of actions are the *act*, where people state what was done; the *scene*, in which people ask where and when actions were done; the *agent*, who engaged in the act; the *agency*, in which people examine how the act was done; and the *purpose*, in which people ask why people engaged in that action. The pentad provides a logical basis for examining activity by commencing with establishing what, who, where, when, and how. These questions, asked of any action, help explain the action. After these aspects of the pentad are determined, the next step involves examining the emphasis each aspect of the pentad is given compared to another aspect. Is one element the priority or dominant feature in the account?

This second step explores a ratio between the aspects, such as the ratio of act to scene in the account. One element in a pentad is more dominant than another. As an example, I am a fan of the television show *The Walking Dead*. The most important motive of action in *The Walking Dead* is the scene because the zombie-infested apocalyptic surrounding is the impetus for acts. An apocalyptic surrounding drives the action, the survivors, the means they have for carrying out acts, and the purpose of their activity. The pentad provides a basic schema for analyzing human drama. People can understand the "grammar of motives" of dramatic activity by stripping down that activity into constituent elements and then analyzing them comparatively.

We can adjust the pentad scheme to organize a more sociological analysis of dramaturgical actions. Figure 1.2 presents a variation on Burke's pentad as an example to guide the distinction of nonfictional dramaturgical actions into constituent parts for sociological analysis. The adjusted figure's purpose also identifies sequential questions to ask about observed dramaturgical scenes. The circle structure and alphabetical lettering indicate an investigative order.

Imagine a restaurant dining room, family dinner, or classroom meeting. Analyze the interactions occurring there in an ordered and systematic way. You can begin that examination by addressing the sequence of

Figure 1.2 Systematic Categories for Analyzing Nonfictional Dramaturgy

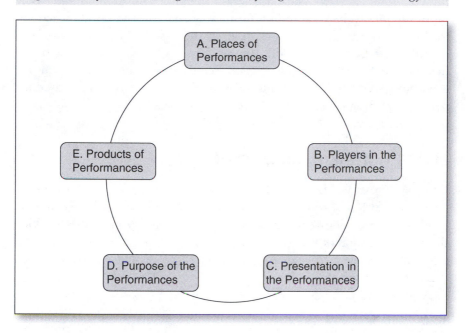

questions that this figure identifies, starting with (a) *places of performance.* These places refer to venues of people's performances that are comprised of the physical locations where people perform. Virtual stages are also places of performance. A setting "contains" interactions. Here we analyze where performances occur and how a given setting structures presentations, actors, purposes, and the products of performances. (b) *The players in the performances.* The focus here is on who and what engages in conscious or unconscious acts of communication. Who are the players? Players can include audiences, individual actors, teams of actors, and/or members of small groups held to represent institutions and organizations in interaction. (c) *The presentations that players give.* Here we identify the actions and expressions that players offer as constituting their performances. What nonverbal communications do the players offer? What do they say when they communicate with others? What are they doing? How and what are they performing? (d) Analysts must then establish what the *purposes in performances* are. Are people attempting to save face? Are people attempting to make others conform, are people trying to manage a stigma, maintain a company line, provide a service? Are they obeying etiquette or expected rules of decorum? (e) Analyze *the products of performances*. What do you think are the consequences—intended and unintended—that occur cumulatively from the performances and the audience's reactions to those performances? For example, in the case of job interviews, the cumulative successes of people who perform well are an economic product of dramaturgy. Examining that product is worthwhile. If there was no economic payoff from good interview performances, there would be no need for training schemes in how to interview well.

Erving Goffman and Dramaturgy

Evreinov presents ideas about the human meanings of theatricality in everyday life. Burke provides a guide for systematically exploring dramaturgical actions. Both contributions provide a background that enables deeper exploration of the dramaturgical perspective on social life. Erving Goffman, however, developed the lion's share of analytic concepts in dramaturgical sociology.

Academics can focus more on reinterpreting a theorist's ideas than on why the average person who does not read social theory for pleasure or work should care about those ideas. Erving Goffman, the theorist featured predominantly here, gave his books straightforward titles that signal their relevance for readers, like *Behavior in Public Places*, *The Presentation of Self in Everyday Life*, *Stigma*, and *Strategic Interaction*. These books conceptualize how people present information about themselves to influence the impressions audiences will have of them. Goffman studies the surface appearances that people create, the pressures that inform them, and how to conceptualize the interactions that comprise performances.

Let's consider the subject matter implied in this content in an autobiographical way. Ask yourself the following questions: Do you plan in advance how to influence other people's impression of you, like on a date, at parties with coworkers, or when meeting your significant other's parents? Do you monitor what you say about a controversial topic in front of people? Do you wear distinct articles of clothing as "props" to give a good impression of yourself? Do you try to ferret out gossip while keeping some secrets under wraps? Do you practice presentations in private before you give them in public? Do you follow rules of behavior in public that you do not follow in private? For example, do you spend more time nude in public or at home? Conversely, have you ever taken advantage of the anonymity that public spaces offer to act in ways that you would not want your family and friends to know? Do any organizational memberships that you have imply particular things about the kind of person that you are? For example, do men and women try to embody the values of brotherhood or sisterhood associated with a particular fraternity or sorority?

The dramaturgical perspective offers insights into performing one's identity. The key point to remember is that impressions are not just expressions that reflect natural processes. People produce impressions as concerted and social actions, and organizations encourage people to take on certain roles. Yet people do not always analyze the work involved in creating and sustaining such performances. The dramaturgical approach centers on analyzing how people manage these impressions, some mundane, some not, as the focus of study.

Goffman's Six Principles of Impression Management

Goffman identifies six principles in considering *impression management*.

- *People are performers who use impression management to convey a persona or sense of who they are to others.*

To illustrate this idea, Erving Goffman (1959) provides a long excerpt from a novel by William Sansom, *A Contest of Ladies*, in which the author takes us into the calculating mind of the vacationing Mr. Preedy, who is exceedingly self-conscious about giving off and displaying physical expressions and varying personas as he vacations on a beach:

> He took care to avoid catching anyone's eye. First of all, he had to make it clear to those potential companions of his holiday that they were of no concern to him whatsoever. He stared through them, round them, over them—eyes lost in space. The beach might have been empty. If by chance a ball was thrown his way, he looked surprised; then let a smile of amusement lighten his face (Kindly Preedy), looked round dazed to see that there were people on the beach, tossed it back with a smile to himself and not a smile at the people, and then resumed carelessly his nonchalant survey of space. But it was time to institute a little parade, the parade of the Ideal

Preedy. By devious handlings he gave any who wanted to look a chance to see the title of his book—a Spanish translation of Homer, classic thus, but not daring, cosmopolitan too—and then gathered together his beach-wrap and bag into a neat sand-resistant pile (Methodical and Sensible Preedy), rose slowly to stretch at ease his huge frame (Big-Cat Preedy), and tossed aside his sandals (Carefree Preedy, after all). The marriage of Preedy and the sea! There were alternative rituals. The first involved the stroll that turns into a run and a dive straight into the water, thereafter smoothing into a strong splashless crawl towards the horizon. But of course not really to the horizon. Quite suddenly he would turn on to his back and thrash great white splashes with his legs, somehow thus showing that he could have swum further had he wanted to, and then would stand up a quarter out of water for all to see who it was. The alternative course was simpler, it avoided the cold-water shock and it avoided the risk of appearing too high-spirited. The point was to appear to be so used to the sea, the Mediterranean, and this particular beach, that one might as well be in the sea as out of it. It involved a slow stroll down and into the edge of the water—not even noticing his toes were wet, land and water all the same to him—with his eyes up at the sky gravely surveying portents, invisible to others, of the weather (Local Fisherman Preedy). (p. 5)

The quote illustrates the nonverbal actions that Preedy takes that he thinks will produce particular appraisals of him as a result. Goffman (1959, p. 6) wrote, "When an individual appears before others his actions will influence the definition of the situation, which they come to have." He notes that individuals may act in a "calculating manner" just to manipulate reactions or they may act unthinkingly. He further comments that audiences may interpret a performance accurately or not understand and reach conclusions other than the ones that the performer aims for them to have. There are *calculated impressions*, which are impressions that a person seeks to make as a result of her or his performance, versus *secondary impressions*, which are the impressions left in the minds of an audience, and that may or may not include the calculated ones that the performer sought (see Leary, 1995, p. 11).

Goffman (1959, p. 6) clarifies that what matters is "in so far as the others act as if the individual had conveyed a particular impression, we may take a functional or pragmatic view and say that the individual has 'effectively' projected a given definition of the situation and 'effectively' fostered the understanding that a given state of affairs obtains." Audiences interpret and understand performances as meaningful communications that define situations and what a "given state of affairs" is, which provides insight into how to treat people in that particular situation.

- *People perform in different social spaces referred to as regions of performance.*

For the most part, people perform in the *front stage* region, where they are "onstage" in front of an audience. Front stages are where actors expect to give performances and audiences expect to appraise them. People prepare those performances in the *backstage* region, which is any area where actors take a break from a persona that they have been performing and/or is where they are rehearsing and preparing for a future front stage performance.

A person may give a great impression in front of a date. While out of view and earshot of that date, they might use a mirror in the bathroom to touch up their appearance. Maybe they will talk to themselves about how to act and what to say when they return. What different adjectives do they hope to embody, such as charming, beautiful, fun, a good listener, and so forth? What strategies and actions will they use to try to get those impressions to take hold in others?

A front stage is where performances occur, but that is only a starting point. The terms front and backstage have a conceptual basis and comprise more than physical locations where people perform or practice. A front and backstage in the sociological sense reference situations where people anticipate meaningful social judgments to be ongoing about expected performances. Consider in daily life how often just being watched alters behavior, as people change their naturally occurring actions, because they worry about other people judging them. Research methodologists refer to this problem as *reactivity*, and this issue is an intrinsic component in dramaturgy. If your boss is watching you, you feel on front stage. When your office door is closed, you have a backstage where you feel freer to surf the web or text someone. People often try to transition from the front stage to the back. A simple move to do so is by closing a door or asking someone to shut the door. If you want a quick example of a signal in conversation where a front stage switches to a backstage, just think of moments at work when a coworker approaches your office to talk, and the first thing he or she says is, "Do you mind if I shut the door?" An open door can make a front stage and closing the door can make a backstage.

The composition of an audience also defines front and backstages. Suppose, for example, that you have a wild sex life, but "pass" as a humdrum type to coworkers, other students, and family members. Knowing that particular people may observe you in particular situations impacts your approach to your own behaviors and determines whether you are on the front or backstage. If in front of individuals who know and share your secret wild side, you may be able to relax (backstage). In front of people who are not wise to your secret, you may perform to fit whatever actions you think characterize a staid person.

A person, and to a lesser degree a place, for example, may determine when a situation is a backstage or a front stage for the person. Before people who share your fraternal or sorority membership, you also may be on front stage, because you do not want your brothers or sisters to know that you keep your affiliation secret from employers or professors. Unlike the front stage being in one physical location for performances in actual theaters, front and backstages are fluid and variable in social life.

Goffman (1959) describes many examples of people conducting impression management on the front stage while acting differently back-stage. He famously quoted George Orwell's observation of a dining room in *Down and Out in Paris and London*:

> I remember our assistant maître d'hotel, a fiery Italian, pausing at the dining room door to address an apprentice who had broken a bottle of wine. Shaking his fist above his head he yelled (luckily the door was more or less soundproof): *Tu me fais chier.* Do you call yourself a waiter, you young bastard? You a waiter! You're not fit to scrub floors in the brothel your mother came from. *Macquereau!* Words failing him he turned to the door, and as he opened it he farted loudly, a favourite Italian insult. Then he entered the dining room and sailed across it dish in hand, graceful as a swan. Ten seconds later he was bowing reverently to a customer. And you could not help thinking, as you saw him bow and smile, with that benign smile of the trained waiter, that the customer was put to shame by having such an aristocrat to serve him. (p. 123)

Backstage, an enraged assistant maitre d' yells insults at an apprentice. Once front stage, the same person transforms into a polished, refined but servile "aristocrat." Workplaces typically have identifiable front and backstages, such as being out with customers or back in the office. Have you needed to provide service "with a smile" that required a front stage performance that you did not feel like giving? Have you seen anyone relegate anger at a customer to swearing backstage, while they remained polite on the front stage?

- *People work in teams and collectively to express the characteristics of social situations.*

So far many examples provided involved individuals acting alone. Yet most dramaturgical events involve individual actors who perform together as a team. *Performance teams* refer to individuals working together as a team to create and sustain performances for one another and for an audience. Athletic teams demonstrate team spirit through various ritual chants and huddles. Family members will act as a team to conceal secrets from outsiders by relying on other family members to act as if nothing is wrong and to backstop an acceptable story (Goleman, 1996). Maybe family members will say that someone is having a procedure done or visiting relatives when he or she has committed himself or herself to a psychiatric hospital. Workplaces expect coordinated activity by employees to conduct their jobs and serve the organization's interest. Disney World, for example, supports actors playing characters interacting together in order to sustain a marketed fantasy image for guests visiting their parks. Disney employees even refer to themselves as cast members. Many workplace groups, from White House cabinets to local businesses, rely on employees to camouflage disagreement privately and to agree to appear to support whatever the "party line" is publicly.

Individuals must coordinate actions with others to define social situations. Defining a situation means more than just knowing what the "state of affairs is"; defining a situation allows people to understand what they should do in that situation. People must share a common interpretation of what a situation requires from each person, so that together they can act as a team to produce a recognized and ordered situation.

For example, if a teacher and students meet in class, then they may implicitly agree to accord their behaviors to the prevailing definition of what is expected in that situation. Students and a teacher will then perform typical actions that comprise a class meeting. For most situations of this kind, a teacher stands in front of a screen or a blackboard orating, while students listen in silence, appear to or do pay attention, and write notes. If students are actually not doing any of the above, they may hide their lack of interest or their texting to avoid publicly disrupting the class "situation" and being confronted. A class that is out of control has participants who ignore these niceties, and the definition of the situation changes. When students are polite enough to camouflage inattention, they allow the defined "show" of the class situation to continue. As students, you may have witnessed such collusion. There is the game of making sure to look up at the teacher occasionally to nod as if you follow, while one's mind is otherwise occupied. The teacher, while assuming a persona appropriate to describing whatever information is on tap, will also sometimes pretend not to see a distracted student or two nodding off or hiding their texting.

In a doctor's office, patients stay in a waiting room until a nurse or physician assistant beckons them to a small room behind the reception desk. Patients are ushered into examination rooms, which usually have an examination table covered with the same crunchy white wax paper. The medical assistant collects information and takes some small measures of bodily functions, like one's temperature and blood pressure readings. Patients are then told to wait and that "the doctor will be right with you." The staff choreographs patient actions to make them reactive. The staff does the same things over and over each visit to make the ordered situation of the doctor's visit possible. The receptionist and medical assistant constitute a team that maintains the routine social situation of the medical visit by corralling patients and heightening efficiency on the doctor's behalf. The visit is not a moment of social improvisation. It is a predetermined situation in which people know and are told collectively how to act.

- *People prioritize giving credible performances.*

As described previously, the goal of impression management is to embody a persona credibly. To give convincing performances means taking steps to appear authentic. I refer to tactics that people use to build up credible performances as *authentication practices* (Shulman, 2007). In the past, I described these tactics as steps that people take to create believable deceptions and to pass off lies as the truth. Yet people use authentication practices in more circumstances than just to make lies appear believable. People use authentication practices to also reinforce that a performance is credible and honest even when they are *already* being honest, particularly when they tell the truth in circumstances where people are suspicious of them. Credibility is the key goal in those performances. To persist in affiliations with social groups, people must appear credible to garner trust, maintain social order, and receive desirable responses from audiences. Even when people do tell the truth, they have to worry about appearing believable. Credibility is a dramaturgical must.

- *People avoid communicating "out of character" and taking any actions that could contradict the requirements of a performance and spoil it.*

People should stay in character when they perform. As an example, I have had a few students e-mail me stating that they were too sick to attend class. If they call me instead, they usually cough and hack on the phone from the "flu" that keeps them from attending my fascinating class. I have then sometimes seen those same students running around outside with their friends on the campus quad or working out at the gym, definitely not appearing sick.

Professional wrestling promoters used to make wrestlers act in real life according to the storylines of their characters. If a villain and hero were feuding, they had to appear to detest each other at all times, including when traveling across the country to shows, in front of reporters and after matches. A bad guy had to taunt fans, and a good guy had to smile and be friendly. In a famous incident, wrestlers "Hacksaw" Jim Duggan, who draped an American flag on his back and took a 2-by-4 to the ring, and the Iron Sheik from Iran, who carried an Iranian flag with him, were supposedly bitter enemies involved in a feud. Then the police pulled them over when they were driving together after a show and found hard drugs and marijuana in the car. Both were fired immediately for drug use but also for exposing their actual friendship and communicating out of character with their storylines. American patriots and Iranian tough guys just don't drink and get high together when fighting each other for the honor of their respective nations.

- *When people produce "spoiled" performances or someone spoils their performances, they try to repair any damage by engaging in curative steps.*

Goffman described many cases where people had a "spoiled identity" that they needed to repair. Think about occasions when you observe people apologize or give excuses to get out of trouble. "I'm not myself today." "I'm cranky because I haven't been sleeping well." If someone acts stupidly at a party, he or she may explain that they were drinking too much.

A classic example from popular culture is when a person who is involved romantically with someone is caught with a different person and says, "This isn't what it looks like" in an attempt to avoid trouble. Sometimes people anticipate having a performance spoiled, so they issue disclaimers in advance to avoid negative judgments.

As another example, stand-up comedians are paid to make people laugh. Sometimes they confront audience members who heckle them by interrupting them and insulting them during their acts. A successful heckler breaks up the comedian's rhythm and tries to steal away the audience. Good comedians thus have put-downs ready to use on hecklers to preserve their legitimacy and avoid spoiling their identity as the comedy professionals. They may respond quickly with a line like "It's alright,

I remember the first time I had a beer" and "Do I go where you work and tell you to flip the burgers faster?"

Erving Goffman described *defensive practices* as efforts that people make to defend their claims of having a particular identity or persona. When stand-up comedians shut down any hecklers who disrupt them, they use defensive practices to prevent their identity from being spoiled. People use *protective practices* when they try to help another individual or team sustain the integrity of a persona that they perform. An example is when someone's child does not meet the criteria of being a great athlete. Parents then offer up a parade of reasons to "unspoil" the youth's identity as a gifted athlete by telling the child that he or she was just "unlucky" in that game or that the coach is wrong not to play him or her because he or she is better than the other players who get more playing time. Students that have worked as counselors at sports camps have told me that when they rate the skills of campers who are not that good at a sport, they soft-pedal criticisms to preserve the child's identity. They may write comments like "good heart," which is a laudable trait, but not an athletic skill like how good your fastball is or how well you shoot free throws.

Defensive and protective practices help people sustain reputations. Think of public relations professionals whose jobs involve rehabilitating the public standing of infamous celebrities. How do you convince people to vote Barry Bonds or Roger Clemens into the Baseball Hall of Fame after steroid use tainted their athletic identities? When one's repute is at stake, personally or professionally, people employ defensive and protective practices. You need only look at past political elections, or any election cycle really, to observe myriad political consultants suggesting defensive and protective practices on behalf of their clients while trying to stigmatize their political opponents. Scholars of impression management describe the use of *attributive tactics* versus *repudiative tactics* (Leary, 1995, p. 17). Actors use attributive tactics to express something about themselves, while they use repudiative tactics to disassociate themselves from unwelcome attributions.

To sum up Goffman's six principles of impression management: (1) people perform; (2) specific regions of performance exist in the front and backstage; (3) people often perform as teams; (4) performing credibly is a key priority; (5) people try to avoid communicating out of character to maintain effective performances; (6) if a performance is spoiled, people attempt to repair the damage. More complex aspects of each dimension exist to explore later. For now, these basic points offer an orientation to key conceptual aspects of dramaturgy that Goffman articulated. Additional concepts are introduced through discussion of recent research. For now, these basics should establish a footing into the dramaturgical approach.

The Self

Goffman states presentation of self in the book's title. What is the "self" that people are busy presenting? A self is not a specific thing that some set of psychological reports and studies capture, nor is it equivalent to a person's physical body (Hewitt & Shulman, 2011). Individuals can perceive themselves in the third person, as objects out there in the world about which other people have opinions. Thus, the self is a key object in people's thinking about their behaviors. The ability to imagine ourselves as a collection of characteristics that other people judge helps guide our conduct. People also have a socially derived sense of self as we use the input from other people's judgments to help determine what to think of ourselves.

Because human beings can consider themselves as objects in the third person, they can take potential reactions to their actions into account and estimate how actions they take will reflect on them. That is, if they can imagine themselves acting in a particular way, they can then imagine how others will act toward them based on what they do. This knowledge helps people consider how alternative ways of acting would affect themselves and others. That consideration involves a projective extension of self, in terms of hypothesizing, "Doing X will lead people to think particular things about me."

G. H. Mead (1934) used the personal pronouns "I" and "Me" to describe a process whereby people create and recreate a sense of self from social feedback. Individuals have a sense of self that incorporates the views of other people about who the person is and what he or she is like—those attitudes are the "Me" that others see. The "I" is the sense of self that wants to act in advance of receiving those attitudes—the "I" is the sense of self before the attitudes of others impact the "Me." The "Me" arises as people grasp the meanings that their own acts will have on how others interpret them. The "Me" is always situated, which means that a "Me" arises in specific situations, or in terms of dramaturgy, as a result of specific impression management and performance. The key aspect of this process, and vital to the symbolic interactionist approach, is that the experience of self rests on the capacity to see ourselves from the vantage point of others. The individual human being acts as a subject and is also an object of thought in his or her own experience. Our actions and identity are self-referential, which in turn means that we develop a sense of self from taking in, integrating, and reflecting on the views that others have of us.

People pursue a sense of security and social identity by integrating themselves into group life. Individuals also want to attach a positive value to the self, to regard themselves favorably, and to maintain and enhance their self-esteem. The self is an important focus of social conduct. From this vantage point, projecting a desirable identity is a social process and not just a naturally occurring and unconscious behavior. So a first aspect to consider about performing onstage is that people care about what audiences think of them. That concern extends beyond people who we know well or who have some power over us, even to when an audience is composed of strangers. Psychologist Mark Leary asked why people care about looking good in front of strangers and others who have no relationship or a negligible one with them (see Leary, 1995, p. 42). Why care that much whether people who we don't know hear a fart or see that food spilled on a shirt, or that everyone (who we may not know) is "looking at us"?

Leary answered that people are so conditioned on a routine basis to connect performing and being judged with how they feel about themselves that they experience lower self-esteem whenever they look bad, even in front of strangers, or people that don't figure in that person's daily life (Leary, 1995). If people feel bad about themselves just from having an off appearance in front of an inconsequential audience, then judgments in general, both from strangers and from consequential observers, really do impact us. The reverse also holds. Do people mind receiving compliments, even from people who are inconsequential in their lives? The impact such reactions have on an individual's self-esteem makes the quality of impression management a priority all the time.

Individuals have a *dramaturgical* self and a *psychological* self (Schwalbe, 2013, p. 77). Performing a self to an audience is a social act that is external to the person's imagination. People can think of themselves over time in their own minds as an "invariant self"; that is, they see themselves as the same "psychological" person with a bundle of characteristics who goes through different interactions and events in his or her life. That invariant person represents a more psychological sense of self. Our interest here is to examine how individuals perform situational selves where they try to come across to others as certain kinds of people in certain kinds of situations, roles, and statuses. This self that is presented to others is a dramaturgical self. Who a person is to herself or himself as a continuous psychological self over time is a different question to explore. How people perform a persona in a given situation to others is the aspect of self examined here.

Hare and Blumberg (1988) note that a "self is in effect a personal role." People switch between selves in their own minds. A fictional example that Hare and Blumberg use to make this point is Dr. Jekyll and Mr. Hyde. One self is kind and gentle while the other is aggressive and nasty. In our own minds, we can chide ourselves for being a certain kind of person or thinking some particular thoughts, like "Why am I so (nervous, mean, worried, grumpy) today?" Sometimes those personal roles we play to ourselves spill out into public observation. Have you ever heard a person remark that someone you both know has "changed"? A woman may complain that her boyfriend acts differently when his male friends are around than he does in their absence. Who the self in effect is, at a particular time, is a situational role that a person plays. A psychological sense of self is more continuous and biographical and runs through all kinds of different encounters that people have. A dramaturgical sense of self is much more situational in nature. People can have the same worries over time that remain backstage, so anxiety can be a feature of a psychological self and emerge across situational roles, but for now, we focus on what happens in performances, as opposed to what people think of themselves in periods of solitary introspection.

Good sociological thinking analyzes the social conditions under which individuals act and that constrain their actions. The social feedback that people receive affects their self-esteem. People also consciously associate their sense of self with some images to bask in reflected glory and detach themselves from others to cut off reflected failure (Leary, 1995, p. 27). One such presentational strategy is when people associate themselves with hometown celebrities or successful sports clubs or talk about how their kid went to Harvard. An example of people cutting off their sense of self from a troublesome association is when some Americans clarify that, yes, they are Americans, but did not vote for Bush, or in the current era, that they do not support Obama.

Symbolic Interactionism

Psychologists often are interested in how inner motives explain the presentations that people make. While acknowledging these influences, we must also look to identify how social forces can affect presentations. How people behave in final form is influenced by a combination of individual factors and social forces. Focusing on the social forces side requires asking under what extant conditions people make decisions and take actions. That emphasis investigates research topics such as how certain social contexts, circumstances, and settings tip the balance in how people act and feel. How do different social backgrounds influence people's outcomes? How do larger social processes, such as local cultural preferences, lie behind and affect what otherwise appears to be random individual decisions that people make? For example, research shows that the willingness to accept a gift can connect to local cultural influences on people (Watts, 2012). In some cultures, people accept a gift because they want to accept the gesture or because they are acquisitive. In other cultures, people reject some gifts because they want to avoid reciprocity, meaning they don't want to accept an obligation to owe the gift-giver a favor later, as to them gifts are not "free." To explore how individuals present themselves to other people, we must learn more about how social forces can pull people's presentational strings as if they were marionettes.

Symbolic interactionism is a sociological approach to understanding human behavior that provides theoretical propositions that support the dramaturgical perspective. Symbolic interactionist thinkers supply conceptions of the *self, role, symbols,* and *definitions of the situation* that clarify dramaturgical interactions between actors and audiences and connect social acts to larger scale patterns of behaviors across groups of people and in organizations. The connection between individual interactions and patterns of human behavior is an important concern for sociologists.

Individual acts are just the tip of the analytic iceberg of larger, more complex, and socially coordinated activities that apply to multiple people. Shaking hands, for example, means more than two persons extending their hands to each other. Shaking hands is a normative and socially coordinated activity where past experience and established social conventions matter. A handshake to seal a deal ("shake on it") is different from the message people convey when they shake hands in a situation instead of hugging to express formality. There are correct and incorrect handshakes (firm versus weak) and secret handshakes for private groups. To only assess the individual's part of an action (two people shook hands) without considering the more extensive social ramifications of acts explains far less about the social implications and meanings than exist in that action. In America, a bow might be a casual gesture that an entertainer makes after he or she performs a song. In Japan, bowing is considered a complex and socially meaningful performance with incredible nuances in how straight the back is in the bow, how someone looks, and the level of respect that a particular kind of bow implies. Proper bowing in Japan takes experience living in that society and is a more complex socially coordinated activity than can be captured by just stating that someone bowed.

Individual actions do not emerge out of thin air. People know and anticipate social meanings for the acts that they select across a repertoire of available acts (when they have a choice). They know common interpretations for actions; they choose an action and then they act. To sociologists, the potential interpretations and reactions to our activities push our individual actions out the door, not primary biological impulses. This sequence is not always so. For example, fight or flight is real, and people will flee danger because of an inherited instinct to survive and not become something's dinner. Yet social agents can train people to overcome running away in terror by training social interpretations into them to stay and fight dangers.

Like other sociologists, symbolic interactionists emphasize the impacts that cultural norms have on human behavior. People are born into an already existing society and culture and directed right into a flow of how to act. Other people define actions, objects, and obligations for us as part of socialization. People do not always follow those instructions to the letter, but they do form part of a repertoire of responses that people can have to social influences. Sometimes patterns of how to act are unchanging, and other times people innovate new behaviors. The key point is that people do not act or perform in a social vacuum; they respond in common to social context. How?

According to symbolic interactionists, a "significant symbol is a vocal or other kind of gesture that arouses in the one using it the same response as it arouses in those to whom it is directed." Because people can use significant symbols, we can interact with one another on the basis of shared meanings. How we respond to one another depends on our negotiated and shared interpretations of symbols. Think of how people read one another in social interaction. We anticipate how other people can act based on what symbols they manifest. Language is a phenomenal social accomplishment. People can understand what words mean in unison and know that they create similar reactions and responses between people. The predictability that language offers is vital as we can usually depend on people responding to words in common. Thus, the word *hello* should get nearly the same response from you as from other people.

People's capacity to use symbols allows them insight into how other people will respond to their actions. If they use a symbol in a particular way, they will receive a specific reaction. The knowledge that meaning is captured in symbols allows people to be strategic planners of interaction and to be conscious of us as other actors out there.

Two

Persona Watching

Catching Impression Management in Action

Whenever you do a thing, act as if the whole world is watching.

—Thomas Jefferson

You can observe a lot by watching.

—Yogi Berra

Introduction: Reverse Engineering Dramaturgy

Goffman's basic concepts are excellent to think with, and many scholars examine them empirically. This chapter illustrates how readers can situate a range of dramaturgical concepts in the social world around them, beginning, for example, with how people act on a front stage and prepare on a backstage. We move from a basic introduction to observing impression management and ratchet up the complexity of examples.

Reverse engineering refers to taking an object apart to analyze its inner workings. Instruction booklets, for example, sometimes provide schematic and cutaway diagrams of disassembled objects. Reverse engineering entails dissecting an object, process, or situation to determine how the separate parts of the system work, alone and in cooperation, in order to sustain a functioning whole. In this chapter, I reverse engineer dramaturgy by disassembling some sample performances to observe these concepts in action. The goal in doing so is to offer a primer on observing dramaturgical concepts as they play out in real life.

Social life does not operate as predictably as natural processes do. If you combine two known chemicals in specific amounts, under controlled conditions, you should always get predictable chemical reaction X. Social life is messier since people's actions are not as invariant as chemical reactions. While we can still apply a reverse engineering approach to analyze human activities, we must be wary of some risk of error if we want to generalize a conclusion to a wider audience.

As a thought experiment, first consider how people move through different interactions and situations in everyday life. Pick a situation or interaction and imagine cropping out that encounter and placing that scene on a slide. First you can identify the situation as constituting a specific kind of activity, like meeting a friend or having a job interview. Then you can start detailing exactly what occurs in that activity. This approach examines smaller acts, including ones that seem mundane, for example, like waiting in a line. Analyzing microsociological acts can reveal them to consist of complex and systematic behaviors that are discovered through observation.

Detailed rules exist, for example, in "normal" line waiting in the United States. People form lines in multiple ways. Sometimes people stand immediately behind one another in a straight row or ones curved around in an ordered way, or they assemble in seats. The physical pattern a line takes is situationally determined. Lines in non-fast food, more expensive restaurants tend not to manifest as a long line going in one direction but as an assemblage of people waiting around a room or at the bar for a table. In popular diners, a mob of people stands near the cashier until a name gets called out, and that person goes up front. People wait differently in doctor's offices. The line there does not look like a line, as people sit around indiscriminately on chairs and couches waiting to hear their names called. Yet the space is called a waiting room, and people still wait there in a chronological order to see a doctor. They just don't wait in linear rows. Possibly, the more high status or expensive the event for which one waits, the more dignified the waiting process is, to the point of elites never having to even wait.

Then there are numerous unelaborated rules to recognize for standing in lines. For example, there is the "can you watch this for a moment while I go somewhere" request, which is accepted typically when the person has already been in line waiting with you. There is a rule of joining, in which if a person clearly knows someone in front of you (family or friend), who has already been waiting in line, and joins him or her, then it is okay for that person to join the line in front. The joiner receives this exception because friends or family who already have been waiting in line and have earned their place are "allowed" to reserve a place for someone expected to join them but who just isn't there yet. Otherwise, there is a strict don't cut the line rule in place. Line cutting is a severe breach that triggers hostile reactions. There is an expectation that the first people in line should be the first ones served and that the rest of the line follows in consecutive order.

A line is a miniature form of social order worth studying. During occasions when people all want the same thing, they take turns and establish rules for the situation, rather than just the strongest people or people with weapons automatically taking what they want first. Lines also function as status-revealing devices. Sometimes lines appear democratic, and other times they show how exclusionary social groupings can be. For example, one aspect of traveling first class is to not have to wait and to have a special line or lounge dedicated to your special class, such as when boarding planes. A snarky statement attributed to celebrities is stating, "Don't you know who I am?" to avoid waiting in line with "the little people."

Let's consider a figure that helps reverse engineer the dramaturgical regions involved in service interactions. Please consider Figure 2.1, reprinted from the work of Grove, Fisk, and John (2000). In each region, there are numerous small mundane behaviors that make up the scene. Businesses care about interactions between service-line employees and customers. To that end, scholars of marketing employ the dramaturgical perspective to understand encounters between customers and business providers. Figure 2.1, provides an analytic template to examine front and backstages in service encounters.

Figure 2.1 Services as Theater Graphic

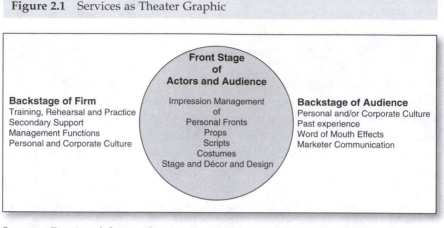

SOURCE: Reprinted from: "Services as Theater: Guidelines and Implications," by Stephen J. Grove, Raymond P. Fisk, and Joby John. Chapter 1 in *Handbook of Services Marketing and Management*. Edited by Teresa Swartz and Dawn Jacobucci. Sage, 2000

Organizations need to communicate their messaging on their front stages. For example, Disney promotes their theme parks as places where "dreams come true" and as "enchanted" and "magical." Consequently, as a business, they have an intense dependence on fronts, props, scripts, costumes, designs, and décor to embody those claims. A claim to be enchanted is irreconcilable with an unadorned location. Performances and sets must be staged to match the marketing promises. A first analytic step is to document how the front stage appears. Props are displayed; actors need costumes to play characters, and they are visible performing scripted lines in interacting with guests. Character breakfasts, parades, and photo opportunities are all staged to make "magic come alive" for guests, whether in visiting Cinderella's castle, going for a simulated jungle cruise, or journeying through a haunted mansion. Crop a scene from that front stage. What do the characters say to customers? What are they wearing? What are the tones of voice, demeanor, and nonverbal movements in their interactions?

Now consider other dramaturgical regions the figure identifies. Workers labor in backstages to structure front stage performances. Workers prepare with rehearsal and training regimens. Backstage teammates support characters and performances by providing services ranging from security to set design. Décor experts manage the stagecraft. Managers instill an organizational culture in the product's backstory regarding the enchantment that the park offers, so that performance synchronizes to thematic guidelines. People can analyze backstages to establish what actions and resources make those effective performances possible. Analysis can then transition to seeing how performers make their characters come to life on the front stage. The reciprocal relation between front and backstage is vital.

The figure emphasizes another dramaturgical feature, which is how audiences also help create and sustain the shows that performers give. The audience has a backstage that impacts the expectations they bring to bear on the upcoming performance they observe. How often do parents wind their children up to anticipate when Mickey or Cinderella appears, urging them to react with amazement and wonder? We can examine what expectations guests bring with them for these performances. What is the marketing to consumers that shapes their hopes for their front stage experiences at the park? How has Disney's marketing affected the backstory before guests even arrive?

Many people have affection for Disney characters. Children view their movies and TV shows and play with their suite of consumer products. Consumers are encouraged to use that suite of products in more than passive ways—even actively eating, sleeping with, and wearing them. For example, a child may wear Disney characters on their clothes, sleep in sheets with characters on them, play Epic Mickey on their game consoles, eat *Toy Story* themed healthy snacks, watch Disney TV, listen to a Disney singer while reading a Disney book or magazine, and play with their Disney character stuffed animals and toys. These actions and items build expectations for what people want to see in the Magic Kingdom. These objects connect guests to the content the company offers.

Disney prepares front stage performers formally by insisting that actors playing character parts and other employees go through orientation and training. Much is at stake in meeting the audience's expectations. A Disney University exists to offer classes to that end. The backstages of Disney, in its university and other components, offer rehearsal, practice, management, and cultural training to support the front stage. Following up the dramaturgical analogy further, as indicated on the reprinted figure, we can then start to ask bigger questions, such as how performances shape products for a market, how workers enact brand relationships with consumers, and how market communications create expectations for brands.

Regions, Actors, Performance: Some Service Examples

In another example, consider a typical layout of any hotel reception area. Break down the physical properties of the stage. In real life, or nonfiction performance, a *set* is a descriptive term for staged elements in settings where performances occur. Props, lighting, boundaries, and seating

Figure 2.2   Hotel Reception Area "Set" as Sample Stage for Performance

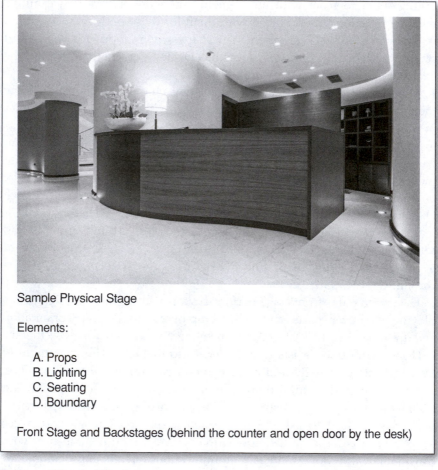

Sample Physical Stage

Elements:

    A. Props
    B. Lighting
    C. Seating
    D. Boundary

Front Stage and Backstages (behind the counter and open door by the desk)

SOURCE: Rilueda/iStock

preferences are all aspects of that staging. Props include objects such as personal props, costume props, and stage props used to adorn a stage, like books, vases, and paintings. Boundaries like doors, high desks, partitions, and walls are also important to see as barriers between a set's front and backstages. Pieces of furniture and large objects can also suddenly transition into backstages such as when someone hides something under the bed or the rug to remove the object from an audience's view. Examine the elements of the visible front stage in different hotels. What is the look of the furniture, the messaging of the light fixtures, or the purpose of choosing open glass doorways versus ornate magisterial doors?

Seating preferences, for example, are interesting because they carry social messages that are intentional though not spoken aloud. For example, when people sit at the back of the school bus or at the front of the class, they are communicating a message (Leary, 1995, p. 33). In some hotels, the seating is open and luxurious but also under the watchful eye of the reception desk. Lighting may be dim or bright and is encased in higher end fixtures to better dignify the hotel. The higher the quality of seating is, the greater the claim of a stage's social status to transfer as a measure of the status of its temporary denizens. There may be a large space between the seats and the reception desk to allow for passage of individual traffic without people bumping into one another. The reception desk has an open field of view on the front stage and usually multiple doors opening up to a back area where internal business is transacted out of view of the customers.

The actions reserved to front and backstages are so important in the hotel business that specific areas sometimes are referred to as "front of house" and "back of house." This distinction is a functional one. Front of house is where the customers live and business is transacted. Back of house is where all the hidden or obscured work occurs to meet customer demands and keep the enterprise running. For example, housekeeping is supposed to take place when guests are away. Workers maintain the stage and performance in the front of house and work with one another in the back of house to maintain the front of house. You can often see this distinction visibly. Areas meant for customers are prettier, shinier, and well maintained. Areas for employees are more dingy, smaller, and designed for un-ornate efficient function. Less money goes to decorate the back of house than the front of house.

One can move from the physical aspects of regions to examine the physical movement of actors within each area. Physical actions and expressions in performances lend themselves well to reverse engineering analysis the more that they are repeated and routinized. For example, repeated physical movements can be put into notation as dance choreographers do, as illustrated in Figure 2.3 in the dance notation for *Castaguettes*.

Stage blocking is a theatrical technique that outlines movement and interaction in a detailed way. As an example, consider a common social event that professors often use to illustrate the dramaturgical perspective: job interviews. In interviews, people seek to make a positive impression to pursue an opportunity, whether for a job, admission to a school, or to come off well to a media outlet. Before the encounter begins, sociological contemplations ought to occur. Why did this opportunity occur for that person? Did the opportunity result from combined social influences put in place by the person's own efforts, class origins, or some network of social connections, like who knows who? Who gets approached for such interviews? Given whatever education or experience the person needed to get this chance, does he or she now have the resources and experience to succeed in the interview? Can the person afford the right clothes to wear for the interview? Is the interviewee familiar with the kind of person conducting the interview? These questions illustrate a confluence of sociological issues regarding how class, economics, and social knowledge impact people's capacity to even get these auditions for opportunity. Before attending to these big issues, which address

Figure 2.3   Castaguettes

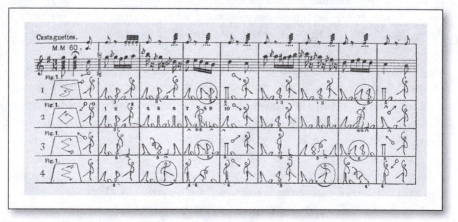

Source: Wikimedia Commons/Zorn_ Cachucha

Figure 2.4 Sample Codes for Interview Performance

Area/Object Identification	Performance Goals	Line Readings & Movement
DT = Desk/table	DL = Dramatize listening	SL = Speech length
C = Chairs	RC = Redirect conversation	E = Exclamation mark on key points (arrow up for voice)
D = Distance from each other	ABCs: Actively covering biography and credentials	AL = Animation level in speech
FL = Furnishing level	AH = "Achilles heel" detection question asked to probe possible weakness	PC = Posture check
PI = Types of personal items evident on desk	TC = "Triage" comments and responses for unexpected inquiries	H = Handshake firm at start
DR = Door	DA = Dress appropriate	EP = Exchange of pleasantries
W = Windows	SPQ = Sense of personality question to establish more of what this person is like.	CV = Resume burnished in hand
D = Décor statement	RKQ = Repeating of key qualification	EC = Eye contact

how larger sociological variables can influence performances, what actually transpires in the interview situation must be considered.

After getting this opportunity, people prepare backstage in anticipation of the upcoming performance. They think about what to wear and research potential questions and answers. They ask friends for advice. Career planning and "acing the interview" type books exist, videos can be consulted, and guidance counselors and career services offices, if they are available, and they have the sense to use them, help people prepare and practice for these events. Now, during interviews themselves, a person plans to act like "herself," but a more fine-tuned, prepared, and intensely focused version of herself. She avoids outright lying, an ethically problematic tactic, and a risky one, as she might get caught. She just concentrates on coming across well. Her body language demonstrates attention, and the seriousness and respect that she bears for the propriety of the interviewer and interview situation. There is no slouching, and she focuses on looking into the interviewer's face when speaking, and she picks up on verbal and nonverbal cues. She nods at the right times, considers the conversation's flow, and is talkative but not overtalkative.

The figure on the preceding page illustrates some features that you could notice during interview performances, from basic issues of posture and pitch, to how the stage is set for the interview, to goals for particular actions. View the people involved as actors communicating. What message is the person trying to get across, with what tactics? Does a voice arc up in agreement and go low for emphasis? Should that pattern be echoed? Does the interviewee look intently at the interviewer when the interviewer is speaking to demonstrate interest? If interviewing at a clothing company, does the interviewee wear an article of clothing that company makes? If an interviewee tries to make a good impression, we can analyze what the interviewee says and wears to learn what recipe they perceive makes for leaving a good impression. We can inventory and catalog those characteristics. We know that interviewees and interviewers comprise the audiences for impressions, so we can observe the ping-pong match inherent in how they cue up and react to each other's responses. Does the candidate arrive a little early, signal interest in the position, demonstrate knowledge about the employer, and discuss her or his credentials in the best possible light? How?

One could analyze such events through integrating video recording to dissect movements piece by piece. Some analysts collect video for later study. Sports teams, for example, employ reverse engineering by videotaping past games and then showing critical actions in slow motion. For example, a football videotaping session may show how a lineman missed a blocking assignment or a receiver ran the wrong route, and as a consequence, the play broke down. If you play a musical instrument, you might try to learn a new song by listening to it over and over until you can identify the different chords in sequence to the song, playing your instrument along with the song as a test of fit. Companies can reverse engineer worker productivity by recording and analyzing keystrokes to examine the amount of labor completed per hour.

Social scientists conducting ethnographic research immerse themselves in the activities of a group that they study, or they observe them more passively. Their observations attempt to break down different components and motives of actions to understand more about how the group operates. Ethnographers are in place to watch activities and learn about the cultures that inform those actions. Reverse engineering means asking what processes make an object or performance work instead of leaving those operations as a mystery to take for granted. The most predominant research methods used in studying dramaturgy are ethnographic methods and interviewing.

The theatrical analogy is useful as a descriptive tool but risks oversimplification if people do not explore why people do what they do more deeply. We must go beyond documenting actions. People can state that "life is like theater" and mention Shakespeare's quote, "All the world's a stage and all the men and women merely players," but considerations of this analogy must move beyond that realization. To appreciate how using the dramaturgical metaphor can reveal important sociological insights requires reverse engineering sets of related social interactions. Life is also not a theatrical production. There is a difference between actresses onstage who ask audiences to accept fictional portrayals with a suspension of disbelief versus giving nonfiction performances in everyday life. A person conducting impression management tries to fit within a social persona that is part of accepted and routinized interactions in social life. Goffman also noted that people have creative potential and some spontaneity in managing their impressions. People do not go to parties, unfold a paper, and read off a set of instructions of things to say to other partygoers. Instead, there is a guiding sense that people have of how they hope to come across and of how they might act to deliver a desirable impression, as there are structured but flexible ways to perform.

People act as individuals but not necessarily under circumstances or directions that they choose autonomously. Much social life involves repeated actions, performances, and statements. A receptionist repeats the same greeting to customers; teachers offer similar, if not identical, examples to explain concepts. Over time, people "fly" through the same familiar and patterned interactions. We greet people in accustomed ways. We eat with a fork and knife. Even within pairs, we grow into patterns. A spouse hears the same old rationalization for some inaction by her or his partner. Individuals enter into established personas and perform for other people seemingly on autopilot.

Unpredictability does occur when a normalcy is disrupted by an improvised action that departs from a typical pattern. For example, an interviewee can arrive drunk or a service worker can be rude to a customer. Predictable scenes do get hijacked. Yet most of the time, situations follow expectations, and people move from established pattern to established pattern. We can anticipate actions in routine situations. Most of the time, for example, when you enter an elevator, the people there will stand facing the elevator door, stare at the floor numbers going down or up, or look at their cell phones, and are unlikely to speak to strangers. You will not see someone place their back to the door or sit on the elevator floor or panhandle the other passengers.

Thinking of Performances as Cumulative: Social Order, Norms, and Rules

Predictable patterns of behaviors represent a form of social order. Social order exists when stable, predictable, and repeated behaviors, interactions, and interrelationships exist among individuals and within social institutions. Sociologists study how social order exists. How do people integrate themselves into perpetuating a range of predictable activities that help produce a functional collective life?

Social influences exist that encourage individual behaviors that abet social order. Sociologists use some specific terms, such as statuses, role, values, and norms, to identify these influences on behavior. A *status* is a named position within a network of other statuses, such as son, grandfather, woman and man, doctor, patient. Statuses come with specific expectations, rights, obligations, behaviors, and duties. *Roles* refer to how people perform obligations, behaviors, duties, and feelings associated with particular statuses. For example, a drill sergeant is a status, a named position within the military, which involves a role requirement of demonstrating authority in training new recruits.

Prevailing norms and values affect how people perform roles. *Values* are standards of judgment that people use to determine desirable goals and outcomes. Values help inform what norms should exist in everyday life. *Norms* are directions for how people should act and are conceived of in types such as folkways and mores. *Folkways* are more informal expectations that constitute taken for granted rules that guide behavior in small groups. *Mores* are stronger dictates, more like "official" norms in a society, closer to laws.

People can disagree on what values to support and what norms to obey. Yet many norms and values exist that are noncontroversial, often ones at a microlevel. For example, abiding by etiquette helps maintain a stable social order. People in U.S. culture try to avoid invading personal space because the physical borders of individual privacy are an important value. The repetition of compliance with such folkways and mores cements an affinity and obligation among the participants that helps order the interactions that they have with one another. For example, men in fraternities may greet each other with a secret special handshake as a folkway intended to promote the value of their brotherhood bond.

Sociologists investigate role performances and their underlying norms and values by connecting them to different groups, organizations, and institutions that influence them. People mostly act in specific, concrete, and usually well-known situations. Being familiar with the situation we encounter, such as greeting family members, talking to a coworker, or walking in public, presents us with a recognizable configuration of possible acts and identifiable objects. This configuration, which enables us to understand what is expected of us, is the *definition of the situation* Goffman references. The definition of the situation provides an overall sense of a particular setting, what activities happen there, what objects to take into account there, and what kinds of people and roles exist there. Hewitt and Shulman (2011, p. 49) described the definition of the situation as "an organization of perception in which people assemble objects, meanings, and others, and act toward them in a coherent, organized way." How people act is situated in these preexisting social meanings as definitions of situations constrain behavior and guide performances. Our attitude toward social situations of all kinds is to organize or structure them into schemas of how to act.

A role crystallizes how someone performs obligations, behaviors, duties, and feelings associated with a particular named status in society in a given situation. Roles represent a preformed conformity in a persona. Situations contain roles and statuses. For example, the drill sergeant or law enforcement officer performs a role that demonstrates authority. Being in a role influences how people perform and comes with expectations for how people are to act. These expectations are triggered when people see themselves in circumstances that activate taking on a role and when others accord them to be inhabiting that role at a given time. A police officer in uniform or a person at work now occupies a role other than their "civilian" individual personality. Who hasn't heard someone state, "Hey, I'm just doing my job," to indicate the role is responsible for an act, as opposed to the individual personally favoring that act. People sometimes seek *role distance*, which is a distance between a putative self associated with a role and you as a separate self from the self that must perform that role (Goffman, 1961). When not at work or off duty, people are out of the role. Roles offer specifications from which people can construct lines of conduct to fit situations and dovetail our conduct with other people's anticipated actions. Roles provide frameworks for people to use to construct a reasonable performance to meet the needs of a particular situation.

Knowledge of who is likely to be doing what, and how roles structure actions, permits people to make reasonably accurate predictions about how they are expected to act and what will occur in situations. When a child hears, "Go to the principal's office," they are expected to be intimidated and reprimanded in the dreaded principal's office and to avoid acting rebellious. There, the child is being sent from the run-of-the-mill teacher as disciplinarian to the "heavy hitter" of discipline, "the principal's office," which invokes the role of serious punisher that resides among the principal's suite of role obligations.

Individuals are not mindless robots who just fulfill roles without autonomy. People in roles do not just state lines word for word from a script, with every action preordained, and with no latitude in what someone can say and do. Such programmatic situations for role-play may exist, where intense prescriptions about roles are enforced, like in prisons, but these are less common than hybrid situations, with some expectations but also some fluidity in how people assume a role. A principal can be more or less lenient, a yeller or a whisperer, a bureaucrat or more flexible. Definitions of the situation, norms, roles, and values preexist individuals and play the tunes to which people dance. How individual performers dance in response reflects individual agency, but dance they will. People conform in countless ways in everyday life to repeated performance requirements.

The key to making sense of dramaturgical actions is to unpack how known roles and statuses become evident in how people act. A doctor may wear a white coat and stethoscope while police officers wear distinctive blue uniforms, badges, and weapons that telegraph their authority. People play roles with some flexibility. For example, some doctors avoid white coats because patients get nervous and their blood pressure jumps when seeing a white coat. Doctors will otherwise fulfill their role by asking diagnostic questions about health and have offices and stages that look like every other doctor's office.

The dramaturgical approach conceives of people embodying statuses through performing social roles. The impressions that result from those performances reveal personas associated with appearing as a doctor, mother, father, and so forth. Conceiving of people as "actors" fulfilling social "roles" brings in societal elements and the idea of factory specs. We do not usually perform roles blindly, without knowledge of what actions are expected with what roles. We can perform without that knowledge or mess up when we know what to do; but usually, social experiences are foreshadowed by a sense of what is to be expected when we play certain roles.

In addition to dissecting performances, we must advance analysis to think about what performances mean to the social body. Roles and statuses exist to make collective living possible. Playing roles well and reaffirming statuses help maintain social order. There are good reasons to research why playing roles in a particular way is considered expected as opposed to playing the roles in an alternative manner. The role expectations that prevail have societal consequences. Which expectations win or lose also will mean that some sets of performers win and some lose and that some types of actors will be favored to play dominant roles over others. These kinds of dramaturgical inequalities are examined in more detail later.

As a present example though, if assertiveness is considered more a "male" capacity in playing a role, but assertiveness is discouraged as not being "feminine," women face an obstacle in pursuing leadership roles. Roles can involve gender, race, and religious aspects in ways that comprise expectations that others demand people meet when occupying particular statuses. Consider the tale of a white, male middle-aged friend who graduated from a prestigious culinary institute. He applied for a job as a chef at a Thai restaurant. He had the training to prepare the food, knew the right recipes, and how to make the dishes in an "objective" cooking process, such as how to season, how to combine ingredients, the chemistry of cooking, and proper preparation techniques. However, he was told he could not be hired because he was not a Thai person, and he would be unacceptable as a legitimate preparer of Thai dishes. While having the ability and knowledge to cook dishes, not being Thai, he was perceived to lack the dramaturgical appearance required to be a legitimate chef cooking Thai cuisine. Lacking this "authentic" background made him *role ineligible*.

Audiences interpret racial and ethnic identities as important criteria for eligibility to play roles and occupy some statuses. If this sort of circumstance is generalized to a much wider range of lost performative opportunities for predominantly minority groups who are denied opportunities for being viewed as role ineligible in a racist society, discrimination looms as an aspect that is influenced by impression management concerns. As Schwalbe and Shay (2014) note, analyzing "dramaturgy can . . . yield insight into the microsociological foundations of macrolevel inequalities" (p. 155).

Sociological analysis jumps a level when moving from who and how someone performs to asking more cumulatively, why that "who" and this "how"? First, there are consequences to some groups for not getting to audition for some roles. Or if they inhabit them, audiences may be perceived as unwilling to bestow credibility on them as legitimate performers. Why? Such inequities bring in issues of cumulative social effects emanating from performance, not the least of which are discrimination in hiring on the basis of age, ethnicity, gender, race, religion, and sexual orientation.

Role ineligibility affects many people who have all the technical abilities to be competent to play some roles and occupy some statuses yet are perceived as not meeting some role eligibility criterion that is required to play a part persuasively, from not being of the same ethnicity or nation as a restaurant's cuisine to being a particular gender in a job traditionally associated with the other gender, such as being a male nurse or female bouncer. Analysis can go deeper than describing just the action of a particular performance. We ought to consider how observed performances connect to social issues of broad significance. Is a performance judged more harshly because of the demographics of the performer? Is the role altered because of the inhabitant? Are the resources granted to the performer variable depending on who is cast?

People consider themselves to have invariant personalities and to just naturally be themselves in most social situations. This perspective downplays social influence to the extent that people must sometimes act in ways to create the "right" appearance that differs from how people really see themselves. A person can define their "real" self in all kinds of ways that they do not want many others to know. Who has to go a further distance from their own self-image in a performance? They may be angry and hide anger because demonstrating anger in a particular role is inappropriate, like yelling at a coach who is berating you or a customer who is stereotyping you negatively. How social pressures enable people to repress some legitimate anger is a powerful means of social control. If communicating out of the character, role, or persona that one is assuming is the cost of defending yourself against insults, people may have so much loyalty to carrying on the performance that they subject themselves to mistreatment.

However, people are not always being "fake" in circumstances where they do not act like "themselves." We live in a world with expectations for behavior that mandate people to be "ourselves" in a given situation, but to "be" what the expectation is for persons in that role and status. Social life is full of moments where people learn not to spoil occasions by acting out of order, and Goffman argues that this "systematic desisting" occurs routinely in social life to avoid disrupting society.

Systematic desisting is important in understanding how social forces affect individuals. For example, at work, we agree to take on certain roles and behaviors and to give certain impressions to customers in exchange for a wage or other reward. We may be told when treated poorly that because of that role, we should not "take it personally." People interacting with us may define "us" differently than the "us" we think of ourselves as comprising. "We" are not people who would normally let ourselves be pushed around, but at work, maybe clients can get away with treating us rudely. Army basic training, for example, takes individuals and socializes them into the status and role of soldiers, who learn to act in a collective role and not just as random individuals. Outside forces impose an order on performance that then has larger societal-level implications. Appearance is not always reality because social norms and personal goals sometimes clash and constrain actors.

Not all performances that emerge involve deception or fierce external social pressure. A person on a job interview wants to give a good impression but that does not mean that he or she lies or poses as something that he or she is not; it is more that he or she wants to come across honestly as effectively and well as possible. Individuals who become soldiers may believe in that role and want to play it as sincerely as possible—the same with other roles, like being a good father, mother, leader, or supportive colleague. There is genuine *role commitment*, which Goffman referred to as sincerity toward playing a given role and learning to perform authentically and with genuine feeling in a particular status. You can be constrained to play a role against your will or committed to play a role with all your heart. Your performance may be cynical or sincere, meaning that you know your performance to be a put-on versus expressing a genuine, believed commitment (Goffman, 1959).

Ratcheting Up Sociological Analysis With Dramaturgy

To use and view dramaturgy as a more complex and fruitful sociological perspective, we will consider cumulative issues such as how dramaturgical behavior reflects the social order or who is included or excluded en masse by role requirements. When you are not purely "yourself," but playing the "you" judged appropriate for the circumstances, you can notice dramaturgy in action. People have very good motivations to influence the views that others form about them, and not because someone is being craven, phony, or superficial. Just being an interacting member of a social body makes this conformity inevitable. Now how we choose to act when we confront a tremendous range of different expectations and tasks, whether we perform to expectations well or poorly, and how others affect us through their responses to performances; those issues are important, interesting, variable, and complex.

Here I caution that presenting a more sociological treatment of dramaturgy's significance is trickier and more complex than people concede. Yes, a main premise that people perform in social life just like actors do onstage is straightforward enough. However, what must be unpacked afterward are the social conditions that orient people to perform in the particular ways that they do. Connecting microlevel individual acts to larger social patterns of behavior is the most important initial issue in transforming dramaturgical analyses into more serious contributions to sociological thought.

Social class and other background resources and variables discussed in the next chapter meld into a form of cultural capital, which distributes knowledge for performers to draw on that leads them to perform variably and with different consequences. How audiences establish criteria on which to reward or punish performances, finding some credible and others not, is a vital issue because performing before others is a means to achieve important outcomes and better opportunities in life. In other words, the sociological study of dramaturgy is more than noting that you can examine people's actions using the metaphor of acting onstage. A truly sociological dramaturgy should examine social components that shape the ability to perform effectively before others. The next chapter pursues this agenda.

As a concluding note, when I write that a perspective is more "sociological," what I mean is that the perspective integrates the impacts that social forces have on individual behaviors. C. Wright Mills (1959) argued that people should cultivate a sociological imagination and consider how larger historical and social influences affect events in their individual biography and not just assume that outcomes in a person's life are solely due to his or her own private doings. For example, a person might explain another person not getting a job because of some individual failing that the person had, such as being a poor interviewer or not trying hard enough. However, an initial step here might also be to ask what is the labor market like around the individual in terms of available jobs? Is the person in a time period of disruption of available jobs from technology or outsourcing? There are many talented graduate students applying for scarce academic jobs today, who in the heyday of hiring for academic jobs in the 1970s would have found work. In the 2010s, where institutions of higher education are cost cutting by reducing tenure-track hiring and by staffing with adjuncts, an opportunity to get a full-time academic job is a long shot, more so than in the past, despite the availability of many candidates with excellent credentials.

Cultivating a sociological imagination requires overcoming tendencies to explain behaviors and outcomes in people's lives using biased information or conventional wisdom. For example, consider an individual-level conclusion like people are "fat" because they lack willpower. Such a flip response can lead people to overlook meaningful causes of the problem that interest them. For example, can we explain mass rates of obesity without taking into account a surrounding environment in which fast food is everywhere, where a sedentary life is more prevalent, and a host of other social factors? There is no doubt that some people would explain excess weight by stating reasons such as the lack of willpower or genetic predisposition. However, such individual level explanations alone offer incomplete answers to en masse weight gain over the last few decades. A mix of considering social forces in combination with individual ones offers a more thorough explanation. For example, maybe willpower is an issue, but economy and technology also create pressures that erode willpower and create more opportunities to overeat. Advertisers tempt, agricultural productivity leads to unprecedented eating options, transportation systems enable more and more food to be available whenever you want and more cheaply, and chemists work to make new snack foods as close to addictive in taste as they can. Plenty of people can say no to overeating, and plenty overeat, but the point is that people do not make these decisions in a social vacuum; social forces, in addition to their own individual agency, influence their behavioral choices.

This same sociological imagination is also required to analyze how social forces contribute to dramaturgical choices. So how do you develop a more empowered social theory out of a soft analogy of people being like actors? Ramping up the analytic possibilities requires a few steps. Taking Goffman's dramaturgical model more seriously depends on conditionally accepting a few assumptions about our social worlds. First, dramaturgical theory posits social interaction as composed of performances that people offer to each other to demonstrate esteemed social values and hide discrediting information. People must communicate and translate their goals into actions and behaviors that other people can understand. People must learn to show that they abide by social norms, that they are good at their jobs, that they are attractive romantic partners. Demonstrating these features does not just "happen"; people must communicate to others in an understandable manner so that others can even get the message. Just consider the amount of self-help books that exist to help people attract partners or to influence others on the job, and you have a sense of the need to communicate effectively in daily life. Such books are premised on the idea that people can learn to put their goals into demonstrable practice. People pay a price for failing to demonstrate credibly or for not being accorded to possess an esteemed trait. That lack of success carries meaningful consequences.

A second assumption behind dramaturgical theory is that a person's identity is a "product" that emerges from social interaction. Having, and being attributed to have, some identity as whatever sort of person, is a social process and not just the result of naturally occurring and unconscious actions. Performances exhibit actions that in turn produce attributions by an audience. Performances offer a crucible for producing situational selves and definitions of situations. Whether a characteristic is imputed to others or not depends on the audience and performance in scene. Goffman (1959) wrote,

A correctly staged and performed scene leads the audience to impute a self to a performed character, but this imputation—this self—is a *product* of a scene that comes off, and is not a *cause* of it. The self, then, as a performed character, is not an organic thing that has a specific location, whose fundamental fate is to be born, to mature, and to die; it is a dramatic effect arising diffusely from a scene that is presented, and the characteristic issue, the crucial concern, is whether it will be credited or discredited. (pp. 252–253)

People need to perform, and the product of that performance either is accorded credibility or not. There is a false equivalence that just because someone possesses a characteristic, they will perform naturally in just such a way that the audience will attribute to them having that characteristic. Just because a person is smart doesn't alone cause a performance to be smart. What is attributed is to come from performance. Performances are the evaluative mechanisms for social appraisal and judgment.

How is the interactional traffic producing a product from a scene organized? Consider how much we define experiences in a particular way, based on being convinced by others, or convincing them, that the activity is interpretable as living up to social billing. Do people's relationships look like the ones in the magazines? Did the adventure trip get staged like the brochure promised? Did the clothes "make the man"? The adjectives that we apply to describe ourselves do have a litmus test in which others should evaluate whether our actions match those descriptive terms. For example, "saving face" refers to other people recognizing that someone will be attributed to have some positive quality and acknowledges that someone risks embarrassment and shame if something happens to make people think he or she no longer has that quality, such that he or she has lost "honor" in some way. Eleanor Roosevelt referenced the importance of individuals trying to withstand the definitional machines all around them, when she urged people to remember, "No one can make you feel inferior without your consent."

Third, the dramaturgical study of social life focuses on a micro-sociological level of analysis, such as how people interact with others in everyday conversations and their nonverbal behaviors. Take how people indicate romantic interest in one another or how people act toward each other while waiting in line. These kinds of interactions between people should not be overlooked as too "mundane," but viewed as performances that people offer to meet ordered and meaningful social expectations.

Many businesses, from airlines to Disney, for example, care about how people behave in lines because that factor affects their efficiency and economic success with customers. Customers who wait too long in lines may become dissatisfied. How people interact romantically matters to people's happiness, but also commercially as well. How many Hallmark stores, jewelers, tourist sites, and restaurants depend on providing the setting and trappings suitable for marketing the "romantic" to customers? Studying mundane interactions and performances can center on diffuse but meaningful subjects, such as how do people try not to look like jerks, or getting someone to realize you are a good friend, or that you are doing a "job" but are not just about the "job." The key point is that the strategic dramaturgical actions are a stable infrastructure through which people live their lives. Dramaturgical actions are a medium through which people demonstrate important social values, are viewed as social products, organize interactional traffic, and live. How do social forces influence these values, venues, and outcomes?

THREE

Sociological Influences on People's Performances

Face is located not within an individual but in the flow of events that constitute an encounter; it is "on loan" from society.

—Erving Goffman

Hermits have no peer pressure.

—Steven Wright

Conventional people are roused to fury by departure from convention largely because they regard such departure as a criticism of themselves.

—Bertrand Russell

Introduction: Learning How to Act in Everyday Life

From a sociological standpoint, conformity within societies is a complex and stunning accomplishment. Conformity is why social order exists.

Conformity in this sense refers to people engaging in specified, set, repeated, and expected patterns of activity as the price for being integrated into social groups. A more typical definition of conformity is that people conform when their behaviors and thoughts are induced and judged to meet a powerful individual or larger group's expectations and standards. Conformity can be a Dr. Jekyll and Mr. Hyde phenomenon. In disastrous outcomes of this binding social force, people live in an oppressive state reminiscent of Orwell's *1984*. In benevolent applications of this social force, people end up sharing positive social values that benefit social integration and make an uplifting social order possible.

The word *conformity* usually has a negative sense in everyday life, as in the term *conformist* referring to people who obey, follow, or imitate others blindly, and lack autonomy, independence, and empathy for difference. "Conformists" are pathetic robots, and all rebellious artists, brooding teens, intellectuals, romantics and writers ought to scorn them. That negative label is geared toward maligning a kind of person and not to describing the general sociological process of socialization. Some people urge trying to live in an "I don't care what other people think" state of independence, and parents will still ask their teenage children whether they would "jump off a cliff if your friends told you to" until the end of time. Yet people conform in mundane ways, many of them beneficial, and they have little choice but to do so.

People live in a world with preestablished expectations about how to act, from learning a language in order to communicate, to being children under adult sway. This mundane conforming is not about scenarios where conforming means consciously ignoring right and wrong, like going along with a peer group in bullying someone when you know better, or giving into a harmful ideology or oppressive actions. Such cases represent conformity gone wrong. People conform and work to meet social expectations in everyday life because doing so enables people to live together, understand one other, and predict the actions that others take in advance. This more sociological view examines conformity as individuals acting to meet a wide range of expectations, under different social constraints, for purposes of social integration. Conformity is a resource and background from which individuals draw knowledge, lessons, and practice in presenting themselves and understanding situations.

As individual actors, we must know what expectations and roles to perform and how to perform them. Goffman (1966) wrote that people's copresence involves mutual monitoring; people must present themselves to others in a "situational harness," meaning that they must dress, speak, and otherwise enter their interactions in normatively appropriate ways. Think of this harness as like being expected to drive a roadworthy car that can pass inspection. Fortunately, people have background knowledge gained from a lifetime of experiencing conforming, starting in our childhoods. We conform to expectations of eating with utensils, using language, and wearing clothes. Cooperation with rules is rewarded and lack of cooperation is punished. Toddlers get taught to do what parents say or get spanked, put in time out, or yelled at. Parents encourage conformity to rules from the start for essential safety reasons, like don't eat that or touch something hot. Children must learn and abide by basic rules just to be safe.

As you age, more organized collective conformity is thrust upon you because you interact with more social institutions like schools whose work centers on integrating people into the social body. When you enter school, there are now more kids around, and you become something to be processed to help the school maintain order. Now you cannot get up from your seat during class, and if you have to go to the bathroom, you need to request permission. You line up by last name. You speak when allowed. You become something called and treated as a "student" and not always as an autonomous individual who can follow her or his discretion. You eat when told and not when you are hungry. You have to read books and learn things that you don't choose. If you act unhappy or don't comply, you are disciplined. You learn that if you don't follow the rules, you ought to at least appear to follow them because you are watched for compliance. You start learning how to perform acting innocent whether you are or not because performance quality can make the difference between getting caught and going free.

Being showered in pressure to conform all our lives teaches us expectations and how to perform in anticipation of judgment. "Smile!" "Sit up straight!" Individuals have differences in agency that impact their capacity to meet a more complex range of expectations. Even then, people wish to appear in idealized ways, rather than to meet the bare minimum. People also don't want just to conform; they want to appear to embody social ideals. Who wants to go back to a high school reunion as a less successful adult? Do college professors want peers to perceive them as just "smart" faculty members or as "geniuses"? We pin many aspirational hopes on appraisals of our personas.

So people conform mundanely in the real world because they need to, and they are rewarded for conforming or appearing to conform.

Throughout life, influencing how others assess and control us matters because there are vital stakes that impact us if we are assessed poorly. Don't listen to mom and dad and get punished. Outcasts in high school understand with great bitterness what not fitting in means for how they are treated. Interview badly for a job and you are not likely to get that job. Form good relationships and network in business or make less money. You exist in a world of embedded and cued reciprocal expectations for how people act with one another. Agents of social control enforce expectations. The world contains individuals, members of organizations, and social institutions that all have power over us.

Conformity is also nuanced, for example, and includes appearing to go along with expectations. Someone may define the standards he or she conforms to differently than how others think the standard should be met. For example, maybe drinking or gambling, in a person's view, is how they "relax" and is not a "problem." How many students think they did "A" work despite receiving a lower grade? People can believe, sincerely, that their divergent interpretations are the genuine ones and not understand how others miss that truth. Individuals just disagree on what counts as meeting the standard. People must consider conformity, and whether a specific act constitutes appropriate conforming, in terms of a phenomenon to be interpreted.

This interpretability issue ratchets up the complexity of conforming. People can fake conformity, like when a teenager says he or she is going to a friend's house to study, only to sneak off to a club. These teenagers know what conforming to dad and mom's dictates requires; they just don't want to, so they fake their compliance. Another difficulty occurs when people may want to conform authentically, but they lack the ability or knowledge to conform successfully. You want to feel at ease speaking in public but can't. You try to lose weight but fail. We cannot always conform, even if we would have been better off doing so.

Further, people need to appreciate that some actors have more power than others to decide when attempts to conform succeed. Powerful people and social institutions often have latitude to decide what counts as meeting a standard of performance. There are also more nuances in individual relations beyond the pure coercive power that institutions have. For example, a person who wants someone to like them in a situation is less powerful than the person being courted, who can give thumbs up or down to entreaties for their affections. On the other hand, an institution can send a small army to coerce people.

To further illustrate a connection between conformity and performance, think of the signs in front of amusement parks and mall entrances that post directional maps with the designation "you are here." "You are here" maps identify where people are standing to look at that sign and specify their spatial relations to adjacent and sought destinations in a setting. People look to these signs to get their geographic bearings and to identify a route to a destination. Those maps help people navigate physical environments.

Imagine now if people had social versions of those maps available that provided equivalent direction about how to act in social environments. What would "actions you can do here" maps look like for charting out the different actions that are available in social settings to get to a desired end? Options for action would be laid out, and potential responses and paths clarified. Though I wrote imagine if these maps and signs exist, they already do exist in our heads; we just usually do not draw them out on paper except in self-help books.

These detailed social maps require knowing specific roles, values, and norms for social situations to orient people about options to act appropriately or to get away with acting inappropriately within particular settings. When we study dramaturgical actions, we may sketch this map mentally. Pick an established social setting, like a classroom, party, or doctor's office. Consult a mental map, and choose among behaviors that fit your immediate goals. Social "you are here" designations must capture unspoken realities of social expectations, demeanors, and understandings that different people see as routine behaviors in these settings. We don't write out social "you are here" maps in every social situation normally; we should just know them. However, if you want examples, we sometimes do write them out for unfamiliar scenarios, such as for travel outside our nations, or for visits to particularly sacred sites, such as religious shrines, and for participating in sacral rituals, where conformity to protocol is considered as a sign of respect for enshrined values.

As an illustration, consider the instructions for visitors to religious shrines in Japan, as evident at http://www.mustlovejapan.com/manner/shrine.html. This site contains images and instructions akin to "social maps" indicating where people should do what particular things when visiting the shrine. There are instructions about how and where to bow, where to walk, how to clean the body at the water place, and how to pray. Parents whisper similar kinds of instructions to children to teach them proper actions. When adults are unfamiliar with settings where some behaviors are very important, like during occasions where silent respectful behavior is valued to the point of being ritual, the instructions are formalized. You can write "you are here" maps for infinite social settings. When you do, you detail appropriate impression management and persona manufacture for a particular stage.

While conformity dictates much of our performances, we cannot predict every scenario or contingency of a performance. We do not know what the essentials of all situations are, such as ones new to us or ones where we do not trust the people involved to represent events accurately. In uncertain situations, we must appear to understand the situation with guesswork. We employ our best inferences and guess because we cannot always know all the facts in front of us, such as what people really think of us and a host of other unavailable information. Conformity is a good guidebook but an incomplete one. *Bounded rationality* exists in terms of limits on what information is gatherable and on human capacities to process that information. We live in a world where sometimes, no matter how much we think we know, or how we are trained to react, we end up guessing about what is going on around us to decide how to act.

Figure 3.1   Torii Gate

SOURCE: Cristian Baitg/iStock

People guess, sometimes because human brains cannot host endless information, sometimes because necessary information is unavailable, and even more complicated, sometimes because what information is available is twisted intentionally to encourage inaccurate inferences. Life might be more straightforward if all appearances reflected reality with complete honesty but that outcome is neither universally possible nor guaranteed. Further, people are unpredictable about when they want honesty. Sometimes people want appearances and reality to agree, and sometimes they do not. For example, when people fish for compliments, they do not want to hear criticisms. They want to hear that they look great in what they are wearing no matter how they really look. You want your idea for a business to be brilliant or to hear that your speech will be a hit, whether true or not. Other times, people want reality, like to know what problem to fix in their understanding and performance to get a higher grade on an exam or paper.

People use schemas to address problems of having limited or uncertain information (Hewitt & Shulman, 2011). Schemas refer to specific background knowledge that provides information about objects, and ideas about the relationships between objects. Schemas can center on specific types of people, situations, social roles, social groups, specific events, and the self. You might think of them as customized social flash cards, though they are not scripts. In movie parlance, they are like background notes on character relations or situations. A given individual might have schemas about a spouse, office parties, workaholics, bosses, celebrities, professional athletes, or the millennial generation. People walk around with schemas that inform their knowledge base for performances.

Social Structural Forces That Impact Dramaturgical Actions

In previous chapters, I considered how audience reactions help shape an individual's sense of self, which motivates the impressions they might make and what rewards might flow from them. Social norms structure the expectations that, in turn, signal what actions people ought to perform, and in what manner. In this chapter, I addressed how conformity and the goal of social integration are sociological processes that shape performances. There are more complex sociological forces to describe that further represent how social forces affect impression management. These forces, which have overlapping influences, include cultural capital, demographics, socioeconomic status, rituals, social mindscapes, status and role, social control, and trust.

Cultural capital refers to the general cultural background, knowledge, disposition, and skills that people pass down through generations (see Bourdieu, 1986; Lamont & Lareau, 1988; McLeod, 1987). Cultural capital is a "catch-all" term that describes a comprehensive set of dispositional resources that people draw on to shape their everyday actions and performances. Those resources within cultural capital are drawn initially from the experiences afforded by parenting and a family's socioeconomic background. This background instills certain cultural affinities and habits that affect one's shot at upward social mobility in the mainstream American economy. For example, did the family teach the child to value doing homework, stay in school, and pursue higher education? To relate effectively to authority figures? Such social values are more valuable for upward mobility than less privileged alternatives.

In Philippe Bourgois' (2002) book, *In Search of Respect*, he contrasts the cultural capital between white affluent workers in Manhattan's financial and real estate echelons and poor drug-abusing Puerto Rican residents of the barrio in Spanish Harlem. Ray, a drug-dealing boss, is an excellent businessman in a competitive, rough, and demanding sector of the underground economy. He has organized his business and employees successfully and made himself a lot of money. Yet Ray is at a loss in knowing how to deal with public bureaucracies and municipal red tape in order to pursue legal business opportunities. Astute streetwise business skills exist on one side against complete bafflement with working within public bureaucracy on the other. Another subject in the study, Candy made a court appearance in what she thought was a fancy respectful outfit, but to the judge, the outfit choice was read as inappropriate and disrespectful.

Cultural capital of different genesis and content helps inform individual performance, deference, and demeanor, with a range of consequences. The entrepreneurial skill to run an enterprise in an underground economy is formidable; at the same time, dealing with everyday bureaucracy baffled that person. The skills do not transfer. Cultural capital can encompass one's education level, speaking with a particular accent, amount of exposure to high culture, and taste in clothing. As an example, if people think of certain actions or objects as low class or high class, that value judgment is significant because of potential negative responses. A person who manifests "low-class" clothing in a high-class venue is thought of more poorly, even if performing well.

Demographics refer to the influence of social groupings like gender, ethnicity, race, employment status, and religion that are part of classified human populations. Demographics impact dramaturgy in that audiences react differently depending on one's background demographics, which can form important criteria for judging a performance in advance, even overriding a performance's content. Demographics can also affect how someone acts in that members of different demographic groups may perform differently. If someone is racist, they may automatically object to a performance or accept one, depending on race, no matter what the quality of the actual performance is. Someone in a segregated environment, for example, may have less knowledge of how to perform and work with an audience they have not encountered previously. Background demographic status can affect a person's capacity to perform and subsequent treatment. For example, a person with a particular religious background may not be able to play a certain role on a given day or wear an outfit associated with a given role. Many colleges work to enhance diversity because they believe that encouraging students to have more interactions with people of different backgrounds will benefit their future interactions with other groups.

Socioeconomic status refers to social factors that comprise a person's economic attainment and assets. Incomes, types of job, and education level are characteristics that comprise a person's socioeconomic status. Socioeconomic status affects the material basis that people have from which to perform. The quality of clothes that someone can wear, as an example, is a matter of money, not just taste, which in turn impacts the reception that a person receives. As in the case of demographics, audiences carry assumptions with them about how kinds of people will act and are expected to act. Those assumptions constitute a form of stereotype and self-fulfilling prophecy and affect performances before they even unfold. A person's social class background can limit their exposure to certain opportunities to perform, factor into how they think they should perform, influence an audience's judgments, and provide material resources.

Trust is the expectation that a person will meet a future obligation in good faith, such as keep a secret or pay back money. In a more sociological sense, trust is a social mechanism that reduces life's uncertainty and complexity and allows people to feel that they can predict someone's future actions (Luhmann, 1979). Trust levels affect how well people work with teammates and whether people judge performances as credible or not. The reliable repetition of activity also inspires trust. Since people base trust levels on familiarity, reputation, and how routine, reliable, and predictable dramaturgical activity has been in the past (that there is repeated past proof of being trustworthy), there can be more trust in future interactions. An important issue people confront in performance is whether trust exists prior to the interactions that actors have with an audience. Some performances are predicated on prescreening and other actions to try to ensure that an ensuing performance should be considered trustworthy, such as when people do preemployment screening. The mechanics around guaranteeing trust are important precursors to performance and sometimes filter down to whether people are even allowed to perform.

Rituals refer to prescriptive social traditions that have emotional and moral meanings for people that connect and integrate them as individuals to a larger social body (Collins, 2004; Durkheim, 1965). Social norms encourage people to participate in rituals. Rituals are traditional sets of organized behaviors through which people also demonstrate their conformity to the social body, for example, through participating in hazing or religious ceremonies. Rituals reference patterns of meaningful and sequenced social encounters, all of which usually have rules that govern what people do, such as in religious rites. Rituals and social norms are both prescribed, but their meanings are not synonymous. When a person disobeys a minor norm, like by jaywalking or speeding, an intense feeling of moral lapse is unlikely to result. However, when people fail to participate in a ritual, the result is more a negation of belonging to the social body and of a moral break with society. For example, not standing for the pledge of allegiance or talking during a prayer service is seen as rejecting social integration and affiliation with meanings that have a powerful symbolic grip on people. People participate in many rituals that have powerful emotional and moral meanings. That people respond to such rituals and traditions indicates that moral systems associated with belongingness and inhibition influence people's dramaturgical activities and impression management.

Randall Collins is a well-known sociologist who developed a theory that builds on dramaturgy and ritual that he called *interaction ritual chains*. As Collins (2004, p. 1) explains, "A theory of interaction ritual (IR) and interaction ritual chains is above all a theory of situations . . . human bodies charged up with emotions and consciousness because they have gone through chains of previous encounters." Collins (2004) references a famous quote from Goffman's work, describing "not men and their moments, but moments and their men," when he describes the power of situations to define people:

> In gender-neutral language: not individuals and their interactions, but interactions and their individuals; not persons and their passions, but passions and their persons. "Every dog will have its day" is more accurately "every day will have its dog." Incidents shape their incumbents, however momentary they may be; encounters make their encountees. It is games that make sports heroes, politics that makes politicians into charismatic leaders, although the entire weight of record-keeping, news-story-writing, award-giving, speech-making, and advertising hype goes against understanding how this comes about. To see the common realities of everyday life sociologically requires a gestalt shift, a reversal of perspectives. Breaking such deeply ingrained conventional frames is not easy to do; but the more we can discipline ourselves to think everything through the sociology of the situation, the more we will understand why we do what we do. (p. 3)

Focusing on situationism detaches people from an egocentric tendency of explanation, through acknowledging that situations structure individual performances more than individuals can voluntarily structure all the situations in which they find themselves. Collins does not deny individual agency and argues against an oversimplified dichotomy of individual agency versus social structure. The point he urges is for people to note the determining power of situations while also considering that situations and individuals infuse one another with meaning and power. The connections between self and situation matter as opposed to consistently arguing one against the other. What is relevant here for dramaturgical theory is how situations and rituals precede and help determine the nature of dramaturgical performances.

Collins argues that, over time, participating in rituals and the emotional energy emanating from them builds into greater social integration and a "society," as partaking in interaction rituals "chains" people to the larger social body. The inverse also occurs in that interaction ritual chains "gone wrong" can produce negative energy and damage the social body. For Collins, there are some preconditions for interaction ritual chains to exist (Baehr & Collins, 2005). The first condition is that two or more people are together in a significant exchange; they see themselves as bonded insiders; they "focus their attention upon a common object or activity, and by communicating this focus to each other become mutually aware of each other's focus of attention" (Collins, 2004, p. 48); they also share "a common mood or emotional experience" (Collins, 2004, p. 48). Performance in rituals can generate intense emotion, such when people cry at a wedding. These moments are powerful emotionally, and dramaturgy is one of their binding engines.

IR chains produce outcomes of increased solidarity and common cause; an infusion of emotional energy, which is motivational and provides a feeling of enthusiasm; a creation of new symbols and empowering of old ones that store energy; and a moral code that punishes people who violate the sanctity of rituals. As an example, consider moral code through the prism of how religious groups view those who violate their precepts. Consider how tied to a sense of being "sacred" a performance of a rite is in creating emotional and symbolic power. People performing rites wear ceremonial garb, walk in certain progression, and have sacral oaths and minute choreography of events. Events can become closer to radiating a sacral nature when pursuing a ritual in a pure and painstaking way. Weddings, graduation ceremonies, and initiation rites are all examples. These events have social norms and values, but they are also bonding rituals. When people undergo initiation rites, they cement an emotional tie of belonging to a group with almost sacral power, creating symbols out of objects and charging them with the energy of everyone's attention and commitment to the ceremony. People become "brothers" or "sisters," enter a "priesthood," become a "husband" or "wife," or otherwise undergo a rite of passage. For now, consider the obvious point that existing ritual chains create preexisting instructions for people that dictate their performances and actions in advance.

Status and role: Statuses and roles are preexisting instructions akin to schemas that influence how people perform. Statuses and roles vary in nature, and there are differences in how people choose to fulfill them, but they are determinants of the kinds of actions that are required. Paramount here is that roles and status preexist people and are out there in society waiting for people to perform them and make them come alive. They are the social facts of existence that people wear as commonly considered identities.

Social control: The sense of social control to keep in mind here is that of pressure people experience to abide by the rituals, roles, and situations in which they find themselves. There are implications in not abiding by instructions for how to act in situations. These social controls vary from embarrassment and losing face to quarantine from society (incarceration) or violent punishment. Social control exists powerfully in interactions between individuals in how much people dread potential embarrassment and negative judgment.

There are multiple levels and types of social control. There are agents of social control who patrol and do surveillance for deviant behavior, officially, like police, and other informal agents, like friends, who tease someone for violating a norm. Levels of social control can be self-control, group social control, and institutional social control. An individual may be controlled by fear of looking bad or by concern with being expelled from an organization. The point is that anticipated negative consequences are a prime mover guaranteeing performance or a feigned legitimate performance in a social situation.

Social mindscapes: Eviater Zerubavel (1997) is a prominent sociologist of *cognitive sociology*. Social mindscapes is a concept he developed to conceptualize the categories of shared meanings that people have and use that enable them to understand and define objects and phenomena in similar ways. In his words, "As we learn to see the world through the mental lenses of particular thought communities, we come to assign to objects the same meaning they have for others around us and to remember the same things that they do" (Zerubavel & Smith, 2010, p. 323). A social mindscape refers to having a shared collective meaning so that performances are understandable to others around us because we share the same meanings. The mindscape concept argues that people have similar cognitive knowledge and categorize meanings in the same way. A shared social mindscape is a requirement of basic interpretive competence. A shared social mindscape is a precursor to effective impression management.

Think of Social Forces as Interweaving Clusters

The preceding discussion presented social factors in a general way. In action, these forces interweave and are not understood properly in isolation. There is no exhaustive list of social factors in combination.

Consider the impacts social forces have on dramaturgy as "clusters." *Repetitive monotony* enables people to live together in a normal state of predictability, in overwhelmingly familiar patterns of interaction that are routine at work and among family and friends. In the largest sense, repetitive monotony is vital to an efficient society. Knowing that people may engage in routine actions predictably enables mass planning and organization, which is highly productive, whether on an assembly line, in bureaucracy, or in interpersonal interaction. Social theorists like Karl Marx and Max Weber note that such efficiency also produces alienated people, so what is good for us on a large scale in some ways can also be bad for us as individual experiences. Bureaucracies are an incredibly efficient organizational form, but to work within one can be mind-numbing and stultifying.

Why does repetitive monotony matter in self-presentation? Familiar situations train people to know how to manifest situationally appropriate selves. A fraternity brother understands the sort of public self that a party calls for; a member of a subculture knows to use jargon with other members present; mom and dads use guilt like a welcome old friend. Situations call forth certain kinds of predictable responses.

People march to the beat, rhythm, and cadence of social routines. There is variety in the different kinds of routines that people have, depending, for example, on their cultural background and social class. There is likely less variety within type than between types. Both airplane pilots and flight attendants, for example, follow routine beats, but they respond to different instruction. So while people do manage their identities, they do not always work to improvise new ones or even think about doing this work all the time. For many interactions that are now repetitive, identity management is just going through the motions because people are so well socialized to the routines that they perform. Having stated this point, we still must not gloss over work that people do to present routine selves. People must still perform so that an audience can create attributions about what those individuals are like, and the work people do to make performances lead to scenes that produce a sense of self.

Presenting a persona effectively also requires controlling the specific information that is disclosed while preventing hidden information from leaking out. How many times has a friend told you "don't say anything" or have you urged a friend to keep something "between us"? What about times when you concealed a negative aspect of your biography while accentuating the positive? Have you ever omitted information to save face? To project an identity or characteristics of a situation to others is a social process that is impacted by the knowledge of being observed because people make conscious choices to influence what others will see. Conscious work is involved in presenting personas and situations, and people all do and know about this work on a more subjective level. Where the dramaturgical approach is useful is to reveal how sociologists can analyze that work in conceptual terms. Goffman's analogy of people in social life being like actors performing on stage provides an initial metaphorical framework from which he devised theoretical concepts that aid those analyses.

Conceiving of individuals as actors and performers is not meant as an attack on people's ethics and morals or to claim that people are all "fakes." The dramaturgical perspective is criticized as being too cynical and as asserting that people are inauthentic and shallow morally. This criticism is debatable but one to leave aside at this early point in the book. Maybe people are more or less thoughtful and conscious of strategizing the images they present. Perhaps acknowledging that people try to manipulate and shape what views others will have of them is an unseemly acknowledgment about how people act in everyday life. However, objectively, people assemble performances to meet social purposes, and examining how they accomplish that work is worthwhile.

Realizing the Analytic Potential in the Dramaturgical Perspective

I hope to use the applied cases in this book to promote the benefits of greater application of the dramaturgical perspective. While some teachers use the approach mostly to describe social activities, while extending on dramaturgy as a means of comprehensive sociological analysis, sociologists should be and are applying the perspective more to modern circumstances to analyze contemporary developments like the Internet. Erving Goffman proposed the dramaturgical metaphor in 1959. Since then, the Internet has produced a cyberculture that has created new contexts for examining people's activities as impression managers. Though many scholars conduct empirical research using a dramaturgical approach, they publish their insights mainly in specialist journals for other scholars, so their findings do not reach many lay readers and students. This book explores a range of contemporary insights from applications of the dramaturgical perspective in order to help promote new dramaturgical research.

Erving Goffman's dramaturgical sociology, though extolled here, also received blunt criticism. Meltzer, Petras, and Reynolds (1975) argue that Goffman's work has

> no explicit theory, but a plausible and loosely-organized frame of reference; little interest in explanatory schemes, but masterful descriptive analysis; virtually no accumulated evidence, but illuminating allusions, impressions, anecdotes, and illustrations; few formulations of empirically testable propositions, but innumerable provocative insights. In addition, we find an insufficiency of qualifications and reservations, so that the limits of generalization are not indicated. (pp. 70–71)

These criticisms are accurate. Goffman did not summarize all of his dramaturgical ideas into one grand theory. While he christened many new analytic concepts, he did not organize the concepts that he coined into a unified categorical system. He also did not present his ideas in a hierarchical order so as to add up to a comprehensive interrelated set of social theory. Dramaturgy has no evolutionary stake or historical development or a neat 2 × 2 table that summarizes key points.

Goffman's modus operandi was to dissect social interactions and devise concepts to capture significant activities within the performances he observed. Yet he did not organize the resulting concepts into a formal order, as testable propositions, with explicit directions regarding generalizability and scope conditions. As a consequence, his work appears more as collections of ideas and complex analytic assertions on distinct themes, such as types of social frames.

In response, scholars of Goffman's ideas often try to organize and systematize his work into themes that synthesize different concepts into new categories. Those scholars then produce groupings of key take-away ideas. Those groupings offer interpretive pathways into Goffman's work. For example, in Lemert and Branaman (1997), Ann Branaman describes Goffman's four main ideas as (1) the self and society relationship; (2) the relations of power, status, and self of "normals"; (3) the contribution of analogies Goffman uses to analyze social life: drama, game and ritual, and their relations to morality and manipulation; and (4) how frames, described as situationally based interpretive patterns, influence social structure. Phillip Manning developed the

SIAC schema to categorize the sociological significance of Goffman's work centering on (1) situational propriety, (2) involvement (or lack of involvement) in ongoing social activities, (3) accessibility and inclusion in activities, and (4) civil inattention to others (Chriss, 1995, p. 178). Scholars of Goffman's work often contribute some anthologizing and systematizing of his key ideas (for examples, see Brisset & Edgley, 1990; Burns, 1992; Edgley, 2013; Fine & Smith, 2000; Lemert & Branaman, 1997; Manning, 1992; Scheff, 2006).

In teaching, I believe that the dramaturgical approach is treated in a more simplified way. Students may not move much beyond an analogy of people as actors. They may accept that they can describe the utility of the approach on an exam or paper with an illustration or two, and depending on their interest, they may just explore a few more examples of people as performers. The complexity that is possible may be ignored because in a sense, dramaturgy is a victim of its own ease of application. People can apply the concepts of dramaturgy so easily and readily that once they describe a social performance using dramaturgical terms, they do not pursue the full analytic potential that this approach offers. That people perform during a date and that a worker acts nicer to a client than he or she really wants to are initial observations and starting points. They are not conclusions, even when they describe impression management techniques perfectly. They represent an unfinished sociological assessment that could occur if gendered expectations are added to the mix of dating dramaturgy or if the impression management of workers is translated into a higher or lower dollar figure based on client feedback.

Once people can determine what a performance encompasses, those revelations can lead to addressing deeper questions. For example, what are the ramifications of having the appearance of deference as a routine expectation for workers? That question is different from noting that workers perform in front of customers. How is deference alienating, and why is deference so embedded in hierarchy? How the quality of service affects a company's bottom line is a question of vital interest to managers and involves analyzing dramaturgical performances. People can figure out that a store or a restaurant has a front stage. Yet analysis might stop once they attach a concept to a performance, rather than consider bigger questions about what those performances mean in a more cumulative sense, such as how the store benefits economically from good service performances. Analyzing interviews is more complex when considering how some people have huge disadvantages in social interaction if they have to camouflage some discrediting aspect of their identity, like having been incarcerated or fired from a previous job.

In general, scholarly writings on Goffman's works can be collapsed into four types: (1) collections of Goffman's own writings, (2) brief presentations of dramaturgical ideas in introductory primers, (3) specialist interpretations of the ideas, and (4) applying adherents. The first category includes excerpts of Goffman's writings, ideas, and examples. The second category refers to scholarly works that introduce Goffman's dramaturgical approach to students in brief as part of anthologies and textbook readings for courses and which usually involve a mix of introductory passages and some descriptive examples.

The third category consists of analyses by various theorists who interpret Goffman's articles and books as sophisticated scholarly products, identifying what he "really meant." Specialist interpreters are less interested in writing for lay readers, as they frame their writings for other specialists who also debate the meanings of Goffman's ideas and their connections to other theoretical traditions. These specialist interpreters offer an exhaustive analysis of Goffman's ideas and their contributions to sociology. This theoretical debating is sophisticated and important but not for beginners. If someone is uninterested in how Goffman's ideas relate to other theoretical schools, in how his biography and scholarly career shaped his work or in debating what he should have done more of, and other more internal theoretical housekeeping issues in social science, these works will not be your cup of tea.[1] The fourth type of literature references scholars, both in sociology and that carry out interdisciplinary scholarship, who apply a dramaturgical approach in their research, collecting relevant data and publishing their findings with an aim of expanding applications of the dramaturgical perspective. These works examine dramaturgical activities across diverse settings.

Dramaturgy has tremendous contemporary relevance. Dramaturgical analysis has also become an interdisciplinary perspective on social life, with anthropologists, humanists, marketers, sociologists, and psychologists all contributing ideas. The goal here is to integrate some

---

[1] Alternatively, if that approach to scholarly work is your cup of tea, this book's reference section will interest you, as it lists works by some of the leading scholars of Goffman's oeuvre. You should also access the website *The Erving Goffman Archives*, curated by Professor Dmitri Shalin at UNLV. This website has a collection that shines a biographical light on Erving Goffman's life, teaching, and the development of his ideas and a full bibliography of Goffman's writings.

of these interdisciplinary works in focusing on the applicability and sociological usefulness of the perspective while highlighting insights that the perspective offers into contemporary commerce, popular culture, workplace life, crime, and the Internet. This book will turn now to considering updates in dramaturgical sociology for interested readers by focusing wholly on how a dramaturgical approach sheds light on aspects of contemporary life. A big motivation behind writing this book is also to present great works from scholars who have developed ideas that capitalize on dramaturgical concepts, but where those connections are lesser known across disciplines.

Dramaturgy is considered a microsociological approach, meaning that the focus is concerned with small groups and individual behaviors, rather than large-scale societal phenomena, like comparative crime rates in Western Europe or how public policy affects poverty rates. Some sociologists hope to use microsociological insights to offer a greater understanding of more "big picture" issues, an effort Gary Alan Fine (2012) identifies as *sociological miniaturism*, in which people can analyze how larger social orders are composed of many intersecting "tiny publics" or organized small groups. According to Fine (2012, p. 5), the virtue of studying intersecting tiny publics is that "within these spaces" are "the core features of social organization, features that are often attributed to larger institutions. Through an interaction order—*a field of performance*—phenomena that we attribute to external, trans-situational forces have effects."

Gary Alan Fine (2012) has developed an argument for sociological miniaturism that will feature in this book. The argument is as follows:

> The miniaturist approach posits three fundamental claims about social reality: transcendence, representation, and generalizability. First, social reality is *transcendent* in that social processes operate on multiple levels. Processes such as justice, inequality, or communion that apply to one level of analysis (for example, the interpersonal) can also be observed on other levels (for example, the institutional) but within different structural contexts. Second, this approach treats the behavior of individuals as *representative* of social order in larger entities. The individual can stand for the group and, more important, *is taken as* standing for that group by individuals and institutions that thus recognize and respond to the individual actions of an actor as those of a *collective* actor. So, for example, the behavior of clerks can—and often does—reflect on the store or government that employs them. While experiencing bureaucracies

through the individual actions of clerks, clients consider these clerks to be representations of the bureaucracy or sometimes even reflections of the states or institutions in which the bureaucracy is embedded. Thus, a citizen seeking to renew his driver's license decides—based on cultural representations and on the perceived typicality of the interaction— whether the clerk behind the desk represents herself, the Department of Motor Vehicles, or the entire state government. The behavioral options and motivations of individual actors have recognizable parallels in attributions of behavior to groups, organizations, and other collective units. Although individuals need not always represent organizations or be taken as such, this behavioral synecdoche is routine, comfortable, and grounded in commonsense assumptions. The third component of the miniaturist approach is the *generalizability* of social processes. (p. 6)

Nine Contributions Dramaturgical Thinking Can Make to Enhance Sociological Thinking

This book treats transcendence, representation, and generalizability as reasons to consider dramaturgical analysis as potentially offering significant sociological contributions. Yet sociological miniaturism is a broad starting point. There are other contributions that dramaturgical analysis can make to enhance a reader's sociological thinking.

1. Dramaturgy provides a conceptual vocabulary for analyzing the microworld of social interaction (Scheff, 2006). People notice and observe patterns of minute microlevel behaviors but may lack an existing terminology to encapsulate and examine those activities as a type of social interaction. Goffman identified analytic terms and a vocabulary to use to describe these activities.

   For example, Goffman coined the phrase *civil inattention* to describe when people give a superficial acknowledgment of one another but then purposely decline a more detailed interaction with each other. So, for example, people in crowded city spaces may acknowledge the presence of others in proximity to them but make clear through nonverbal cues that they wish to maintain a non-involvement with them. We may further manifest a concerted ignorance of people's problematic behavior, no matter how obvious that behavior, to avoid interaction or as a protective practice not to embarrass or spoil someone's performance and disrupt the situation. People purposively pretend not to notice people or things to avoid having to deal with them, which they might have to if they signaled being more aware of them. In a deeper sense, civil inattention is to some degree a form of social and self-preservation because of the costs involved in breaching interactional boundaries. People perpetuate some blind spots on purpose.

When people are taught to attend to distinct actions, we learn that those actions carry social importance. When we learn not to notice certain actions in particular, "out loud" in given situations, we reflect having bought into a message to not highlight something as a socially important task and a vital component of social integration. I've learned not to express my actual view that you must have had work done, or that you obviously have inherited wealth but want to pass as a "working stiff," or that person X is a hypocrite. Thank goodness that others around me accept an implicit mutual truce of not exposing my contradictions either. Much social life between resourced equals operates like a mutually assured destruction form of deterrence based on each party agreeing not to notice "flaws" in publicly embarrassing ways.

There are many concepts like civil inattention and concerted ignorance in the dramaturgical lexicon that enable readers to gain a greater analytic purchase on what the smaller actions that people engage in everyday can mean in a larger sense. For example, engaging in civil inattention is important for keeping the peace in interactions with strangers. In addition to empowering people's capacity to conceptualize actions around them, establishing a conceptual vocabulary for the microworld is also useful to organize larger-scale analytic investigations. Goffman coined many terms for practices that everyone immediately recognized existed but that had heretofore been unnamed. Goffman kicked an analytic door wide open by enabling people to conceptualize the microworld that they know is out there but that needs an orienting conceptual map to allow people to discuss these ideas and happenings more clearly.

2. Dramaturgy offers an approach to examine and identify *idiocultures,* which are cultures that small groups develop. In a sociological sense, idiocultures reference shared meanings, norms, understandings, and values that small groups create, share, and sustain, that organize their activities (Fine, 2012). The thinking here is that values that are important pillars in a small group's culture are embodied and made visible through their dramaturgical performances. A Greek

organization has an idioculture of initiation and rush that is meant to socialize people into shared values that make that organization distinct. Groups that range from carnival workers, deans at colleges, and *World of Warcraft* players all have expectations and values for behaviors that cohere into and comprise that group's culture.

3. Dramaturgical activities demonstrate an infrastructure and order of organizing that are building blocks for larger societal activities and rituals. *Meso-level* theories incorporate microsociological data to reach conclusions about larger social phenomena. In lay language, a successful meso-theory level connects the everyday and large-scale social implications. Several sociologists have developed meso-level ideas that build on dramaturgy, so greater familiarity with the idea of the meso contribution will provide readers with more insights into the claims that these theories make. Examples of these approaches include Cultural Pragmatics (Alexander, 2004); Frames and Interaction Orders (Goffman, 1974, 1983); Inhabited Institutionalism (Hallett, 2010); Interaction Ritual Chains (Collins, 2004); Negotiated Orders, Tiny Publics, Sociological Miniaturism (Fine, 2012); Performance Circuits (Wherry, 2012); and Dramaturgical Infrastructure (Shulman, 2007). While these concepts differ in nature and scope, they all reference dramaturgical actions as representing routinized means of social organization among small groups and organizations that have cumulative, more macrosociologically relevant products as results. Dramaturgical actions reveal routine means of social organization among small groups and organizations. We can analyze how these actions work, how they are routine, and what implications result from them.

4. Dramaturgy offers an analytic basis for exploring how people control information in their conduct with others and why they might conceal some types of information while expressing others. This issue is particularly salient in Goffman's (1963) book *Stigma*, which addresses how people manage interactions with others when a discrediting or discreditable social attribute (homosexuality, illness, for example) exists that strains social interactions. As people both keep secrets and try to access them in others, the ideas dramaturgy offers in this area are useful to know. These ideas also link to related topics such as deception and trust, which also interest many.

5. Dramaturgy is a perspective that yields insights into social interactions in the workplace. Dramaturgy and impression management can help people to understand institutionally required emotional labor on workers' parts and also how emotional labor affects how people display and react to aspects of gender, race, and

other demographic features while working (Roberts, 2005). Emotional labor is a thriving subject of inquiry in sociology with numerous scholars researching the sociology of emotion. How does that work draw on strengths of the dramaturgical perspective? Further, how do people perform effectively as leaders in a full range of human relations activities such as interviewing, mentoring, and recruiting, all of which integrate dramaturgical actions?

6. Dramaturgy can help examine the mechanisms through which contemporary marketing activity works in an economic period that now some reference as an experience economy. Daniel Boorstin (1962) has written that the use of imagery and illusion is ascendant in modern business practices, and George Ritzer has noted that the rationalization and reenchantment of society is pervasive in what he calls "cathedrals of consumption." Dramaturgy and staging are key in these aspects of contemporary business, and people are well served in being able to analyze these settings using this approach. There is a *rationalization of symbols* now, in which increasing organizational and bureaucratic rationalization of signs has led to a corresponding *rationalization of dramaturgy* in everyday life.

7. Dramaturgy offers a valuable perspective for analyzing the new empirical "stages" that online social interaction represents. Dramaturgy is a perspective that helps analyze these new empirical settings and stages in everyday life that technology brings, such as in online life and in the new contacts and social processes that accompany globalization. How do people communicate with each other in different ways attributable to technology, such as texting? How do people use these new mediums to do impression management? In terms of globalization, people have new forums to understand in conducting business in settings that offer them more diversity than they have previously encountered and must manage.

8. The dramaturgical approach is excellent in helping people transcend taken for granted and kneejerk explanations for behavior. Where people might think that individuals behave in specific directions only because of biological impulses or that they act unthinkingly, the dramaturgical perspective requires studying people's decision-making about actions rather than assuming that people do not plan them strategically or without a modicum of thought.

9. Dramaturgical activities comprise mechanisms through which some groups exert dominance over others (Schwalbe & Shay, 2014). For example, the presentations of self that people enact are perceived as more or less creditable depending on the reactions that audiences

have to the categoric identities (gender and race) of the actors (Schwalbe & Shay, 2014, p. 159). Expectations of deference and demeanor and people feeling that they must hew to established social conventions in their actions also maintains existing inequalities and disadvantages (Schwalbe & Shay, 2014). How people control information selectively in interaction can be motivated by a desire to gain power or avoid stigmatizing. Groups that are depicted negatively relative to others lose ground to them, such as in the case of gender and advertisements (Goffman, 1979).

Other important insights can be taken from applications of the dramaturgical perspective. The above list is not meant to be exhaustive but to reflect some choices of interest as regard to this book.

FOUR

Workplaces as Stages

Individual commitment to a group effort—that is what makes a team work, a company work, a society work, a civilization work.

—Vince Lombardi

I want to share something with you: The three little sentences that will get you through life. Number 1: Cover for me. Number 2: Oh, good idea, Boss! Number 3: It was like that when I got here.

—Homer Simpson

Introduction: Dramaturgy in Organizations and Workplaces

Have you ever felt compelled to accommodate a difficult boss or cranky customer? Deliberated over what outfit to wear at work? Strategized with family and friends over how to impress colleagues? Have you (surreptitiously) not followed an onerous rule and hidden that violation? Allied with coworkers to form a covert team working against rivals? Rummaging through memories of past employment experiences can make people appreciate just how much impression management occurs in workplaces.

This chapter begins by outlining how Goffman's dramaturgical ideas help conceptualize interactions inside workplaces. Following that section, the chapter surveys how scholars of impression management have illustrated and advanced these concepts. Two areas of emphasis are research into how people display emotion in the workplace and the concept of the *total institution* as an evolving organizational form. Overall, this chapter's purpose is to showcase and update insights that the dramaturgical approach offers for analyzing people's experiences in the workplace.

In *The Presentation of Self in Everyday Life*, Erving Goffman (1959, p. xi) stated that his study was of "the way in which the individual in ordinary work situations presents himself and his activities to others." Analyzing presentation and performance in a workplace was the original focal base of Goffman's dramaturgical analysis. Many examples in his book come from his ethnographic research in the Shetland Islands, where he observed interactions between guests and employees. Goffman (1959) analyzed how people worked in what he called a social establishment.

> A social establishment is any place surrounded by fixed barriers to perception in which a particular kind of activity regularly takes place. I have suggested that any social establishment may be studied profitably from the point of view of impression management. Within the walls of a social establishment we find a team of performers who cooperate to present an audience a given definition of the situation. This will include the conception of own team and of audience and assumptions considering the ethos that is to be maintained by rules of politeness and decorum. We often find a division into back region, where the performance of a routine is prepared, and front region, where the performance is presented. Access to these regions is controlled in order to prevent the audience from seeing backstage and to prevent outsiders from coming into a performance that is not addressed to them. Among members of the team, we find that familiarity prevails, solidarity is likely to develop, and that secrets that could give the show away are shared and kept. (p. 238)

This quote identifies prominent points that apply to any dramaturgical analyses of workplaces. Goffman notes that places of work have particular kinds of activity occuring there, with physical and aesthetic boundaries in place regulating who can access what activities. Performances occur for customers and other observers in the front region, and back regions exist where preparatory work occurs for these front region performances. Backstage areas are sensitive and privileged places that are usually reserved to particular team members. One goal of preserving this space is to avoid communication out of character on the front stage and to maintain privacy for workers.

Teams of workers cooperate to present particular lines regarding work that constitute prevailing definitions of the situation of the social establishment's purpose. There is an ethos at hand, sometimes formed as workplace mission statements or in training about the organizational culture, that sums up values and actions that define the "lines" that teams support and that constitute "face" for the establishment. Team members develop loyalty over time from sharing performance work. Teammates have stakes in the impressions audiences form about the social establishment and its offerings.

Goffman's extended quote presents a basic summation of how the dramaturgical approach addresses different aspects of workplaces. Further analysis can explore how definitions of situations form and how workers perform in the front region. Another focus is maintaining team cohesion and morale. The organizational back region is a feature that impacts productivity. How is work produced? How much people really know about how work gets done is exposed when access to that backstage is granted.

Examining face-to-face interaction between customers and workers is our starting point. Face-to-face interactions are the means through which larger scale interactions operate in workplaces and a key forum through which people experience organizational impacts. As Goffman (1983) wrote,

> A great deal of the work of organizations—decision making, the transmission of information, the close coordination of physical tasks is done face-to-face, requires being done in this way, and is vulnerable to face-to-face effects. Differently put . . . as agents of social organizations of any scale, from states to households, can be persuaded, cajoled, flattered, intimidated, or otherwise influenced by effects only achievable in face-to-face dealings. (p. 3)

Taken further, this perspective suggests that face-to-face interactions accumulate to help comprise organizations. Consider interactions like admissions counselors meeting with prospective students, professors teaching classes, a college president speaking to administrators, development officers calling donors, cafeteria chefs preparing food, groups of students talking about a class, and maintenance workers repairing a building. Such actions, among countless repeated others, constitute in total the large-scale daily organization that is a college. An impression management perspective does not consider an organization as an abstract monolithic entity. There is no examining organizations as depopulated entities, or as empty shells that somehow do things, while the actions of people inside organizations are taken for granted and remain ignored or unexplored.

For example, a college could launch a development campaign as an organizational initiative. One could speak of colleges as having different endowments and following different investment strategies, and at that level, the category of all colleges constitutes the analytic unit, based on comparing the actions of different large-scale organizations. Yet to understand how any single campaign or investment decision in this category is built, one must understand how people work to attain those outcomes. You can compare donations, but you don't understand how donations happen unless you unpack the dynamics of doing "the ask." For people operating within the impression management perspective, analysis starts from the bottom up and examines ongoing face-to-face interactions as studying organizational activity. This choice comes with some obvious analytic limitations. Many interactions occur in organizations, and they all cannot be examined or even known. People can cherry-pick, under sample, or accidently miss interactions that bear on their analyses. There are also means of delivering actions and decisions not based in face-to-face interaction. Knowing whether one has captured the right interactions from which to generalize is a problem. These concerns noted, the dramaturgical approach emphasizes examining what people (the actors) do together inside the social establishment using props and facilities associated with their work there.[1] Start with the physical front that exists in workplaces. There is usually a servicescape where services are delivered. There are boundary settings that organize work into private and public regions, such as signs on doors stating, "For employees only." A front

---

[1] Not all actions by organizational actors are limited to a single physical plant. Organizations also exist as entities outside a physical headquarters, as there is "working from home, business trips, conversations over the phone, all of which constitutes forums for interaction in which organizational and personal matters get sorted." See "Organizational Analysis: Goffman and Dramaturgy," Chapter 12 in *Oxford Handbook of Sociology, Social Theory and Organization Studies: Contemporary Currents*, by P. K. Manning, 2008, p. 289.

stage uses equipment intended to induce a particular impression, like outfitting an office luxuriously.

Goffman (1959, p. 27) notes that many fronts preexist us in that people can be assigned to roles. Fronts can be well established and already pre-assigned and trained as de rigueur in workplaces. People in workplaces, for example, wear uniforms as a part of that social establishment's front. Some uniforms imply seriousness like ones worn by militarized guards. For others, like athletes, models, and personal trainers, their bodies are also the "uniform" and part of the front stage. Many different fronts exist in workplaces. Consider how offices are decorated and the accoutrements on display in waiting rooms. Car showrooms entice buyers to explore the vehicles. Some retail stores pump in smells to induce a state of mind that attempts to prime purchases.

A "reception" area, for example, is a designated location where people receive clients. The name alone communicates that a reception space is also a venue for shaping a front calculated to produce a particular impression. An advertising agency might sport a "cool" exterior in the reception area that exhibits the company's creativity and inventiveness. Many restaurants have themes. Websites ignore the appearance and design of home pages at their peril, as people are impatient browsers and want to see what they want quickly and efficiently. Hence the *Google* home page uses a minimalist design that allows people to search for a link they want with no delay.

Fronts encompass appearance, manner, and setting. A workplace works to unite these elements, which should cohere in performance. People judge individuals by how consistent the appearance, manner, and setting of their performances are. Police officers sometimes stop people who wear heavy clothing on hot days where there have been burglaries. Politicians running for president are coached to "appear presidential." Sometimes they make mistakes. Michael Dukakis posing in a tank during the 1988 presidential campaign was a mistake. Former President George W. Bush passed himself off as a country, NASCAR-loving good ol' boy, yet he went to Harvard and Yale and spent time in a family compound in Maine, which are not exactly folkloric characteristics of "good ol' boy-ness." Observers scrutinize the coherence between appearance, manner, and setting in businesses. For example, if we perceive that "things just don't look right" at a business, we may move to an alternative. We could plan to go to a restaurant, but on arrival decide that the restaurant is too empty, so the food must not be good. This conclusion would not be based on actually tasting the food; nonetheless, we judge that product by what we think of the surroundings. We can work in the reverse way. Sometimes people want to experience a "hole in the wall," where the décor is horrendous but the food may be on a much higher level. That inconsistency can work to help some businesses.

Performance Teams: Dramaturgical Circumspection, Discipline, and Loyalty

A performance team refers to "any set of individuals who cooperate in staging a single routine" (Goffman, 1959, p. 79). The routine staged is the activity associated with the social establishment. This idea of staging acknowledges that people perform rather than just "are." This point is magnified within a business context. As Goffman (1959) writes,

> There are many sets of persons who feel that they could not stay in business, whatever their business, if they limited themselves to the gentlemanly means of influencing the individual who observes them. At some point or other in the round of their activity they feel it is necessary to band together and directly manipulate the impression that they give. The observed becomes a performing team and the observers become an audience. Actions which appear to be done to objects become gestures addressed to the audience. The round of activity becomes dramatized. (p. 251)

To perform successfully, a team must proceed through different processes. They must establish a "party line," maintain loyalty to the team's performance, and sustain that "line" effectively during the show. To carry out those tasks, participants must trust partners. People cannot switch teams mid-performance, meaning that they betray one team to side with another during the show. Imagine, for example, a car salesperson switching from selling a car for the dealership to buying the car for the customer in the middle of the sale, telling the customer what to pay and taking on the manager. To organize performances, teams try to control as much of the performance setting as possible, with a person serving as a "director" and some division of performative labor allocated among different members during shows. Directors and team members will assign "parts" and work together to bring wayward performers back into line, avoid disruptions, and repair them as much as possible.

In *Presentation of Self in Everyday Life,* Goffman (1959) analyzed some of these processes under the terms *dramaturgical circumspection, dramaturgical discipline,* and *dramaturgical loyalty.* Management duties can mean being in charge of *dramaturgical circumspection.* Dramaturgical circumspection involves focusing and taking the steps needed for the best performance to emerge out of the team. People want to arrange the best setting, cultivate the appropriate audience, and eliminate factors that might impinge on giving a successful performance. The manager must always keep a wary eye to encourage the best possible outcome. Great examples of dramaturgical circumspection exist in planning political campaign events. For example, a Republican candidate might speak at a rally organized by a senior citizen group of NRA members and take only prescreened questions. A Democratic candidate might take only prescreened questions after speaking at a pro–environmental regulation rally. In both settings, campaign managers work to ensure a positive reception that in turn helps produce a successful performance.

Dramaturgical discipline refers to team members being in control of all facets of performance possible during the show. That discipline extends, for example, to expressing no unmeant gestures, being poised, composed, and ready. In conjunction with teammates, discipline also encompasses keeping on top of and managing any disruptions to performances. Members of teams are to demonstrate this discipline during performances. An example Goffman cites is when parents believe they can take a child to a nice restaurant and count on the child's dramaturgical discipline in that formal situation. A different example is when coworkers worry about depending on a "loose cannon" on the team to hold her or his tongue when the team meets with important audiences.

Dramaturgical loyalty refers to feeling obligated to fellow performers on the team, which encourages them to perform appropriately in the mutual performance and not ruin the show. This loyalty hopefully develops over time through positive relations between coworkers. However, organizations also exercise social control to try to monitor and ensure dramaturgical loyalty. Coworkers will observe other workers to detect whether anyone is not fully committed to putting forth the best work performance for the team.

Goffman coined several concepts to describe interactions within teams. The term *treatment of the absent* refers to how teams speak about those who are out of earshot. *Team collusion* involves the staging work that team members engage in to carry off performances. An interesting example is that professional wrestlers will often, unbeknownst to fans, "call" the match while performing, whispering to the other wrestler what move is coming for them to respond appropriately in order to choreograph the match. The wrestlers are working together to offer the audience the best show, so the more experienced or senior wrestler calls out different move sequences to appeal to the crowd's mood. These communications occur during close-up holds so that audiences cannot see the communications. The result is a team collusion that makes the most out of "staging talk" to put forth a good performance.

Organizations and Order

In the dramaturgical model, a team is not a social organization like a company or a social structure as a whole. The team is a small group that, through interaction, stages the business of larger entities by defining situations in their behalf. In his study *Asylums*, Goffman (1961, pp. 175–176) defined a formal organization as a "system of purposively coordinated activities designed to produce some overall explicit ends. The intended product may be material artifacts, decisions, or information, and may be distributed among participants in a variety of ways" (cited in Manning, 2008b). Face-to-face interactions constitute the "purposively coordinated activities," with actors in the form of "singles," "withs," and "teams" animating those interactions. Ideas motivate and coordinate those actions, with persons being jointly focused on managing the situation at hand in the encounter between them. As Goffman (1983, p. 5) writes, "Orderliness is predicated on a large base of shared cognitive presuppositions, if not normative ones, and self-sustained restraints."

People follow a loose recognizable plot of sorts that is at hand in their encounters with others. Most interactions between people have already had the table set, meaning that people mostly know what to do in these situations, or what is expected that they appear to do in the situation, although they may or may not meet that expectation or may fake the appearance or intent to do so. That interactions are coordinated reflects order in the organization. People approach their interactions with others knowing that in most situations, the forthcoming actions are preordained, those actions being laminated by the shared frame that people have about "what is done in situations we decide are like this one." That order does not mean that people *do* exactly what norms might urge. People approach situations with self-interests, and the structure in which they are embedded has its own interests. These individual interests in the interaction order and the social structure of settings in which they occur are "loosely coupled"—meaning that neither side automatically yields full compliance from the other. People can conflict, concede, change norms, and try to resist the order imposed on them. Interactions are ordered and entwined with social structure, but there is flexibility, as people are not automatons and order sometimes bends if not breaks.

An orderly situation produces, and is produced by, subsequent interactions in a mutually reinforcing relation. As a small example, we understand the need to greet someone appropriate to the situation. Each time we do further demonstrates that order to others and ourselves and reinforces that activity as "what is done." That people work together in this way to manage greetings is clear. People exchange high fives, fist bumps, hugs, kiss noises, handshakes, nods, cordial greeting utterances, and formal greeting utterances in appropriate forms, which mark understandings between all present of the nature of social relationships between the involved parties. The exchange expresses that one understands those relations, and the exchanges express a working consensus to acknowledge them before others, whether someone truly wishes to be as friendly or formal as indicated.

What is shared publicly in this kind of example and with many others (with or without private disagreement) is a working consensus of public agreement to meet accepted ends and protocols, often organizational ones. Just watch a youth coach meet with her or his charges at a team talk, and see the team members nod and visibly assent to the coach's claims and instructions. You can see that team members understand that a coach's injunctions are not to be challenged openly, even though private conversations afterward could reveal a cascade of disagreement.

At work, there is a "party line," and usually, no public disagreement with that party line emerges. Workers empower the working consensus by giving public fealty to that line, which demonstrates fealty to the social order there and reinforces that others should conform, which they may well sincerely do or wisely appear to do. Order and working consensus are evident in actions, but they are not actions alone, even though they are evident in them. Order and working consensus are ideas and motivations that inhere in personas and situations that people engage in when joining and working within an organization and in work as a team in everyday life. These ideas are manifest, for example, in organizational scripts, managerial cultures, and employee aspirations and ideologies.

The Dramaturgy of Meetings

Consider the example of meetings. Organizations favor the appearance of having a united front, where all employees are solidly committed to the mission at hand. An embassy, as the official representative communicator of a country's interests, must have coherent, clear, and uniform messaging across both home and host country (Van Praet, 2009). Ellen Van Praet (2009) examined how an embassy staff fashions that front during staff meetings, as meetings serve as a locus for shaping those fronts. Meetings constitute occasions where face-to-face interactions reflect and form power relations in an organization more generally. Van Praet sought to understand how that power surfaces at the face-to-face level, by seeing how people create influence and dominance over others, through ongoing, moment-to-moment, organizationally set activity. While Van Praet studied staff meetings in her case, keep in mind how many kinds of meetings work out power within an organization. For example, events like stockholder meetings and meetings of "the Board" are highly significant, and they also often involve stage-managed performances (Biehl-Missal, 2011).

Van Praet revealed how influence flows during interactions at meetings. For example, when a powerful person entered the room, attendees stopped talking, fell silent, and paid observable attention to the authority. Those actions clarify to all present what individual gets to command the room. A pronounced form of that situation occurs when a judge enters a room and people in the courtroom rise. Van Praet comments that this kind of display of "formalized respect is a staging that clearly establishes power." At other times, meetings are occasions when people with different levels of power coordinate together to achieve goals. That end may require overcoming differences in status so that people across the hierarchy can give each other enough mutual support to overcome status-based impediments to achieving effective action. Van Praet notes, for example, that pursuing common causes at work successfully "needs to overcome resentments" that could bubble up at meetings.

A hierarchy typically exists in who talks and in what order. There are formal procedures that govern the meeting's structure. Yet people can also speak freely in some conversations. People work out a united front to project to audiences outside of the meeting. They inspect arguments and test different strategies in anticipation of how others outside the inner circle will react to them. The ambassador demonstrated power in organizing all the work to arrive at a "front"—an official position and line for all employees to be cognizant of and follow. Meetings are venues during which people direct traffic in comments, and in which some people police others. People watch others to make sure that they pay attention and appear engaged. Yet there is common cause, as meetings are also a backstage space where people work on preparing later performances.

Capturing the social complexity involved in such occasions is a virtue of the dramaturgical approach. A meeting can be a social occasion where there is a nimble accommodation of different types of social traffic. Meetings integrate hierarchy, status, policing, and rule over others, while at the same time, a democratic component can emerge in some interaction, as people work together to arrive at the best way forward. People build a common front and generate the lines a team is to take, along with additional strategies intended to get an audience to accept proposed lines and react accordingly.

Examining face-to-face interactions between participants offers a means to understand all the above goings-on. For example, people offer different impressions to audiences depending on their status levels. They usually care more about impressing high-status people than low-status ones. Organizational settings offer opportunities to examine how different types of audiences connect to different types of self-presentation. People experience a heightened self-consciousness when the stakes of an interaction increase. Other audience factors include size and whether the observers are familiar or unfamiliar, insiders or outsiders, or hostile or friendly (Gardener & Martinko, 1988).

Contemporary Takes on Dramaturgy in Organizations

Scholars of organizations have developed a range of analytic directions built on dramaturgical concepts. For example, David Boje (1989) has categorized different kinds of performances in organizations:

> *Performance programs*, which are "stored repeatable programs" of performance that organizational participants put on to control the social order in the organization, like a bartender bantering with regulars; *games* between employees which are routine social interplay between employees, like teasing in familiar ways among accustomed characters; *linguistic* choices intended to give impressions, like using big words for one audience and

slang for another; *storytelling*, which refers to tales like war stories that workers tell to make sense of and influence activities, like suspicions of administrators based on "what happened when"; *ritual* events that are typical within the organization. (pp. 84–89)

Peter K. Manning (2008a, 2008b) has also identified appropriate foci for a dramaturgical theory of organizations. His list includes dramaturgically analyzable phenomena such as (1) displays of organizational action, (2) impacts of rules and records, (3) organizational rhetoric, (4) exercises (and non-exercises) of power in organizations, (5) organizations as career crucibles, (6) trust, (7) material components of organizations, and (8) organizations as partners in processes of according honor and status (and presumably of not according status). Lest people view organizations as purely rational venues, Manning (2008b, p. 281) also notes that organizations can be "seething cauldrons of emotion, rivalries and passions," where constraints on performance and people's hidden agendas infiltrate interactions.

Boje (1989) and Manning's (2008a, 2008b) ideas demonstrate some directions for analyzing people's performances in organizations. Scholars of organizations disagree, however, about how far to take the theatrical analogy. Some view dramaturgy as a metaphor that brings organizational processes into useful analytic relief, but they hesitate to conceive of organizations operating *as* theater. Boje, alternatively, rejects the dramaturgy as metaphor approach. For Boje, organizations *are* theater, in the simultaneous enacting of scripts across what he calls the "meta-theater" of organizations. For all individuals, impression management in organizations matters. Here performance comprises means through which people achieve more power and ingratiate themselves with others (Gardner & Martinko, 1988). Face-to-face interactions process people and actions in an organization's work and serve as paths to downward or upward mobility.

For Boje, many diverse performances are all ongoing inside organizations. Hence, he suggests that organizations be appreciated as sites of "meta-theater." From this vantage point, organizations are theaters with many overlaying performances occurring at any one time. Boje's perspective builds from Kenneth Burke's work on dramatism. Burkean adherents refer to drama as practiced activity, not as an initial analytic metaphor, as a dramaturgical analogy does. According to Boje and Rosile (2003),

An organization is assumed to be a multiplicity of stages on which different plays are acted out by organizational members (actors) simultaneously. There is a metascript composed of the integrated senior executive's scripts combined with scripts from the less powerful to be pieced together in a narrative and set of stories that compose the organization. (p. 24)

The Interaction Order and the Negotiated Order

Goffman (1983, p. 1) used the term *interaction order* to describe a "loose coupling between interactional practices and social structure." He noted, "The workings of the interaction order can easily be viewed . . . as enabling conventions, in the sense of the ground rules for a game, the provisions of a traffic code or the rules of syntax of a language" (p. 5). These interactions establish an order that offers benefits of predictability, reliability, and legibility (Misztal, 2001, p. 314).

Workplaces have interactions that represent ordered situations; within them, face-to-face encounters repeat themselves predictably. Those interactions build up nested inside an enabling social structure. Because given environments have definite expectations that are repeated over time, those settings contain predictable enabling conventions. Social structures come with a sense of situational propriety that participants recognize. They can read what is going on in an encounter and what to do. That cognition and enabling knowledge, along with similarly clued-in other people, come to provide an order to subsequent activities. A single interaction can become a strand that over time and repetition becomes a web organizing activity. That web links social structure and behaviors. The interaction order allows people to reconcile structural impingements and shared definitions of reality, so that "everyone knows what is to go on here."

The level of workplace dominance runs a spectrum from what Goffman called *total institutions*, which seek to control all interactions by individuals (like in prisons) and resocialize them to an organizational ideal, to organizations that are mostly free of controlling expectations for its denizens. Again, the ideas that inspire order may be sourced in the organizational host, but the spontaneity that workers have gives organizational routines some variability, so a governing idea can be transformed in interaction orders that follow. As Manning (2008a) writes,

> Internally, organizations are clusters of work routines, dense interactions, cliques, and embedded groups that are constituted and reconstituted over time. The "place" of such standard conceptual paraphernalia as roles, selves, groups and even persons are negotiable in interactional sequences and are not free standing or incontrovertible. (p. 687)

While predictable compliant responses are important, variation in how people actually act, and as a consequence, what organizations produce, are resulting effects of interaction. There is a raw material and base structure in what people do to constitute the organization, but the best-laid plans evolve and morph, attributable to varieties of agendas among people in an organization. To capture that complexity, the analytic focus of the interaction order is fixed on how individuals act within and inhabit organizations. Sociologist Tim Hallett (2010) is spurring institutional and organizational analysts to move more in the direction of researching how people's work, and their understandings of their work, "inhabits" institutions.

The point here is complex. An analytic understanding must account for people accepting fixed routines—the party line—yet improvising off those routines in multiple ways and offshoots. A sociological tradition referred to as the *negotiated order* approach examines how people adjust formal rules and individual affinities. Developed by Anselm Strauss and colleagues (1963) and developed further by Gary Alan Fine (1984) and David Maines (1982), the negotiated order perspective stresses the socially constructed nature of formal and informal administration in the workplace. Strauss (1978) argued that the negotiated order

> could be conceived of as the sum total of the organization's rules and policies, along with whatever agreements, understandings, pacts, contracts, and other working arrangements currently obtained. These include agreements at every level of the organization, of every clique and coalition and include covert as well as overt agreements. (pp. 5–6)

The negotiated order approach "emphasizes the construction of organizational culture, through analyzing how workers create the meanings that are embedded in routine organizational activities" (Fine, 1984, p. 247).

This tradition analyzes how people organize themselves to accomplish work "by the book" and how they "freelance at work" by negotiating informal working arrangements within a given organizational structure (Fine, 1984). This orientation was a response to criticisms of formal understandings of how people work. The negotiated order theorists believed that traditional explanations were at odds with how people actually negotiated and put into place informal understandings of how to do their work. Documenting these arrangements is a hallmark of organizational ethnography. No organizational sociologist is surprised when people state one set of official procedures for working while in actuality following others. In Melville

Dalton's (1959) *Men Who Manage*, for example, workers consistently bypass "onerous" regulations through shadow administration. These informal systems of administration exist to distribute unofficial rewards to valued executives, to forgo safety requirements, and to stave off disputes between union and management. The interaction order and negotiated order approaches demonstrate that consensus can be a mirage and an apparent community just a temporary illusion. For example, people can comply with a rule, but that does not mean that they always will or even that they actually support the rule though they abide by it. People can camouflage inappropriate intent and action while still appearing to comply. Someone can conform 10 times and then act against the rule a different day or help someone else resist an imposed rule. An apparent rebel, a tough government investigator, or a union member can be a double agent secretly in cahoots with management. Not all workplaces bubble over with minor intrigues, but they are also not full of norm-driven robots who perform like marionettes.

People work to get others to do things that they do not want to do, or that are not in their interest, and pass off those requests as being in the mark's interest. People will encourage others to follow rules and state why doing so is important, even though conforming may not actually be good for that individual, and the cajoling person avers complying himself or herself (Goffman, 1983, p. 5). We all can recognize the criticism inherent in the adage "Do as I say and not as I do." As a result, inquiring how long systems of managing people last and why they do not collapse under the burden of some noncompliance are great questions. The largest analytic issue at hand, though, remains appreciating the complexity of organizations, which all have stable routines and little pockets of resistance in them, some of which is in the organization's interest, and some of which is not.

A good analytic approach enables us to peer behind the appearance of stolidity in organizational routines and rules to try to make sense of the Machiavellian machinations of all levels of employees that occur in the backstage. The dramaturgical approach to organizations acknowledges that level of organizational underlife (Goffman, 1963). The coexistence of conformity and autonomy and resistance to conformity is an acknowledged part of working. People can feel committed to the organization's purpose, and other times subvert that purpose by freelancing or converting organizational resources and aims to personal use. Straightforward rules and maxims that mean to be helpful in understanding how organizations work are, unfortunately, sometimes unrealistic depictions of the complexity in how organizational life unfolds.

Manning (2008a) observes,

> Goffman's aim is to show how situated constraints work on actions what-
> ever their setting. The moral constraints on "rational choice," on "gaming"
> or any strategic analysis errs because it does not begin with (a) the moral
> meanings imputed to action prior to the first move, (b) the fundamental
> inequalities produced by the unequal distribution of resources prior to
> action, (c) constraints that do not inhere in the rewards at issue—the
> investment of moral stakes in the actions undocumented in the formal
> schemata. Thus, organizational "rationality" cannot be explicated from the
> actor's point of view outside practice-based exchanges. (p. 681)

Individual agendas, moral or otherwise, are not inherent in formal procedures. People's actions inject them into routines, and they are only visible when they affect and alter action and when the interactional level is
examined. The interaction order, as a pattern of interaction, has significant
meaning at the individual and structural levels. For example, the repeated
patterning of interviews as auditions for opportunity helps determine life
chances for individuals, and at the same time, they constitute a gatekeeping structure that restocks occupations and professions. The interview
process is vulnerable to corruption, as some interviews are gamed to
produce a preordained yes or no. At other times, the interview process
is the fairest medium for a winner to emerge for an open position. The
interview process reflects particular "enabling conventions" and rules
that govern how they are to work as a social practice, and they organize how "traffic" of a particular meaningful social interaction flows. The
interactional approach can then address two important analytic inquiries:
(1) How do involved participants structure and present the meaning of
their work and record to others? (2) How do organizations attempt to
control the interpretation and nature of organizational work? Individual
and organizational interests can align or diverge in these interactions.

People have two kinds of identities: categoric and individual (Goffman,
1983). A categoric identification involves placing "a person into one or
more social categories," while the individual form of identification refers
to how a subject "under observation is locked to a uniquely distinguishing identity through appearance, tone of voice, mention of name or other
person differentiation device" (Goffman, 1983, p. 3). In workplaces, people are embedded within a preexisting categoric identity as a worker of
a particular rank and nature. Whatever identity distinguished you as a
particular individual before is now enmeshed in the organizational or
work category to which you belong. In extreme cases, for example, such

as becoming a prison inmate, your individual identity is minimized. For example, you are to act in the category of prisoner and obey that new reality and the rules of incarceration that diminish problematic individuality. Public projections of self tend to be suited to the circumstances and frames prevailing around individuals.

Consider other basic examples. When people join an organization, they gain and are usually instructed in a repertoire of actions to enact as part of their work. They receive an ID or uniform or hear how they ought to appear in their new role. They are asked to identify with an organization's purpose, and being employed suggests that they have committed to that position. They walk into a set of coordinated activities across teams that precede them, whose importance to the organization is recognized through orientation and training to familiarize the new employees with them. Put back into a dramaturgical sense, workplaces supply people with fronts, appearances, manner, routines, and teams, and we can research those organizational features analytically (Manning, 2008b).

In general, people are creatures of the contexts that surround them. If an individual sees herself or himself as being a different person than the persona he or she is to exhibit, that internal judgment matters to him or her. But the external manifestation of self marks what other human beings treat as "real" and what they act toward. Divergent private feelings inside our head can make us feel like individual islands, but the personas we manifest count as the external self, in so far as living in society is concerned, in that observable persona is the one that receives social contact. A waiter can know in his own head that he is a great actor and that he is just working a "day job" for now, but what the world knows is him in the category of being a waiter.

In nonfiction performances, the situation tying together the audience and interaction precedes the self in defining a situation that then paves the way for a presentation of self. Here the interaction order intersects with social structure. Put more at an individual level, a stage and purpose must exist to then structure an act and its consequent personal meanings. Consider a value like saving face. The "face" to be saved or stripped away is held hostage by an audience. A person can think what they want as an individual, but the social identity of the person exists outside of them. Face is not self-defined but belongs as a measuring in the situation around the person. Further, when people enter situations, they save not only their own face, but that of their team and their organization.

In this regard, impression management has deep connections to administering and completing work. For example, in a study of management consultants, "performance was central to the training as clients' perceptions of (name omitted), and therefore future sales and revenues, depend entirely upon employees' performance at the client site" (Poulter & Land, 2008, p. 72). Again a duality exists in employees adopting the persona needed to conduct official work well, while also trying to preserve some independent identity. People must learn the ropes during training, but they may also want to avoid complete overidentification with the organization. Some role distance is helpful for maintaining sanity. A company can pay for time and emotional labor, but people may not want organizations to truly own their inner self to the point of remaking the individual over completely (Poulter & Land, 2008, p. 74). A little cynical distance offers a buffer to keep people, as anthropologists say, from going completely native.

> By adopting the mien of an actor, and consciously *performing* in accordance with expected forms of behavior, employees are able to project the appearance of a competent, enthusiastic and professional employee requisite for a successful career, whilst also sustaining a sense of self outside this game of appearances. (Poulter & Land, 2008, p. 67)

Asylums and Secondary Adjustments

In *Asylums*, Erving Goffman (1962) examined how organizational structure affects people's behaviors. He developed concepts of *secondary adjustments* and the *underlife* of organizations. He acknowledges that

> the official doctrine according to which an institution is run may be so little honored in practice, and a semi-official perspective may be so firmly and fully established, that we must analyze secondary adjustments relative to this authorized-but-not-quite-official system. (p. 193)

His model of secondary adjustments is a concept intended to help capture the duality of formal rules and individual adjustment to the imposition of rules.

Goffman defines secondary adjustments as "any set of habitual arrangements by which a member of an organization employs unauthorized means, or obtains unauthorized ends, or both, to get around the organization's assumptions as to what he should do and get and hence what he should be" (Goffman, 1961, p. 189). Secondary adjustments also can be unauthorized or unofficial means to complete work, all while sustaining the pretense of meeting an organization's assumptions of how employees are supposed to work. An organization also can use secondary adjustments to complete work, while maintaining an official facade that misleads outsiders about what real organizational activities actually are.

Secondary adjustments recognize and thus reveal a hidden infrastructure within organizations and their administrative and social processes. Individuals may manipulate and convert resources to their own ends by subverting rules or amending obstructive rules to do better work. That some secondary adjustments are also in an organization's interests can be a public and legal problem to cloak, as countless concealed government initiatives demonstrate. Secondary adjustments are responses whose purpose is to thwart particular rules governing behavior, whether for individuals or organizations. How secondary adjustments are functional, and cloaked, is a legitimate subject for analysis, particularly for those interested in white-collar crimes. Organizations take their own steps to increase discipline and to legitimate selective worker practices and unofficially tolerate others. The social control of secondary adjustments is complex. This strategic minuet between worker and manager captures the complex dance between the organizational member seeking autonomy and the manager seeking control (Goffman, 1963). Goffman also distinguished between an individual's activities and the organizational landscapes in which secondary adjustments take place:

> An individual's use of secondary adjustment is inevitably a social-psychological matter, affording him gratifications that he might not otherwise obtain. But precisely what someone gets out of it is not the point—what is crucial is understanding not what the practice brings the practitioner, but what the character of the social relations are that its acquisition and maintenance require. This constitutes a structural, as opposed to a consummatory or social-psychological point of view. (pp. 200–201)

Goffman urges people to focus on the social relations that create and sustain particular kinds of impression management. An individual's secondary adjustments, in combination with the secondary adjustments of other organizational members and their cumulative effects, make up the underlife of an organization. Goffman (1963) metaphorically compares the organizational underlife to the role that an underworld has in a city. He argues that there are technological, political, structural, and cultural components to analyze in organizations, to which he adds the fifth of dramaturgical. He then shows how these different aspects are intertwined and that dramaturgy cuts through them all.

The Dramaturgical Infrastructure

In a previous book, I developed a conceptual framework called the *dramaturgical infrastructure* to describe the relationship between impression management, administration, and organizational structure (Shulman, 2007). I developed this framework to address deceptive behavior in organizations, but the framework also applies to studying nondeceptive impression management inside organizations. Deceptions are a subcategory of impression management, but whether deceptive or nondeceptive, people still confront similar situations where they must perform credibly. You can perform in different ways, truthfully or dishonestly, badly or well, but you will have to perform. In social life, as in the theater, the show must go on.

People participate in many "shows" at work. They have to fake or produce the right impressions legibly to others, gain access to and operate within different backstages, be familiar with and competent to manage role conflicts to avoid spoiling their own identities or those of others (unless they want to), and be invested in rationalizing work-related activities and attitudes. People try to look good at work and appear to embody desirable social characteristics if they do not authentically hold them. If they have those features, then they must be able to perform them convincingly enough to an audience in order to make them legible, so they can receive credit and rewards for them.

All kinds of variability must be accounted for in examining impression management. A person's gender, race, assigned work, and place in the hierarchy all influence how they are expected to act at work and what starting points they face in managing the assumptions made about them. A person's external resources, such as money, allies, and experience, also can affect what quality of performances a person gives. Does someone have the resources to fake an air of sophistication or access to superiors or to dress the part? Everyone's desire to embody social characteristics that are prized in the workplace culture structures how people work. People also will act deceptively to meet these demands in the workplace.

Scholarship on impression management requires more than just describing how people act—attention must focus on the results those actions produce. Impression management is a powerful determinant of workplace activities and structural outcomes, more so than people conventionally acknowledge. Impression management can play a crucial role in organizational outcomes such as determining who gets ahead, how well someone sells a product, and whether people get caught breaking important rules. The argument on which this framework is based is that a strategic dance exists between the structural or workplace demands for particular appearances, the subsequent impression management by workers to produce credible performances to respond to those demands, and the results that emerge as an organizational product based on those performances.

As implied in the interaction order concept, a predictable set of expected interactions inside a social structure constitutes an infrastructure that people must operate within to accomplish organizational work. The individual dramaturgy involved in working life can be traced out to administrative processes and their outcomes in organizations. This framework organizes different domains of impression management in workplaces based on Goffman's dramaturgical model and divides the workplaces into four dimensions, each containing a required form of performance.

The first dimension, *authentication and credibility practices*, refers to establishing a credible persona effectively. The second dimension, *subterreanean education and shadow organizations*, focuses on hidden, informal, irregular, or unofficial means of administrating organizational activities. The third dimension, *managing identity and role conflicts*, involves secondary adjustments to move up and resolve role conflicts and turf battles between people. The fourth dimension, *ethical disengagement*, investigates legitimating deviant, frowned upon, deceptive, or illegal actions that may occur at work. The above domains are neither exhaustive nor mutually exclusive. They represent an initial conceptual and theoretical foray into mapping out significant areas of workplace impression management.

The first dimension of *authentication and credibility practices* emphasizes exploring how people construct convincing impressions, sometimes incorporating deception in doing so. How do people maintain a facade of working when they are goofing off? How do they convince others during interviews that they possess sought qualities? Authentication and credibility practices reference a microsociological level of analysis that examines how people produce what appear to be authentic impressions. The idea here is to consider what tactics people use to construct convincing performances, sometimes of lies and sometimes of truth, in ambiguous circumstances. Vince Lombardi once said, "If you are not fired with enthusiasm, you will be fired with enthusiasm." How do people appear engaged when they are unenthusiastic? How do they force on their smiles? How does a quiet person learn to appear like an active go-getter? How do people demonstrate that they are team players so that others "get" that they are team players? All of these impressions require appearing authentic and convincing to others.

The second dimension, *subterranean education and shadow organizations*, connects secondary adjustments, the organizational underlife, and the negotiated order tradition in organizational ethnography. These aspects build on Goffman's organizational analysis in *Asylums*. How people exchange information, advance their careers, use secret means of managing and administering, or break rules to accomplish their work requires a subterranean education and constitutes a shadow administration of work. Here is where workers obtain hidden means to actually do their work and where going "by the book" meets roadblocks that informal arrangements bypass.

Work experience familiarizes us all with examples of how people fight, instruct others, exchange covert information, pursue better jobs, and break rules to complete work. Unofficial information builds into all of these kinds of actions and constitutes a backstage, subterranean education. A subterranean education represents an instructional and practical immersion in the right kind of background knowledge to engage in impression management that suits an organization's required appearances. Performances and teams can form in shadows to manage backstage aspects of organizational administration.

The third dimension addresses *managing identity and role conflicts*. People must use impression management to confront and manage the role conflicts that inhere in organizations. Whereas authentication and credibility practices reference an actor's actions toward himself or herself, the managing of identity and role conflicts refers to managing mutual interactions. People confront different dramaturgical pressures that others thrust on them, to pick sides, to abandon one responsibility for another, to soothe hurt feelings, or to isolate a troubling person. These situations exist throughout the workplace.

One such conflict occurs when supervisors ignore rule breaking by coworkers who are their friends instead of enforcing the organization's rules. People must address conflicts associated with different expectations in their workplace roles and sometimes hide noncompliance with one side of the conflict. For example, a worker may think that a decision to implement a new policy is idiotic, but he or she will appear to assent happily to the policy implementation in a meeting and then work to that end. Working consensus is paramount.

The last dimension, *ethical disengagement*, addresses how people overcome moral inhibitions against disreputable actions. This category references rationalizing untoward impression management. A crucial workplace phenomenon is that individuals and organizations attempt to disown any moral responsibility for acting against situational propriety. Ethical disengagement addresses how people overcome those inhibitions. Identifying rationalizations that individuals and organizations use in their mutual and sometimes competing efforts to disown engaging in deceptive behaviors is a growing area of research interest. Researching why moral inhibitions fail in concrete circumstances and identifying social influences that effectively counter guidelines to act ethically and responsibly is important.

In *Asylums*, Goffman identifies social processes that institutions use to transform an individual's identity into an impersonal organizational one. In his article "Symbols of Class Status," Goffman (1951, p. 303) writes about how legitimate holders of status symbols try to protect them from being appropriated by impostors; hence they develop "curator groups" to help maintain the machinery of status. Goffman clearly recognizes structural incentives that influence adopting techniques of impression management, but he did not always choose to identify and analyze them in his writings. The dramaturgical infrastructure maps out the range of performance arenas that people engage in at work. Workers must use impression management to appear legitimate and competent in their occupational and professional roles (Abbott, 1988; Hughes, 1984). Impression management requires demonstrating desired attributes and concealing undesirable ones. People fake competence strategically to try to appear legitimate. Workers may act deceptively to exclude information that threatens a legitimate appearance while substituting rosier information in its place. Socialization into organizations is often training in learning what impressions are most useful. Later this information informs how individuals pursue upward mobility, as success is based in part on appearances and putting on a facade that reflects organizationally desirable personality traits (Bosk, 1979; Jackall, 1988). Workplaces constitute a social system that demands outward shows of appearance from individual workers. Total institutions constitute the most controlled setting for such presentations.

Total Institutions

As a microsociologist, Erving Goffman did not research organizations as groups, such as analyzing operations at an industry level. He did examine how organizational contexts impact individual interactions, most prominently in his analysis of a mental hospital in his book *Asylums*. Goffman coined the term *total institution* to refer to organizations whose operations take steps to exert a nearly complete control over people's activities under their power. Examples of such institutions include mental hospitals, military institutions, and prisons. As will be noted in the section on emotional labor that follows, organizational contexts help dictate what emotional displays on the part of inhabitants are considered appropriate. However, total institutions move beyond managing the emotions of others to the complete resocializing of inhabitants of total institutions. A prison is to rehabilitate and help deter future crime, a military organization takes new recruits and makes them soldiers, and a mental hospital takes in the mentally ill and hopes to return them to outside society in an improved state.

Goffman noted that total institutions force people to live together in batches. These organizations process people such that they cannot carry out individual activities autonomously. Instead, people inside total institutions do not control their actions, movements, and schedule anymore. What people can wear, how they are addressed, their freedom of movement, and their activities are under organizational control. Goffman examined how people were socialized into this form of control and their attempts to engage in small acts of resistance, which he labeled as "adjustments," against the organization's encroachment over their autonomy. Goffman, using an asylum as a field setting, saw the subordinating interactions that people experienced there in vivid action.

Moving from the asylum setting, the total institution can be considered today as an organizational "ideal type" in the sense of describing a particular organizational form under which people are subject to an inordinate amount of controls (Scott, 2011). Consider the variety of such controls. They include the spaces people can enter; what they can do there, and when they can do so, occurs on a tightly controlled schedule; there is control over daily privileges, constant surveillance, and procedures of degradation that ensure dissenters lose individual status. People who work for the organization manage the process of resocializing occupants into the new batch identity common to the total institution. The staff is an agent of social control over those that inhabit the total institution.

The total institution is a type of organization that may strike people as a threat to freedom. However, some total institutions can be held to operate in the social interest. Some total institutions benefit some against others, and perhaps in cases like hospitals, a total institution may serve the interests of all. A hospital controls occupants for the end of healing. Boarding schools control the actions of its charges to ostensibly socialize their development as the next generation of elites, and some religious institutions have monastery-like total institutions that build religious adherents and staff to spread, in their view, prosocial values. Total institutions teach socialization and appropriate impression management to their occupants. A total institution is an overt arbiter of interaction. Individual choice and freedom of behavior are impeded, and orchestrated performances emerge that fit the institution's goals. Refusals to comply are punished. Goffman was interested in uncovering how people attempt to resist control. A key point for organizational analysis then is to examine ways to control the performances of people under organizational sway and, in response, how people resist. Some techniques of control include bribing. Or people assimilate or face an escalating series of punishments. Reduced individual autonomy in the organization includes speaking only when spoken to, wearing a uniform rather than the individual choosing clothing, and picking one's own schedule.

Think back to how some people experience high school as an institution that aims to control impulsive youth and put the clamp down on rebels. Some people embrace the system of control and prestige that comes with going along with the system, while others find rewards in nonconformity. What is clear in the situation is a war exists over the stakes of what identity people will have within the organization. Sometimes organizations win that war; sometimes a wayward identity wins in being insubordinate and finding work-arounds or rebellion. Goffman coined a number of useful concepts to describe the processes through which organizations fight to control the identity of a captive population.

Role dispossession is the process through which new "recruits" are prevented from being who they were in the world they inhabited prior to entry. *Trimming and programming* describe steps involved in a new denizen being "shaped and coded into an object that can be fed into the administrative machinery of the establishment, to be worked on smoothly by routine operations" (Goffman, 1963, p. 16). Personal artifacts that highlight a person's individuality or personal identity, referred to by Goffman as an identity kit, disappear within total institutions. Authorities confiscate or forbid personal items that lend themselves to a divergent identification other than what an institution establishes. Shaming occurs, as do degradation ceremonies that punish people before others by humiliating them. "Privilege systems" exist that reward conformity, some of which pit occupants against one another. For example, one tradition is to punish a group of innocents when a guilty party does not come forward, which then depends on individuals to betray one another or turn on each other for the institution's interest. As an organizational type, the concept of the total institution opened inquiries into forms of social control inside coercive institutions and efforts by occupants to resist that imposition through making secondary adjustments.

Susie Scott (2011) has advanced on the total institution concept by examining what she calls the modern version of the total institution, the *reinventive institution*. A total institution is considered to resocialize an individual self into a new batch identity that suits the organization's purpose. A *reinventive* institution is an organization that a person chooses to commit oneself to in order to be reinvented into an organizationally sponsored identity, typically one that markets a reinvented identity to occupy. In a total institution like a prison, people are inmates who are involuntarily placed in that institution and controlled. In reinventive institutions, which can involve a much larger range of organization, Susie Scott notes that people voluntarily commit themselves to pursue the new identity on offer—they want to throw away an old me and suit up a new self. Scott insightfully sees the reinventive institution arising to match today's new era of people pursuing self-development schemes on offer by organizations. Examples of reinventive institutions include religious and spiritual communities, military academies, secret societies, therapeutic clinics, educational enrichment institutions, and virtual institutions (Scott, 2011). In a DIY era, people are not going alone in their self-reinvention. They are met with a marketplace that supplies institutions that enable them to resocialize and "reinvent their selves" on demand.

Goffman's total institution has an authoritarian air of making the inhabitants comply through various control schemes. In a reinventive institution, people opt in, and that shared commitment to a new identity links the inhabitants of the reinventive institution in a chain of mutual social control. Scott (2011, p. 6) uses the term "performative regulation" to describe how inmates monitor and sanction each other's behavior by sustaining a shared belief in the institutional reality, which they enact dramaturgically. Individuals learn both to present themselves as ideal inmates, doing conformity and seeking to appear committed, and to appraise each other's claims to authenticity, evaluating their progress in relative terms. Where the total institution imposes its power, the reinventive institution involves people choosing to have power imposed on them. They collaborate with their peers in controlling themselves and their ongoing interpretation of their self's "journey."

So what kinds of organizational experiences are on hand here? Time spent in weight loss clinics and "fat" camps, conversions to cult religions and living styles and new age communities, entry into specialized academic communities like music conservatories, and sending a child to a military school. Presumably, any form of specialized batch living qualifies where a common identity and transformation are sought with the willing assent of inhabitants. The key transformation of the individual is not only a process of top-down social control by the heavy hands of the institution. Instead, fellow pilgrims judge the person's commitment to the new identity and his or her progress along the way and help construct the joint reality of the new self being forged in the experience. A person joins a fraternity and becomes an observer of the commitment of others and himself to the new identity.

A person who seeks to have the reinvented self has a new crew to learn from and with, about how to interpret what one feels and how to stay and know that one is on the right path to the new organizationally sanctioned version of self that they seek. Interpretive experts come to rate one's commitment and progress along the ways of the belief system in highly hierarchical reinventive institutions like quasireligious ones, while in other forms like month-long retreats, people are there to prop up the meaning of the "journey" to each participant. The total institution enforces an external dramaturgical self. The reinventive institution involves exerting self-control with the prompting of other committed actors to engage in getting people to believe that they have reinvented themselves.

Emotional Labor

Work on displaying emotions is a key development from Goffman's dramaturgical model. The focus on studying emotions in action as displays to others is often sited physically in workplaces, hence the inclusion of that subject in this chapter. Arlie Hochschild pioneered the growth of this subfield of sociology drawing on the notion of acting contained in *The Presentation of Self in Everyday Life*.

Drawing on Jonathan Turner's (2009, pp. 340–354) review of dramaturgical theories of emotion, Arlie Hochschild (1979, 1983) is lauded for extending Goffman's early work by conceptualizing the role of emotions in social situations. People live in cultures "composed of emotion ideologies about the appropriate attitudes, feelings, and emotional responses in generic types of situations" (Turner, 2009, p. 345). We all understand that there are expectations that dictate what emotions people should display in situations. Hochschild researched how people in certain occupations, like flight attendants, are required to present particular emotions while on the job. This work was identified as *emotional labor* or *emotion work*, particularly if they must perform emotions that they do not actually feel but must depict to do their jobs, such as service with a smile.

Hoschschild developed the ideas of deep and surface acting to distinguish variety in people's emotional displays to others and to draw analytic attention to what people feel when they manifest different or intense emotions. In *surface acting*, people perform an emotion without actually trying to authentically feel that emotion internally. They demonstrate the emotion on the surface in their presentation, but they do not actually feel that emotion. When *deep acting*, people actually try to summon up emotions internally to feel an authentic connection with the emotional part they play. Organizations pay for and regulate performances by employees that involve surface acting. With deep acting, people really try to summon up the feelings so as to be authentic (Grandey, 2003). The connection between surface and deep acting built on Goffman's work and also highlighted a new issue, which is the dissonance people feel when asked to demonstrate feelings that they don't actually feel. What burnout can result from being inauthentic or too superficial over time?

Impression management in general also requires managing emotions, as people must abide by feeling rules, whether due in part to the interaction order or other influences, that dictate what emotions they must demonstrate publicly in certain situations (Hallet, 2003). People should cry at funerals, be happy at celebrations, be angry at insults, and laugh at jokes. People, through emotion management in workplaces, "essentially recreate and reaffirm the appropriate expectations for that role through their interactions with others" (Lively & Weed, 2014, p. 205).

People use strategies to display proper demeanor and emotions. That work also involves authentication practices. Think over some strategies you might have seen people use. People adopt pouty postures and depressed-looking body language. Other people use energetic, go-getter movements. Sometimes people try to think of something sad in order to cry. People will practice expressions in the mirror to capture the right look to communicate the right impression. Modeling is a case where people who have what Ashley Mears (2011) called body capital are supposed to manifest particular looks. Some are never to smile in pictures, and others are to summon up whatever emotion is necessary to connect with a product's image. Thinking back to childhood, or socializing a child, we can remember incidents where parents cajoled the child to approach events with the proper solemnity or exuberance. People learn quickly that they are supposed to make their face the right kind of canvas to avoid trouble with authority. Few smart alecks completed school without hearing some scolding along the lines of "wipe that smirk off your face."

When social settings urge people to feel things that they don't feel and hide authentic feelings, a discrepancy emerges between actual feelings and feeling rules (Thoits, 1996). Peggy Thoits and other sociologists noted the importance of researching social situations where these discrepancies occur. In role conflicts, people may have to put on one face when they would prefer to wear another. Parents have encountered putting on a more serious demeanor at a child's infraction when they actually find the violation that they are punishing more amusing than not, such as when a child swears but mangles the swear word into a comedic work of art. More severe situations occur where people are asked to support political viewpoints that they do not believe in or have belief systems and things that they take seriously that others do not. People may hide their discomfort at encountering prejudice and "hold it all in" because of situational circumstances. If stress involves frustration in being annoyed, blocked, or helpless to change something, that discrepancy can arise from not being able to feel what one wants to feel or in having to feel in public in ways that are not felt authentically. The more people are thwarted emotionally in this way by social situations, including at work, the unhappier they are.

Research on emotional labor and interactive service work (Hochschild, 1983; Leidner, 1993) demonstrates that a worker's emotional performance, whether in an airplane, insurance office, or restaurant, is part of a service landscape in which organizations deliver their products. Employers pay for certain emotional displays that are key to work. As Rafaeli and Sutton (1987) note, emotions can be control moves meant to improve the employer and employee's situation by influencing others, no matter whether the involved emotions are authentic or inauthentic.

Display rules govern the forms that emotional displays take, and scholars of emotions in the workplace are keen to connect such displays with financial returns to the bottom line. A sociological point here is to examine how social situations call for some to control the emotions of others. This point was relevant in Goffman's work, for example, in cases like managing the emotions of inmates in total institutions or in quelling the irate victims of confidence schemes.

People use many different means to incite emotion in others. Lights, music, and smells can elicit emotions such as candlelight dinners or "make-out" music. People try to offer sympathetic displays to deflect anger toward them. In workplaces, people may go through training to simulate and stimulate examples of required surface acting on the job. The idea here also may be that the more people simulate the emotion, the more they might condition themselves to actually begin to authentically feel that emotion. Certainly the area of therapy is a rich forum for such simulations where people are asked to role-play or confront provocations or triggers that target emotional responses. People may be asked to organize their bodies in ways that summon up feelings like hugging, violating norms of personal space, trying to smile, and touch. Thoits (1996), in addition to identifying some of the above actions, also identifies venues where emotion management is used for various organizational purposes, such as military training, love bombing, and hazing—in her analysis targeting the emotions of others is a classic social strategy at hand in courts, meetings, and other occasions (Thoits, 1996, p. 106). Transforming recruits into aggressive people and humiliating people in rites of passage are socially functional examples of organized management of others's emotions to make them conform.

Many workplace products also involve emotional performance, whether in a doctor's display of professionalism, a professor's capacity to reach students, or a river-rafting guide's "aren't we having fun" demeanor (see Arnould & Price, 1993). The emotional labor of workers plays a major part in determining the productivity of services marketing, sales, and workers (Grayson & Shulman, 2000). Turnover in the workplace is also linked to burnout from burdensome emotional labor (Hochschild, 1983; Leidner, 1993). Excessive demands for emotional labor from ethnic and racial minorities (don't speak so "ghetto") and/or women ("just smile, honey") also constitute forms of gender and racial inequality.

A key issue in studies of emotional labor and deception in service provision is the successful construction of a false emotional reality. A good work product may require convincing deep or surface acting. There are many occupations for which convincing lying as one's emotional labor is vital. Undercover police officers must dupe suspects. Professional wrestlers are deeply engaged in the project of crafting collaborative convincing emotional displays as heels or heroes and in expressing pain and righteous revenge without seriously harming one another, if they can avoid doing so (Smith, 2008).

Patwardhan, Noble, and Nishihara (2009) researched emotional labor by workers at call centers based in India that was outright deceptive. They found that employees in many Indian call centers are trained to use Western names and accents because Western customers accord more trust to identities that seem familiar. For scholars interested in exposing techniques of deceptive emotional labor, this study is an informative read. As a start, Patwardhan et al. (2009, p. 321) noted that all agents use pseudonyms for names. They identified four types of deceiving in these call centers. Two were subtle, such as asking customers about whether they were baking cookies around the holidays and pronouncing words consistent with existing practice in the country in question (Patwardhan et al., 2009, p. 322). The company's goal, considered crucial to success, was to convince clients that service agents were not calling from India. Legitimating that deception meant that the employer had to actively support employees lying as a normal part of their work.

The call center example is a deceptive one that involves surface acting and "appearing American." Yet many companies depend on a more benevolent form of Trojan wholesomeness, in which a self-interested profit motive obscures itself within a sweetened facade. Projecting the innocent wide-eyed wonder of a Disney princess or the emotions of a character in the park is an example. Other professions are intended to serve up plates of compassion as their main course of work. Those displays need not be fake and may well be felt sincerely. However, acting authentic still means that the resulting emotion is a product built up and shaped to best serve clients.

FIVE

Modern Life as Show Business

The making of the illusions which flood our experiences has become the business of America, some of its most honest and most necessary and most respectable business.

—Daniel Boorstin

It's the movies that have really been running things in America ever since they were invented. They show you what to do, how to do it, when to do it, how to feel about it, and how to look how you feel about it.

—Andy Warhol

Introduction: The Thicket of Unreality

In his 1962 book *The Image*, Daniel Boorstin predicted that modern businesses would inundate Americans with staged events, illusions, and theatricality, all to sell their wares. These commercial interests would attract consumers by appealing to the "extravagant expectations" that people hold for how life should be experienced. Neal Gabler (2000, p. 5) echoing Boorstin, argued that contemporary American society

111

is now characterized by a "deliberate application of the techniques of theater to politics, religion, education. . . . Commerce has converted them into branches of show businesss, where the overriding objective is getting and satisfying an audience." Gabler goes so far as to refer to contemporary American society as a "Republic of Entertainment." Given these views, how are American social and business institutions promoting these theatrical shows? If modern life is all about "show business," then applying dramaturgical concepts to study contemporary life works well.

The "modern life as show business" assertion refers to people being awash today in what Daniel Boorstin called a "thicket of unreality," where artificial simulations and illusions of real things predominate. Boorstin (2012) referred to an image as "an artificial imitation or representation of the external form of an object, especially of a person" (p. 197). An image constructs a "visible public personality" (p. 187). The idea is that images can be shined, developed, and refined for public consumption. The image "is a studiously crafted personality profile of an individual, institution, corporation, product, or service" (p. 186). Illusions are images that are "mistaken for reality." People go to Disney's animal kingdom and spend time on an artificial safari. Disney dyed a lake in Orlando blue because people expect lakes to be blue and not a natural brown or greenish color (Hiaasen, 1998). Restaurants, stores, cities, and malls project themed versions of realities for people to experience as a draw, like at the Paris or Venetian hotels, Rainforest Cafes, Planet Hollywoods, and a now Disneyfied Times Square. Mainstream print and television journalism focus on tabloid-style coverage of well-known individuals and events, promoting details about celebrities, awards shows, fashion choices, and disseminating publicity as a dominant form of entertainment. People are so immersed in celebrities that they identify them more readily than the political figures governing them.

Museums borrow tricks from theme parks to make exhibits more exciting, and cultural critics bemoan that a need to be entertained overcomes a need to be educated. Laugh tracks bark out canned laughs during TV shows. Politicians debate arguments in an entertainment style, reducing presentations of complex issues, like what to do in health care policy or international relations, to 30-second sound bites of misleading grandstanding. Attention spans dwindle unless people feel entertained, and reality is unattractive unless dressed to kill. American society is awash in illusions, images, retail atmospherics, plastic surgery, Spanx, and unending advertisements, all of which integrate dramaturgical performances.

Erving Goffman used the term *idealization* to describe people acting as if they live up to idealized social standards. Goffman viewed people's performances as constituting opportunities to display their congruence with important ideal social values. They represent chances to "introduce favorable information about oneself," in an effort to be treated as a performed status warrants. Positive idealization involves depicting roles and identity in positively idealized terms, as if one actually lives as the projected perfect image implies. Positive idealization equals giving off a glowing public persona.

Positive idealization also conceals larger inconsistencies between appearance and reality than more mundane dramaturgical performance does. The gap is bigger in pretending to be a rich heir or a Harvard graduate than in acting friendly to a colleague to whom you are indifferent. If you want a quick sense of positive idealization, think of the "perfect" college application essay people joke about writing, something like this: I wake up at 4:00 a.m. to get to my shift at the coal mine to support my family but still found time to start my nonprofit foundation protecting spawning salmon, to captain three varsity sports teams, patent ten inventions, graduate as valedictorian, and be a published writer of a young adult book series about teenagers surviving a dystopian world of supermodel vampire overlords.

More minor examples abound. Applicants to law school may state that they want to attend a top law school to pursue justice for the oppressed when they really want a shot at attaining a lucrative partnership at a well-heeled corporate law firm. A person may rent a Ferrari for a day to appear as someone who can afford that vehicle when going out on the town.[1] Negative forms of idealization also exist, such as in an example Goffman (1959) offers of smart women playing down their intelligence to appeal to men. Some students may say they hardly study when getting good grades to give an impression of their effortless capacities.

People also wish to create some distance from being observed in order to cultivate a sense of mystery about themselves. When people do not know the full details of how someone's persona or performance emerges, they may feel some sense of awe in regard to what they observe. Goffman (1959) uses the term *mystification* to refer to the maintaining of

---

[1] Thorsten Veblen described conspicuous consumption as wanting to exhibit one's capacity to consume as a means to trumpet one's status to others. Neal Gabler, drawing on Veblen, stated that a purpose of acquisition is exhibition.

this "elbowroom" that allows performers some privacy in carrying out a performance that might otherwise be discredited if done in open view (p. 69). As an example, consider how a magician uses a curtain to cover up the mechanics of a trick to heighten the mystery of its accomplishment. To see what is done behind the curtain might expose a mundane reality behind the trick that would otherwise spoil the effect. Similarly, individuals may use means of insulation from observation to seek to maintain a "magical" effect. Goffman cites an example of royalty being advised to remain aloof to maintain a sense of awe and distinction—nothing mundane should be observable, and protocol should be in force to reinforce status distinctions. Mystification occurs down to the microlevel—in personal appearance, for example, a celebrity wears an outer garment that covers up the celebrity's unacknowledged Spanx that makes her or his body look unnaturally great. Mystification also can abet misrepresentation. Goffman notes, "There is hardly a legitimate everyday vocation or relationship whose performers do not engage in concealed practices which are incompatible with fostered impressions" (p. 64). The very awe and distance through which we perceive legitimate occupations helps them engage in misrepresentations. Mystification crafts a blind spot in perception that abets a thicket of unreality.

Social commentators like Boorstin, Gabler, and others consider people living in a thicket of unreality to be our current state of affairs. The thicket of unreality also is a thicket of idealization. Boorstin (1962) argues that images are "salable commodities" that appeal to people because they outdo reality, or what Baudrillard (1994) refers to later as the "desert of the real." B. Joseph Pine and James Gilmore (2011) draw on dramaturgical theory to examine the *Experience Economy*, which refers to brands and organizations producing a variety of staged experiences to attract consumers. Examples of the most elaborate staged experiences are called "brandlands" and are represented by venues such as Autostadt, Hershey's Chocolate World, "Spamtown," Harley Davidson Museum, Goodyear World of Rubber, SONY Wonder Technology Lab, The Crayola Factory, LEGOLAND, the Guinness Storehouse, and the Heineken Experience. These brandlands operate like themed amusement centers, museums, and ride attractions that brands operate to heighten their appeal and encourage consumers to immerse themselves in the brand's imagery. While Pine and Gilbert examine these showpieces, their work is also more comprehensive. They analyze different types of staged experiences and offer background information and advice to businesses on how to develop better experiences for their consumers. They also innovate dramaturgical concepts to analyze how staged images and experiences work in business contexts.

Neil Gabler (2000) states in reference to a changing American culture:

> The new culture of personality emphasized charm, fascination and like-ability. Or as Susman put it: "The social role demanded of all in the new culture of personality was that of a performer. Every American was to become a performing self." (p. 198)

This quote reflects a cultural criticism that in contemporary American society, individuals are fixated on performing. Consumerism can abet this characteristic. A focus on individuals' performances must also include not just consumers but also how individual representatives of social institutions perform on their employer's behalf. For example, Disney must portray an essence of wholesomeness and needs staff to convey that message. Starbucks needs to stage store designs to sell their progressive aesthetic plus coffee message. Image making and image industries, advertising, entertainment, and politics employ many professionals to create influential images that use dramaturgical approaches to craft positive idealization messaging to serve client needs and wants.

This chapter will examine the different cultural, economic, and technological arguments that explain how the contemporary thicket of unreality arose. I outline how Erving Goffman's dramaturgical perspective helps to analyze this historical moment and use examples to dissect how the actual production of unreality operates. A main emphasis is on how scholars of marketing apply dramaturgical analysis in innovative ways that expand the state of the art of this perspective. Who creates images, performs them, and for what ends; these questions motivate dramaturgical analysis and are appropriate to analyzing an era of unreality. Living in a time when image is everything requires a dramaturgical sensibility, because today's advertisers, brands, governments, retailers, and individuals all perform to demonstrate their merits, beat their competition, bewitch the senses, and serve their customers.

Examples of Unreal Images: Illusions, Photos, and Words

Some examples will help clarify the idea of being inundated with unreality. Consider photoshopped celebrities. The site http://www.beautyredefined.net/photoshop-phoniness-hall-of-shame/ offers some examples of photoshopped images from magazine covers. As you view the images, consider how they manipulate reality without stating doing so. An older model, Twiggy, becomes miraculously younger thanks to eye cream; Beyonce's face and body are "whitened"; Kimora Simmons gets taller; Jessica Simpson drops pant sizes. Andy Roddick, a professional tennis player, now finds himself with a much bigger chest and arms. The images offer unreal versions of the real thing. Ask yourself, would you prefer to show the real thing if you were selling a magazine cover? Does *Men's Fitness* want a picture of Andy Roddick with 22-inch biceps or 14-inch ones? Do customers want to buy eye cream from someone older or younger looking, even if the younger image is "untrue"?

The website *Finances Online* http://reviews.financesonline.com/the-art-of-deceptive-advertising-reviewed/ created an infographic containing a number of examples of deceptive advertising. Advertisers use unreal images to promote their products. Consider the examples presented there of fast food advertising. For example, in images of hamburgers, all ingredients seem delectable, large, and depicted in perfect visual symmetry. Sesame seeds are perfectly placed, the buns are thick, and the meat portions are sizable. Consider pictures associated with travel advertising. The pictorial images that hotels offer often portray gigantic pools, beautiful landscapes, and adjacent proximity to key tourist venues to entice your business. The travel site *Oyster.com* collects examples of inauthentic "photo fake-outs" that you can examine. One example there shows the impact of using a zoomed-in picture of the hotel front that makes the hotel appear much closer to the capitol building than the hotel actually is. Other pictures show how the sizes of pools are exaggerated. Taking a wide angle picture close to the height of pool water on a sunny day leads people to mistake the pool's actual size, which is revealed by another photograph taken from a person's standing height. Travel destinations use numerous images of deserted picturesque beaches to attract vacationers. What is not depicted is how crowded those beaches are and that people will not have those beaches all to themselves. Paradise is usually pictured as a solitary slice of heaven for you and yours to enjoy, with no exposure to everyone else there on vacation.

The website *Oyster.com* also did an interesting take on the constant claim that hotels are only "steps away" from tourist destinations that people want to visit. "Hotel 91 is a new 70 room smoke free hotel located in Manhattan's vibrant Lower East Side. Chinatown, Little Italy, SoHo, Wall

Street, and other major NYC attractions are only steps away."[2] Here's the real breakdown: Chinatown: 0 steps (because the hotel is in Chinatown); Little Italy: 1,000 steps; SoHo: 1,600 steps; Wall Street: 2,200 steps. Maybe a thousand steps is minimal, but the implied promise of steps away seems more like a block or so, not a thousand steps plus.

Images are artificial, believable, vivid, and simple (Boorstin, 1962). Everyone can understand them, which is important, because their goal is mass appeal, which requires clear communication. Images evoke ideal versions of subjects; unfortunately, they require artificial creation because many do not exist naturally. Images depict objects with a consummate front stage persona. Consistent with dramaturgy, images provide surface appearances that obscure the backstage, and they also present a more idealized front stage than exists. Images obscure unfavorable reality with overlaid depictions. Images always shunt attention away from unwanted realism. *Mystification* exists here in concealing and obscuring the real so that an image's effect is more powerful and magical. Photoshop use is not acknowledged in many of these images. Some impressions that images offer conform to sets of expectations that people have, such as that celebrities are unnaturally thin and beaches are always sunny and welcoming. However, many real things cannot be as perfect as expected, so they become perfected in representations.

Some images orient less to fulfilling audience expectations. Instead, they define a situation to discourage audiences from believing something that they might otherwise conclude. In using *obstructive images*, the goal is to introduce ambiguity to obscure an otherwise potentially critical interpretation of some subject. For example, people who oppose claims that the globe is warming posted pictures from the freezing winter of 2014, to juxtapose in images the contrast of record low Arctic weather existing simultaneously with a supposedly "overheating" earth. The image begs the question of how overheating is possible when the earth is shown freezing, which uses the image obstructively. Goffman notes that people "pictorialize arguments through images." You should scrutinize images to decipher what arguments are implicit within them, a subject discussed at length later in this chapter in analyzing gender advertisements.

In addition to images appealing to visual senses, images also use crafty words to create illusions (Beard & Cerf, 2015; Lutz, 1989). William Lutz (1989) describes examples of *doublespeak*, a term which refers to words

---

[2] So says its website.

image makers design to camouflage and obscure a disagreeable reality. This obfuscating magic works by introducing ambiguity and avoiding clear communication. Lutz describes four types of doublespeak: euphemism, jargon, gobbledygook, and inflated language. Some examples include describing civilians killed in war as "collateral damage" and bombings as "protective reaction strikes." A company does not fire workers but chooses them to participate in a "career alternative enhancement program." A tax increase is a "revenue enhancement." A famous person was not addicted to drugs; the drug just "established an interrelationship with the body such that if the drug is removed precipitously, there is a reaction." A used car is an "experienced car" or a "previously distinguished vehicle." Companies use jargon in billing statements to make invoiced items harder to understand and perhaps easier to overcharge. Some cite contractors to the U.S. Department of Defense labeling hammers as "manually powered fastener-driving impact devices" or steel nuts as "hexiform rotatable surface compression units" (Lutz, 1989). For a more personal example, find a bill from a cable, mobile, or bank provider and just try to understand what all the named charges are. Chances are you will be uncertain about what some charges mean since they appear in the form of unclear jargon, perhaps to discourage understanding and frazzle people into compliance.

The advertising industry prioritizes using words skillfully to create magical appeals for products. Companies spend time considering how to name products, and they work diligently to build brands. Examples are so omnipresent that examining products to play a game of what image is used for what effect is fun. For example, some commercial products are pitched as "natural" and apply an anticorporate promotion strategy. These products try to appeal to consumers as alternatives to large-scale packaged and manufactured goods. They are promoted to provide better alternatives for protecting the environment and for serving people through their "social responsibility" sensibility. However, somehow omitted from advertisements is that the same large-scale corporations from which these natural products attempt to differentiate themselves actually own some of those natural product brands. Honest Tea and Odwalla are owned by Coca-Cola. Dean's Food owns Silk soy products. Lara Bars are made by General Mills. Kraft makes Boca products. Hiding potentially unpalatable corporate ownership that could contradict advertising messaging is a sly move.

In a similar example, some craft beers are supposed to be from independent producers but are actually owned by large brewing companies that have positioned themselves in the craft beer market. So buying a craft beer may not score one for the "little guy" but may actually put money in the large guy's pocket. Miller-Coors owns Blue Moon. Anheuser Busch owns Goose Island. A marketing message behind purchasing craft beers is that the manufacturing and brewing process is small scale and authentic and really about craftspeople pursuing an ideal. Faux craft beers from big manufacturers gild the lily. What we think we buy is not what we always get in a thicket of unreality.

Robert Jackall (2000) describes "technicians of moral outrage" whose specialty is working people up to identify with a particular advocated political position without much deliberative thought. They do this work through persuasive imagery. These technicians stir up and then channel strong emotional responses from people to garner vitriolic support as opposed to gaining support after encouraging careful deliberation over an issue. There may be pretense otherwise, but using outrage and summoning up of judgmental emotions is not about a reasoned exchange of views. Technicians of moral outrage get people livid so as to immediately galvanize their support for a particular action or view. Support means getting people to "villagers storming the castle" level mad. You can observe these technicians at work across the Internet, Fox News, and MSNBC. Examine them tactically, and you will see fine technicians at work. From Reverend Sharpton to Rush Limbaugh, technicians in moral outrage rant all the way to the bank. Viewing and vicariously participating in these rants is a form of entertainment and, for some, an unfortunate education about how to argue. To bellow, insult, and act self-righteously about points is sometimes the dominant mode of public argument.

In contemporary society, an increased reliance on illusions and unreality for commercial purposes puts people in a world of positive idealization run amuck. Robert Jackall (2000, p. 5) defines such image makers as "interpretive experts skilled in the creation and propagation of symbols to persuade mass audiences to some action or belief." Images encourage some forms of reality over others. Images persuade in a biased form. The interests of image makers shape the information that audiences receive. Objective argumentation is not the goal. Here I should be clear: When people write that some groups use images in a biased way to influence people, you might think that statement comes from someone who wants to start ranting about conspiracies. That is not the argument here; I make no claims that lizard people disguised as humans are brainwashing people.[3] The point here is more that individuals and organizations use images routinely; such persuasion is a commonplace event and may be more about companies delivering what customers want than about fooling them.

I reference commercial actors using images to highlight large-scale techniques of image making, but both everyday people and organizations truck in unreality every day as their business—advertisers, coworkers, marketers, and politicians alike. The sociological point is that *unreality is not just done to people; people make unreality unto others.* Images exist to persuade people into an action (like consumption) or belief (love or hate Obamacare), and implicit in that goal is encouraging people to focus on things that promote the producer's desired impression. When selling people on an idea, product, or action, the aim is to get them to buy into whatever representational eloquence gets individuals to say yes. Images sell potato chips, beauty aids, applying to a college, denying or warning about global warming, and they show images crafted to persuade, not provide impartial messages, like potato chips taste good but are caloric, or this college is good but other ones are too, or people wear lifts and Spanx but height and weight should not factor in judging someone. Be aware that people and organizations of all kinds use images to influence in cases beyond extreme dystopian places like North Korea, where all media are state controlled and extol the ruling family. North Korea is the outlier and not the routine.

A limited and inaccurate understanding results if people view politicians and corporations as the only actors that manipulate. Focusing only on infamous actors switches attention away from examining more routine ones. In a thicket of unreality, using images is unexceptional and almost routine to the point of being mundane. On an individual level, when a person drapes makeup on to look younger, he or she creates an unreal image. When a man or woman dyes gray hair black, he or she alters an appearance. These individuals use images and create unreality as actors performing for their own purposes. The thicket of unreality argument is that people have extravagant expectations of how grand life is supposed to be, which obscures vast discrepancies between appearance and reality, in part because mirages are more palatable than being trapped in a desert

---

[3] See http://www.thewire.com/national/2013/04/12-million-americans-believe-lizard-people-run-our-country/63799/ regarding the percentage of Americans that believe in lizard people and other conspiracies. Seriously.

of less perfect real things. Producers of consumer products that help create unreality abet these hopes, which is a more commonplace use of coercion than the conspiratorial idea that people live in a barely hidden version of Orwell's dystopian *1984*. Multitudes of individuals in isolation from one another, but en masse, buy unreality products and produce profits for companies. They create unreality as part of doing their jobs. Hence Boorstin's argument that American business is about selling illusions.

Appreciate the sociology inherent in the *scaling* of using images that is involved here. Individuals acting in a job interview are a level down from how powerful dramaturgy is when performances involve a large organization leveraging its resources to sustain images to push commercial interests. Larger groups have an increased capacity to produce compelling and powerful images because of their resources and since their image-making efforts reach a large audience. Organizations perform image work on a more aggregate scale than individuals. They can craft effective idealized images for promoted products, and their performances may have more impact because they reach more people.

Can You Detect Unreality?

Unreality causes problems when unreal images are exploitative and focus action, attention, purchasing, and thinking in ways that make people vulnerable to unknowingly being duped. Going to Disneyworld presupposes that people want to suspend disbelief and be immersed in unreality. In other cases, people may be unaware that commercial forces are imposing make-believe upon them. You may rate your skills well in detecting individuals who seek to mislead you. Maybe when scrutinizing individuals on a one-to-one basis, you are an amazing detector of BS. But consider what happens when you pit your talents against an entire team of professionals working together to compose a persuasive image. How good are you at seeing through very proficient dramaturgical work? Teams of advertising and technical staff create and stage convincing images. You can confront occasional "super-lies" and skilled fabrications of unreality in myriad forms. People know how to dress to hide age, use Photoshop to alter their pictures, disguise physical flaws; food presentation specialists handpick the most photogenic sesame seeds for hamburger buns in ads, witty people write "spontaneous" humor for public speakers, or poets are hired to mobilize deep and moving sentiments in mercenary objects like commercials. Can you, audience member, catch all of these contrivances? Or, being embedded in contrivance, do these images fade into a constant sort of wallpaper? Or do people not want to see the illusions because life is sweeter with them?

Let's consider some advantages that groups using unreality have in staging their works, including the money to pursue research into consumer vulnerabilities. Modern highly sophisticated marketing research operations work for and against you. Dedicated researchers use psychographics to understand psychological wants that underlie and encourage different demographic groups to make purchases. That research likely produces great benefits for consumers whose wants are satisfied and good business for companies, yet there is a mercenary motive at hand. Consumers are researched as targets of opportunity that are ripe for the plucking. Researchers pore over focus group sessions to discover triggers that galvanize and entice consumers. Consumer researchers fit eye-tracking technologies on participant's heads to watch where they focus their eyes on retail shelves so that they know where to locate products for maximum appeal. They study contributions from neuroscientists to learn how people respond to stimuli to take advantage of neurological processes. Researchers dissect geographic territories into maps of financial resources and behavioral affinities, for example, by zip codes, to instruct marketers about characteristics of particular buyers in different zip codes. Look up zip codes at Claritas, which breaks markets down into "lifestyle" segments.[4] These market researchers know if you live in a neighborhood where people read *Sports Illustrated*, hunt, or attend theater, or if you are bluebloods, downwardly mobile, or a two-income family with no dependents. Researchers observe how parents shop with their kids to learn what pressure points kids exploit when they nag their parents to buy them things. Called "pester power," market researchers sell strategies to companies to teach children how to pester their parents more effectively to get them to buy things. Companies hire shills to pose as innocent passerbys in locations who "randomly" promote products outside stores but that do not appear to do so as paid advertisers. Sometimes schemes are more clandestine, as when the publicist for a movie based on a Tucker Max book organized protests against the movie (Holiday, 2012). His idea was to galvanize attention to the movie to get free publicity to spur business. Who would think that the book's promoter organized protests to try

---

[4] See https://www.claritas.com/MyBestSegments/Default.jsp?ID=20.

to support the movie? Another alleged example is that teenage girls were paid to scream during Frank Sinatra's early shows to build up hysteria at his appearances.

Impartial strangers are not the only people posting product reviews on websites. People allied with a particular business may post positive reviews on that site surreptitiously or post negative ones about competitors. Groups can pay celebrities to tweet positively about a product, presumably without their knowing much about the product and without stating that they are paid endorsers to fans. Nightclubs hire attractive women to hang out at their clubs without disclosing having hired them to market to men.

As a whole, people must interpret some semblance of accuracy against eloquent and numerous forces of unreality in the forms of designed stages, pictures, cast members (declared and undeclared), powerful scripts, beautiful lighting and makeup, capped teeth, and shoe lifts. Maybe people will catch a few examples of unreality and can recognize and speak that language, identifying who has had plastic surgery to attain physical perfection or that a product is lit unnaturally, but over time, the sheer numbers game involved may overwhelm them. There is too much unreality for some images not to sneak in and come to double for "reality." Further, living in unreality may produce expectations that images are more accurate and lead to disappointment in unadorned, real things.

Technology gives dramaturgical practitioners, especially in professional hands, almost god-like powers to craft illusions. If commercial actors use those skills to sell people on products, values, and ideals, an unprecedented means of representative social power emerges. Historical persuasion once had limited power, given a piecemeal basis of distribution only to those who could hear or see in proximity. Carnival barkers could reach people in a public courtyard or through early print forms, but mass mobilization of sentiment was unavailable, attributable to technological limits. Along come the Internet, TV, and mass-distributed media, and the dramaturgical power of unreality gains more reach. Modern persuasive material can target groups en masse that might have been shielded prior, maybe who lived in remote places, in more isolated and repressive societies, or who did not read. Presently, unreality is bigger than a thicket. Products in today's hyper saturated media context have a seemingly never-ending front stage capacity to bombard audiences.

Many product front stages urge attending to various dramatized problems that are then promised remedies through buying objects or points of views as answers. A danger lurks in "miracle cure" images leading people to overlook an accurate sense of problems that in turn also prevents solving them. An example are advertisements for what are known as payday loans, in which people receive small loans from "payday" providers who charge so much interest that people end up more hurt financially than before the loan. The typical ads show smiling people with giant wads of cash and promises of quick deposits into their accounts and that people with all kinds of credit get approved. Left out of the picture is the high APR and a reality that people will pay much more back than what they borrow. These images encourage people to have a false belief about solving their financial problems more easily when they could actually deepen those problems if they take the loan on the terms some loaners offer them.

Walter Lipmann (2011) writes in *Public Opinion* the important observation that people respond to unreality with real behaviors.

> To that pseudo-environment his behavior is a response. But because it is behavior, the consequences, if they are acts, operate not in the pseudo-environment where the behavior is stimulated, but in the real environment where action eventuates. . . . For certainly, at the level of social life, what is called the adjustment of man to his environment takes place through the medium of fictions. . . . For it is clear enough that under certain conditions men respond as powerfully to fictions as they do to realities, and that in many cases they help to create the very fictions to which they respond. (p. 14)

Erving Goffman identifies a photographic fallacy of conflating "realness and representation" in photographs. This false equivalence extends beyond photographs into conflating depictions across the range of graphic and moving images with reality. The term d*epiction fallacy* may better communicate the need to avoid perceiving any graphic depiction as reality. People must be wary about the commercially pictured world around them because there are vested interests in these depictions, and further, these images are pervasive. When people confront contrived scenes, they must avoid perceiving them as genuine, for as Lipmann alludes, the consequences of the acts that unreality prompts have real consequences.

Neil Postman (1985) described a need to defend against the "seductions of eloquence," referring to steeling oneself against the pull of the perfections depicted in images that can otherwise overwhelm the senses and mislead people. In the worst implication of unreality, people become puppets who dance on the strings of image makers, who force their vested political and economic interests on people through cunning interpretive framings. Assuming a less severe outcome, seductions of eloquence are an effective form of communication that cause people to encounter images that encourage overconsumption and stereotypes in powerful ways. For example, parents and children confront an advertising industry that designs messaging for children that contains powerful persuasive machinations. Those campaigns urge consumers to crave commodities.

Causes of Unreality: Extravagant Expectations and Pseudo-Events

To fully explore all these images and countless others requires understanding how social forces lead people to be embedded in unreality. What social changes caused the thicket of unreality to proliferate? Summarizing insights from various scholars, three interrelated causes can be identified: *technological innovation, extravagant expectations, and economic changes in how consumption is organized societally.*

Technological innovation has enabled a widespread application of images. The growth of media institutions, photography, recorded telecommunications, and increasingly powerful image-rendering technologies produced what Daniel Boorstin called a "graphic revolution." The graphic revolution begat the rise of multiple newspapers, movie studios and theaters, magazines, television, and content storage devices like videotapes, DVDs, and hardware pertaining to the worldwide web. The growth in technological capacity to carry and deliver content provided means and created new demand for content. More content had to be developed, since the world on its own does not supply as much news as is required to interest audiences, or at least enough news to fulfill the same number of pages every day of the year. Soon companies started reporting on constructible phenomena like celebrity doings. Constructible refers to news about celebrities that is easy to construct as needed. The apotheosis of celebrities as "pseudo-events" is evident in *Cosmopolitan*'s feature called "Celebrities Doing Things!" which is composed of pictures of celebrities walking on a street, buying groceries, leaving a restaurant, or entering a studio. Such content can be made to order. Alternatively, reporters must wait to write stories about events like natural disasters, as these are spontaneous events. Abetted by technology, pictures are omnipresent and are now content on their own, not merely visual accompaniments to news stories. Driven by technological capacity and whipped-up demand, a hunt for popular culture content arose as a new arms race between media companies to entertain and feed images to the public. The relationship is symbiotic as celebrity coverage supports interest in the press and media support interest in celebrities.

Cultural change also fueled the growth of image making and hyper-reality. In terms of cultural change, Americans began to have *extravagant expectations*. These expectations require illusions, as the spectacles that illusions invoke are by definition extravagant and not available in run-of-the-mill mundane reality. As Daniel Boorstin (2012) writes,

> We are ruled by extravagant expectations: (1) Of what the world holds. Of how much news there is, how many heroes there are, how often masterpieces are made, how exotic the nearby can be, how familiar the exotic can become. Of the closeness of places and the farness of places. (2) Of our power to shape the world. Of our ability to create events when there are none, to make heroes when they don't exist, to be somewhere else when we haven't left home. Of our ability to make art forms suit our convenience, to transform a novel into a movie and vice versa, to turn a symphony into mood conditioning. To fabricate national purposes when we lack them, to pursue these purposes after we have fabricated them. To invent our standards and then to respect them as if they had been revealed or discovered. By harboring, nourishing, and ever enlarging our extravagant expectations we create the demand for the illusions with which we deceive ourselves. And which we pay others to make to deceive us. . . . Demanding more than the world can give us, we require that something be fabricated to make up for the world's deficiency. (pp. 3–4)

Daniel Boorstin (2012) argues here that American society is awash in pseudo-events and extravagant expectations. The consequence is that people live in a world of constructed images that fulfill these extravagant expectations. Images and simulations arise to fulfill the necessity for illusions that are grander than what life authentically offers. Images require pseudo-events as building blocks. Pseudo-events are man-made, planted primarily to be reported or distributed to others, and are meant to persuade and have an ambiguous relation to reality. Paraphrasing Boorstin, pseudo-events are not spontaneous. They are planned for use as media content. Pseudo-events are not centered in news gathering in the venerated sense of journalistic ideals or to report facts to inform readers. The goal is purely to capture attention and not necessarily to provide vital news coverage (Boorstin, 2012).

To garner attention, pseudo-events are replete with drama. Celebrities are very popular mediums for immersion in unreality. One part of the image here is when audiences become absorbed by the "drama" in a celebrity's life that is also made for that purpose in the form of a pseudo-event. Watch a little reality TV, and you will see all kinds of pseudo-events designed to induce spontaneous drama that attracts an audience. Much reality television provokes and promotes conflict to get people to tune into that week's show. Yet pseudo-events are not limited just to what people dismiss as "trashy" reality TV. What will the celebrity say in her interview with Barbara Walters about her costar? Do judges on *American Idol* really hate each other? People become thoroughly well informed about pseudo-events to the point where immersion in pseudo-events is the entertainment. Awards shows illustrate promotion made into entertainment content as a pseudo-event. Keeping up with gossip is an important driver of staying attuned to pseudo-events and their sponsors. What would Hugh Grant say to Jay Leno about his liaison with a sex worker? How about Justin Bieber's mug shot? What did you think of the Oscar fashions? Pseudo-events become news spinning off more pseudo-events (Boorstin, 2012). Each of these pseudo-events is tied to bringing in dollars through advertisement and merchandise associated with the event.

Extravagant expectations sensationalize the world. The artificial elements in images inspire a false sense of control over the world by pushing the idea that perfect events can be expected. As a mundane example, consider the old show *Crocodile Hunter*, which host Steve Irwin enacted in natural habitats. Viewers could count on the *Crocodile Hunter* always encountering rare and dangerous animals, which were always available, despite people not usually encountering these animals. Absent from the telecast are people on location who found those animals for Steve Irwin to "stumble" upon, as if naturally and not orchestrated, so that he could do the show. Impatience with waiting, not being entertained, and being stuck in a mundane world is unacceptable. People want magical results in disproportion to their likelihood. Boorstin (2012) wrote, "Now all of us frustrate ourselves by the expectation that we can make the exotic an everyday experience (without its ceasing to be exotic); and can somehow make commonplaceness itself disappear." What hidden work happens to meet extravagant expectations? That work is the dramaturgical and professional backstage of images. Dramaturgy abets this false optimism by making make-believe operate as "real-believe." As an example, nature is not supposed to require backstage staging—that is the implied opposite of what nature shows promise in their depictions of the wild.

Pseudo-events encourage demand and fulfill extravagant expectations. People can certainly pay to generate pseudo-events to fulfill extravagant expectations. You can buy radical surgery to look like a celebrity. If you want Beyoncé to play your wedding, you can, but be prepared to shell out lots of money. Stadiums can be rented out for a child's sweet 16. More mundane pseudo-events are available too. Companies use pseudo-events to get business, such as paying a former professional athlete to give autographs at a car dealership as a promotional event. Children can meet Santa or the Easter Bunny to drag parents into the mall. Stores host "beauty festivals" to drive demand and display products. Contests entice consumers' interest in participating. Commemorations are pseudo-events, such as 20th anniversaries, restaurant weeks, downtown fairs, or best-of competitions where people seek press attention to galvanize people to spend money to be a part of things and glorify the celebrated object of the anniversary. These actions are consumption-oriented dramaturgical productions. Pseudo-events provide a cultural lift to induce attention. People are not just shopping; they are at a commemoration of the town or at a 20th anniversary. There is a puppy parade at the mall or craft festival to attend out of interest, not just to shop. It just so happens that you can shop there too. Creating pseudo-events as marketing experiences for consumers connects Boorstin's ideas, and Pine and Gilmore's (2011) notion of the experience economy, as vivid demonstrations of a contemporary relevance of the dramaturgical perspective.

Pine and Gilmore (2011) argue that companies must embrace experiential innovation for their businesses to grow and escape a trap of competing purely on price. They advocate developing CEM, which refers to *Customer Experience Management*. Consider some examples to get a sense of how experience can be the centering focus of economic activity. Think about companies that develop distinctive experiences associated with purchasing their brands. Build a Bear has patrons arrive to customize and experience making their own product. American Girl Place has customers select a distinctive doll with its own story and the chance to make experiences like having tea with them. New trademarked terms appear, like eatertainment, shoppertainment, and shopperscapism. Sports bars like Hooters arrange an experience combining eating and ogling. More extreme experiences are Ninja restaurant in New York City, where ninjas jump out at patrons, dinner in the sky where people eat on a table suspended 150 feet in the air by a crane, and sushi restaurants where people eat food directly from a naked person's body. The goal in integrating experiences is to transform a retail *space* into a distinctive *place* and experience offering. The experience is not naturally occurring but planned, and to hit the experiential theme requires dramaturgical work.

Pine and Gilmore (2011) highlight the interesting example of birthday parties. These used to involve mostly a cake, candles, and cards, with maybe holding the event as a surprise. Now birthdays may involve a themed party somewhere. Birthdays may now be sourced to an outside "experience" provider, which profits from that business, like a Chuck E. Cheese. Weddings now have planners and all kinds of destination weddings and forms of theming. Pine and Gilmore argue that adding experience to any business is a smart economic move to seek profits in a changing business climate. In some cases, if the experience is worthwhile, they suggest charging admission to the store just for the experience. Jordan's Furniture is a furniture business that integrates experiences. Their website has a heading for "attractions" that lists a motion simulator, a light show, a laser show, a winter ice show, and a Tempur-Pedic-sponsored IMAX movie theater. They also charge people to go on the motion simulator. This furniture store now trades on the appeal of an amusement park.

Another interesting example Pine and Gilmore (2011) note is the public library in Cerritos, California. According to Pine and Gilmore (2011, p. 74), the Cerritos Public Library bills itself as "the world's first experience library, employing the theme of 'journey through time' to alter the décor and furnishings of each room. In a town of fifty thousand residents, the library averages more than three thousand visitors daily." Consider the theming and experience built into the design. The picture in Figure 5.1a shows an aquarium and set of oversize book facades as part of the experience of going to the children's section. The picture in Figure 5.1b shows the theming for the area of 21st century collections.

According to the Themed Entertainment Association (TEA), which functions as a trade group for builders, architects, and other professionals involved in developing themed attractions, the market for themed entertainment facilities is booming. The movement to integrate features of entertainment, engagement, and experience into physical design is picking up speed. TEA identified the venues in Figure 5.2 as growing markets for their work.

Figure 5.1a

Source: Courtesy of Cerritos Public Library.

Figure 5.1b

Source: Courtesy of Cerritos Public Library.

Figure 5.2

PUBLIC VENUES	EDUCATIONAL VENUES	OTHER VENUES
Entertainment Centers	Museums	Libraries
Shopping Malls	Collections/ Heritage Facilities	Church Campuses
Mixed-Use Urban Centers	Cultural Attractions	Hospital Wings
Science Centers	Healing Gardens	Restaurants
Hotels and Resorts	Nature Sites	Cancer Treatment
Visitors/Hospitality	Centers Brand Lands	Senior Centers
Gaming Centers	Museums of Industry	Auto Malls
Sports Parks/Franchises	Factory Tours	Alzheimer's Facilities
Music Halls (House of Blues)	College Campuses	Housing
Community Centers	Medical Campuses	Daycare Centers

Interviews with TEA architects published in a trade booklet (Themed Entertainment Association, 2008) stated, "It is an astute business decision to combine retail merchandising with entertainment design. Retail environments must create experiences that translate to sales." Jim Nelson stated, "Universal City Walk is a district branding project that has done it right. Sales per square foot are three times higher than the average retail center" (p. 3). Marty Borko offered another example:

> We're doing a lot of smaller scale customer experiences. A client was look-ing to develop a branded experience. They needed content providers; show designers, technology and lighting. The project has a story, experience map, sketches, content, game characters, and technology show controls. Yet this is a 2,000 square foot project! (p. 3)

Injecting experiences into businesses exists in many forms. Some sales are pseudo-events that drive purchases by encouraging people to respond to a scarce opportunity to pay lower prices. Perhaps the best example of a demand-driving sales pseudo-event is "Black Friday," which is an artificial sales occasion invented to bring special savings to encourage shopping before Christmas. Black Friday is like a holiday all its own, replete with cultural momentum to look forward to the event and to spend on available offerings. Reporters also cover upcoming Black Friday sales, simultaneously getting material to cover thanks to a pseudo-event that they now promote. People join together as eager participants, waiting together to go through the marathon wait to get into the stores at midnight or later to get at the "door busters" inside. Now some stores are even opening early afternoon to grab shoppers such that the pseudo-event of Black Friday now may overtake the Thanksgiving holiday event.

Image Life as Performance

Images take on an *image life* after they appear, as future performances should maintain the stated depiction in continuity afterward. Examples of *image life* are plentiful. A movie star can have an image as a "femme fatale" that is larger than life but not necessarily reflective of whom she is as a real person. Madonna, a star known for conveying a sexual persona, once said, "Everyone probably thinks that I'm a raving nymphomaniac and that I have an insatiable sexual appetite, when the truth is I'd rather read a book." The image life taken on here is of a femme fatale writ large, requiring dressing and acting in certain ways for public consumption, because the image has an important artificial life to maintain for commercial purposes. A male movie star may affect a macho, tough guy image that is far from who he is in his everyday life. Image life becomes a dramaturgical project requiring focused front and backstage management where people guard the backstage as the front stage image must be on all the time. This projected identity is a part that a protagonist plays that has commercial ramifications, as that artificial life may also be a company's property, as are certain characters. Hollywood production companies, for example, used to protect the image life of their stars through all kinds of machinations, such as encouraging male homosexual stars like Rock Hudson to marry women and bribing journalists to not publish stories. Even today, consider the fallout from scandals associated with child stars who get into trouble. A Justin Bieber or Miley Cyrus has tons of young fans, and they are supposed to remain permanent wholesome role models to keep selling products to these kids. Of course, these stars get older and want to pursue adult troubles, like taking drugs and having sex.

The commercial interests that want them to remain wholesome are then furious that because these stars do not manage to sustain their image life correctly, they damage a profitable commodity.

Images can consist of personas treated as real or that incur reactions that are real. It seems silly to state that an obvious image like an animated talking tiger is real in consequences, but cereal sales rose when Tony the Tiger told kids that Frosted Flakes are great. A cartoon or graphic drawing is not organically alive or real in a sentient way but is *absolutely real* in that actual behavior results from people observing those cartoons and graphic images. These images create real actions and money, so they are real in consequence. They also have image lives of their own, even though they are not living beings.

Advertisers create many images and maintain their lives after birthing them. I conducted observations at an advertising agency for a different research project. This excerpt from my field notes draws on conversations with an advertising executive working on feminine hygiene products:

> For (product X), the prototypical identity is of the Alpha girl. She is the "leader of the pack." The identity is "aspirational" because people want to be that person. I asked for a set of examples of the person. She said that the person was a "fearless woman like Amelia Earhart, an edgy trendsetter like Angelina Jolie, and had a smart sense of humor like Tina Fey." The Alpha Girl is also a leader of the pack and a trendsetter. When I asked questions about the age level of the marketing, I learned that the target age is relatively early—maybe 15 to early twenties. The reason why is that with this "femcare" product, the woman is an early adopter who usually stays loyal as a permanent user. This is a "high loyalty" category. This person was also analyzed as a type of person in a given social situation. So for example, the Alpha Girl campaign is "of a young woman playing by her own rules." The subtler message here is that "we understand you" and have empathy and friendship with you. This woman is at a point in time where "she is experimenting with her identity and wants to find herself. She wants reliability in a product that also understands her needs."

Note the image life at hand here. The "girl" referred to as an "Alpha girl" comprises an extravagant expectation and refers to a composite image of women, all of whom are well-known personalities whose reputations are already media driven. This composite woman does not exist but is to be given life through campaigns that associates this image's traits with a femcare product. Consumers are to be motivated to purchase the product through these positive image associations. The image was never alive or a sentient figure, but the image has an artificial life as a commercial actor.

Consider anthropomorphic characters, which offer a good example of image life. These inanimate characters are performers. Anthropomorphism refers to associating human characteristics with animals and objects. During this research project, I was granted access to a style guide for characters who represent different cereal products. Consider the lengths to which the brand goes to provide identities for kinds of cereal (kinds refers to different shapes of the same cereal brand). An inorganic product is provided with human characteristics and an idealized image. A confidential style guide identifies the fictional images that this non-sentient object must depict.

Directions from Style Guide on characteristics of ***.

Original *** is always professional. After all, he's got a job to do: Keep 'em full and focused. But that doesn't mean he doesn't have fun. He loves a good pun, is full of wit and amuses himself with his sense of humor. He's also a bit bashful. Give him a compliment and he just might blush. Ms. *** is the female character and wife to original. All the same rules apply in how she is posed and how her features are treated. Her legs are slightly longer than a regular character and her biscuit is cinched at the waist to show a more feminine shape. She also has fuller lips, feminine shoes and a bracelet all designed to reinforce her gender. She's smart, sophisticated and charming. She is very feminine in the way she is posed and animated but she is never sexy.

The style guide also details how each feature is to be rendered, such as lips, facial expressions, the mouth, their limbs, and so forth. They also have personality characteristics:

They are jokesters, always looking for a good laugh. They're witty. They always reassure mom, encourage kids and help kids. They're excited and energetic. Sometimes they're a bit sassy. They are all about having fun and helping kids do well in school, but there are some things they just don't do. Here are a few things to keep in mind. They never get angry. They're never frustrated, exhausted, tired or sleepy. They never show age, pain or injury. They're not salesmen or shills. They're never shown getting eaten, talk about getting eaten or even eat the cereal—that's just weird.

Where they live in the world, the characters are do-gooders so they often do their very best at all times. They even go to bed early. Their hangouts include schools, offices and kitchens. Can't get into too much trouble there. In fact, they're only allowed to watch movies that are rated G. When they aren't in the real world, they live in their own world where things are their own size. Some things they enjoy doing include bowling, playing dress-up and reading the newspaper next to a warm fireplace.

Ponder the degree of unreality here. First, cereals are gendered. Do you view cereal as being a particular sex when you eat a bowl of cereal? The cereals know human travails and support moms in all their work, which is a nice gesture for the people eating them. They bowl and play dress-up and never get hungry, old, or frustrated. Now if you have cereal at home, take a single piece out, put it on a paper towel, and imagine staging the animation and filming the cereal enacting all of these characteristics and putting them on TV, where they help move sales figures upward. That is dramaturgy to produce unreality—advertising as Dr. Frankenstein creating image life. Advertisers inundate us with these creations.

Performers at Colonial Williamsburg must reproduce colonial history for patrons without giving grievous offense, yet aspects of that history are grievously offensive, such as the cruelties of slavery and efforts to spread smallpox among Native Americans. Dramaturgical rules of presentation emerge that show audiences some things about what times were like but not in full painful accuracy. While the people involved make hard choices about the degree to which they recreate history accurately, and they do their best accordingly, the resulting history is a facsimile. At what point is a facsimile an authentic depiction of the real, as the site claims to bring history to life? Is abridged history, history? What their performances sustain is the life of a simulation.

This history also demands that audiences offer a polite suspension of disbelief. That suspension of disbelief goes beyond simple things like seeing employees garbed in historically accurate clothing while ignoring their texting on phones walking to work. Audiences must forget about the parking lots, all the other people like them "from the future" who are walking around with camcorders, and that how people associate with one another in Williamsburg is different from what was done historically. For example, did blacksmiths spend their days talking about a smithy's life to tourists? Image history is people using old stuff wearing old clothes in old-looking buildings speaking Olde English. Is recreated old stuff "history" when cultural context is incomplete? Image life is performed history in a new artificial format.

Image life as a communicative and dramaturgical form is easy for people to understand, just as images are. What images sacrifice in messaging is complexity. What audiences gain from images are simplicity, predictability, and knowledge. Consider the plethora of rankings and reviews that now inundate contemporary society. Various institutions rank colleges and universities in the United States, with the public viewing the rankings from *U.S. News & World Report* as a key guide. What do rankings mean as images? The mechanics of rising and falling in rankings does not necessarily transfer into students having better or worse collegiate experiences, but the image does lead people to think a college experience and value associates with a generic rank. If ranks change, people may actually feel their experience change for the better or worse, depending on the direction of the rank change. Boorstin connected the idea of image to self-fulfilling prophecy, believing that images could sponsor predictions that people worked to make true.

Rankers tout their rankings as objective and comprised from aggregate data to reassure people that the data reflect complexity and thoroughness. Is having a placeholder number (12, 21, 2, 42) enough to provide a sense that so much information is now clear just from one number? The final ranked numbers must be understood as rounded, but those differences actually could reflect differences between decimal places, like one institution has a score of 4.555 and another is 4.889, but those differences appear on a webpage, translated into unequal summary numbers such as 21 and 25. Round up scores, and ranks now seem more a product of meaningful differences rather than decimal places.[5] *U.S. News & World Report* ranks institutions to sell magazines, guidebooks, and advertising. They are not in the business of developing educational improvements; rankers know that audiences just want the magical answer to interpretation that a rank offers. Who cares about the mess in the making when the resulting image gives you crystal clear instructions on how to view institutions?

A culture obsessed with rankings impacts people, including when they worry about being numerically ranked themselves. Bureaucracies use numerical rankings and assessment, and some companies practice "rank and yank" systems where the lowest ranked percentage of employees are fired annually. As an employee, you do not necessarily pick the standards for evaluation, and fairness is not a guarantee. Some among you no doubt welcome the challenge of being ranked, but that confidence also depends on knowing you can succeed in a meritocratic assessment. Not all ranking is about fairness. If you are evaluated in a workplace and you have some capacity to

---

[5] This point about not highlighting decimal places in rankings is inspired by, but different from, the example offered by Wendy N. Espeland in a lecture she presented entitled "Rankled by the Rankings: Law School and Other Organizational Responses to the US News and World Report Rankings," April 26, 2012, in Easton, PA.

work the rankings, you might be wise to do so. Perhaps you do not commit outright fraud, but if you do not think about how the rank is composed and how to best succeed in that ranking, including by sly manipulations, then you are being unwise. Enter dramaturgy, which flourishes in bureaucratic and popular cultures of ranking. People act to the rankings. In teaching, people can teach to the evaluations. In schools with set rankings from students' test score performances, some teachers just teach to the test while denying doing so. In workplaces, reviews are fought over and contested. Think about reactivity, which is a core engine of dramaturgical performance. Reactivity refers to when people's behaviors are affected by the presence of someone observing them. Reactivity happens just as a result of someone being around you. Now imagine that you know the people around you are explicitly judging you and the reactivity meter will hit the red zone. Businesses are anxious about how websites rate them. Critics can sink entertainment offerings with bad reviews. Imagine how dating would be affected, if after every date, each person handed a score to the other and then published them. Would people's behaviors on dates be impacted more if these scores existed? A culture of ranking produces images that seek to rig reactivity.

An important aspect of reporting ranks is valuing comparison as the key factor. A ranked score captures all kinds of meanings but most significantly communicates a relative standing in comparison to others, as in this place is better or worse than that one. We could examine a place in depth for its own merits and problems or take *U.S. News*'s word for it that you gain specific knowledge of a place because a comparison number exists. Depth of knowledge about the particular is sacrificed to comparative superficial calculability. Complexity is hard, but a single number is very understandable. What is better for cognitively overtaxed people than getting a simple answer to a tough question?

Consider a dating analogy. Forty eligible partners are ranked in comparison with one another about what people think of them, how rich they are, and assessments of their looks. Does your date's ranking impact your judgment of the date before you date? Probably. If you end up liking a person who is ranked in the thirties, even if you are happy, does that rank somehow lessen the experience? What about being dissatisfied with a high-ranked person but fearing the impact of going to a lower ranked person? Who wants to slide down, even if that person could hypothetically make you happier? Rankings predispose. Image life affects real life. Rank becomes an image that takes on a life of its own for the ranked, rankers, and audiences. A ranked institution has a new master when assigned a number and place in a hierarchy of competitive peers. That number has a tyranny because if not good, then people have to move heaven and earth to get to a better number, and if good, then people monitor carefully to see if the number falls. Every person in higher education knows that high-level administrators and members of Boards of Trustees urge moving their institutions higher in rankings, even if they simultaneously decry the rankings as flawed. Organizational changes occur or are debated with numbered ranks in mind. Change is also motivated to benefit institutions, as a higher ranking is often better. Changes to reported class sizes, listing of testing data, salary increases, and new programs—these items become tools to affect changes in a rank. The point here is that changes to these aspects of a college are not necessarily undertaken *just* because they are good to do on their own merits but perhaps also because they are calculable metrics.

People do not experience a rank as something you can always see or touch. A person attends a college or university, not a rank. However, when a person attends an institution ranked 20 versus 39 or 1 versus 10, there is a social meaning about how good that person is because of what rank institution number they attend. Audiences think about rank as a "real" thing, but rank is not alive or made of bricks and mortar. A rank is a compilation of scores that have representative power as an image of a place or person. That number must be fed and becomes a tyrant.

Suppose I asked you to rank your experiences in traveling to Nairobi, London, and New York. How many stars would you give your experiences in each city? As an experience, what does it mean to say that London is a 5 and Nairobi a 10? How much complexity is lost? Hearing a high rank matters because people feel reaffirmed by choosing something more highly ranked than lower ranked. On the other hand, to have experience captured as a number reduces qualities of experience significantly. Does a number capture a city?

Extravagant expectations and pseudo-events are prominent features of cultural experiences and important aspects of unreality's rise. These phenomena spawned off images that then took on lives of their own as illusions with lives that people work to sustain. Advertisers demonstrate maintaining image life using anthropomorphism that gives inorganic items an emotional life and other human characteristics. Extravagant expectations also lead cultures to use lists and rankings more. An extravagant expectation is that the best is what you deserve and should get and a rank provides an easy image guide to the best. People want the world summed up into easy-to-digest versions of the best so that people can make decisions more easily (complexity is reduced) and with an affirmed sense of being right in one's choices (who contests going with the best?). In cultures of ranking, extravagant expectations compare dull options and brighter ones (minus complexity), encourage people to rig the game with dramaturgy, and lead people to perceive the world in simplified terms.

A cost of extravagant expectations is that existing physical objects that interest people may no longer be anchored temporally, spatially, and contextually. Daniel Boorstin (2012) comments that paintings displayed in museums are like animals displayed in zoos; something authentic is lost from the original context, to be replaced by pseudo-context. Events like Halloween and Christmas now have activities (haunted house tours, winter wonderland hayrides) that go weeks beyond the actual day of the holiday. The commercialization of holidays produces a new span of length and opposition movements to "keep the Christ in Christmas." Today, the Christmas "season" now seems to stretch from Halloween to January 2. Binge viewing TV shows on Netflix or other media products on demand is decontextualized from the experiences of going through the anticipation of episode to episode over a season.

There is a dissolving of more complex and longer forms of culture into smaller digestible ones. There were once long stories in newspapers; now there is *USA Today* and, finally, listicles on the web. Think of iTunes as offering a form of decontextualization and reduction from a whole into parts. Songs are made available out of context from what used to be albums that had connected thematic aspects that applied (sometimes called concept albums) to the whole album, like Pink Floyd's *The Wall.* Now songs are available for sale without having to participate in the album's concept. There are upsides, as more songs are widely available, and there are abundant cost savings for consumers. Yet larger themes are now attenuated, and artists and producers receive less payment, which may prevent more artists from earning a living in the medium. Options for consumers are bountiful, but they have less of the whole art available and can damage the industry's viability, which in turn imperils the art's future availability. To Pine and Gilbert's point about embracing entertainment, experience, and engagement as profit centers, the dip in profits from album and CD sales has led many artists to look to frequent touring as offering the best shot to build their wealth.

YouTube posts clips of scenes so that the same stripping out of context process is possible on accessible video, and people can now just zoom to a key scene and ignore the context. The danger here is like the old joke about speed-reading *War and Peace*, a book that is well over 1,000 pages, in 20 minutes. What did you learn from speed-reading the book? It's about Russia.[6] The joke is that the book is about a lot more than Russia. The meaning captured from a brief look is a marginal return. Perhaps an analogy here is imagining a world where just highlights of events are the only priority. Is life just about catching the highlight reels?

The Economics of Unreal Performances and Consumerism

One economic explanation sociologists have developed posits that our present unreality resulted from strategies owners of capital use to maximize profits. With technical innovations and exploitative labor practices ramping up production, more and more objects are available for consumers to purchase. Given this additional surplus of goods, capitalists now seek to ramp up demand to ensure being able to sell more goods. The urgent need to drive demand in the face of that surplus produced *new relations of consumption*, which impact consumer behaviors (Ritzer, 2005). These new relations created significant desire and want for products that lead consumers to fetishize commodities and seek to accumulate goods. Relations of consumption involve comprehensive advertising; a science and spread of marketing strategies, the development of new products, and promotion of lifestyles that integrate consumption as a means; extravagant expectations that consumer goods are to fulfill; and integrating a quality of enchantment and entertainment experiences associated with purchasing.

George Ritzer is a prominent scholar and theorist of these new relations of consumption. The shift to relations of consumption occurred in tandem with large-scale social changes in how people work and live. People now operate in social situations characterized by routine and rational bureaucratic, organizational processes. Ritzer referred to these processes as "McDonaldization," and he argued that these processes have overtaken modern life (Ritzer, 2008). Ritzer developed the term McDonaldization based on identifying the organizational attributes that made the fast food industry generally, and McDonald's specifically, so successful. McDonald's uses managerial processes that guarantee successful duplication of the

---

[6] The original joke, by Woody Allen, goes, "I took a speed-reading course and read *War and Peace* in 20 minutes. It's about Russia."

timing, taste, and availability of the food whatever the facility's location. French fries are supposed to taste the same and be cooked the same way, whether you are in New York City, Mexico City, London, or Moscow. The amazing volume and uniformity McDonaldization produces are attributable to efficiency, predictability, calculability, and control through technology.

The productive potential of McDonaldization also affects individuals and workers. Adherence to effective routine is good for production numbers but not so much at offering people complex choices or flexibility in how they work and sometimes in how they live. A rational world of McDonaldization provides a more abundant world of products but also a prescriptive and more boring soul-sucking world. To combat this languor, companies began to add enchantment to commercial offerings that lay a shimmering gloss over that underlying rationality of production. Consumerism promises imagination products and escape into transcendent lifestyles through acquisition. People want awe and wonder when stuck in a cage of rationalized living, so enchanting qualities offer a respite from stultifying routine.

Ritzer (2005) identified some new means of consumption to observe in contemporary society. One new means of consumption are venues Ritzer calls *cathedrals of consumption*. These "cathedrals," in theoretical terms, are themed containers for hyperconsumption that offer consumers "enchanted" experiences in their shopping. Not too subtly, the suggestion here is that consumption has overtaken religion as the source of enchantment in everyday life. People look for fulfillment in their shopping experiences and focus their aims on purchasing. Has shopping or going to church won more adherents during Christmas?

Themed restaurants, malls, and "Disneyfied" downtowns represent cathedrals of consumption. What is enchantment more specifically? Enchantment refers to injecting meaningful experiences and symbols into traditional processes of purchasing that reward customers for spending time in the venue and for buying. The right enchantment, combined with heightened McDonaldized efficiencies in distribution and unprecedented availability of goods, creates and serves demand. Ritzer (2005) argues that in working together, enchantment and McDonaldization trap people. Enchantment is the honey, and the efficiency of rationality is the ultimately inescapable flytrap. People are stuck in the hyperreal and the underlying rational service economy that produce efficient and symbolic shows to get people to buy more and more commodities while being stuck in an ultimately unrewarding enchantment that can't be real or true.[7]

Enchanting the process of how people buy things sounds mysterious but is straightforward. One place to start is how shopping becomes a form of entertainment. As Pine and Gilmore (2011) clarify, a first move is to inject engaging experiences into locations. Sometimes those experiences are themed. The process of experiencing shopping becomes enjoyable, as there are engaging experiences to be had, complementary service provision, and compelling identities affixed to purchases. The locations are full of fun and excitement. The analogy is as if one watched commercials for the same pleasure that motivates watching the TV show. If done correctly, the experience that accompanies the shopping becomes the incentive and reward, not just purchasing a good.

The enchantment process is embedded in venues of sales. People spend more and more time in themed environments designed specifically to encourage experiences that abet consumption. Casinos and spectacular malls, for example, are not designed on a whim, with planners just putting opportunities to spend money in accessible spaces without thinking about how to design an environment around them to encourage their use. Themed locations are planned to encourage people to consume the products there. "Atmospherics" is about creating a shopping atmosphere that combines aspects of the service and physical environment to encourage emotional and sensory experiences that motivate purchases. In marketing, the term *servicescape* refers to a built environment that strategizes how to use ambient conditions, spatial layout, and symbolic communication to influence customers. That means investigating themed environments as products of processes designed to influence people to understand and react in ways that designers seek. Researchers can spend their lives studying how people consume in these environments.[8]

Here Pine and Gilmore advance the dramaturgical approach in their analyses of the experience economy. Organizations create experiential lands, whether at Jordan's Furniture or Niketown. Pine and Gilmore suggest understanding four types of generated experiences. These are

---

[7] This point is an argument which also has many critics, including marketers who decry this representation of their work and the aims of their client companies.

[8] Sociologists can also analyze the "consumer self": how people seek to meet wants and desires within markets constructed to inspire and satiate wants. Social scientists, who love being in the doomsaying business, can then analyze the negative consequences of a consumer society.

experience as entertainment (people go to enjoy themselves), experience as education (people go to learn), experience as escapism (people go to do), and experience as aesthetic (people go for an aesthetic reward). These domains of experience overlap. For example, some organizations offer classes in stores to get business up, which entertains, educates, and also can provide an aesthetic, such as when a large retailer offers a class on wines or fine cheeses sold there. Casinos teach classes on how to gamble. There is growth in the category of having production facilities also serve as factory tours to show people how products are made (education) which also provides an experience and entertainment. People "escape" into the wild to have a range of outdoor experiences. Pine and Gilmore (2011) argue that companies need to embrace what they call "ing" experiences. How can patrons be more invested in active verb activities associated with the business offerings? Test-driving, traveling—the goal is to incorporate experience more as what a customer will also want to buy. Autostadt in Germany is a car theme park where people test-drive different cars and then pick a car to buy and then take home. These activities integrate people into the product's front stage.

For Pine and Gilmore, the dramaturgical approach is not an analogy but a model of what people do to stage experiences. They focus attention on an enterprise's dramatic nature and state "work is theater." They view people as performing their activities. Pine and Gilmore represent a group of scholars who argue for a literal view of dramaturgy where work *is* theater. Part of that experience work involves staging events like meetings, trade shows, and product launches. They distinguish between different kinds of theatrical traditions that workers must perform. In an experience economy, workers may engage in *improvisational, platform, matching,* and *street* forms of theater. Improvisational refers to improvising performances, and platform refers to strictly scripted theater as if on a classic theatrical stage. Matching theater refers to integrating different components into a performance, much like admissions people and the faculty from a college might bring different components of a college's image together for prospective students. Street theater is more of a democratic, rough-and-ready kind of performance that is about connecting to the masses in public.

Pine and Gilmore (2011) argue for a direct application of theatrical terminology to understand organizing experiences. An ensemble is a team focused on a distinct performance goal, not just a collection of random individuals. The cast refers to workers, and their roles at work equal their work responsibilities. The characterizations workers offer equal their representations of work. Organizational groups constitute ensembles, and the workplace equals the theatrical stage. The human resources department is the casting department. For Pine and Gilmore, the dramaturgical model captures what people do at work. People are not like actors—they are actors.

These actors perform in themed locations where businesses offer experiences. A cardinal rule informing their work is to eliminate "negative cues" that reveal discontinuities in a theme or experience that a place offers, a concern that represents Goffman's notion of spoiled identity to large organizations. For example, avoid having a cast member at Disney World walk around carrying his Mickey Mouse head in his arms. The goal of avoiding negative cues is right out of Goffman, who emphasized avoiding communicating out of character in order to not spoil one's identity.

Las Vegas Casinos as "Cathedrals of Consumption"

Large Las Vegas casinos illustrate themed cathedrals of consumption. Moving away from a more abstract sense of images and themes, let's consider this concrete physical structure as an example. There is a certain "psych-itecture" at work in designing sets that persuade patrons to gamble. Returning to the dramaturgical discussions in earlier chapters, the front stage setting impacts the audience's perceptions. The casino is a themed dramaturgical set on which front and backstage performances occur. The spaces there have meanings and comprise stimuli intended to produce a range of responses in patrons. Many Las Vegas casinos are simultaneously playgrounds and mazes. The atmosphere is euphoric, noisy, sometimes a bit risqué, and built to accommodate all sorts of personal preferences for spending money. There are no clocks or windows to distract people. Patrons are served free alcohol. No stunning artworks, posters, or televisions are near games to lure people's attention from gaming. One exception is television showing sporting events for sports betting. There are no empty banks of seats away from gaming unless the seats accompany group betting like in sports books or variations on bingo games. The atmosphere is loud enough to make the setting undesirable for hanging around to have conversations.

A question to ask in any setting is what information is available to me here? How is information designed for patrons? No strangers are supposed to access the backstage, where staff members focus on observing and managing work to serve customers in the "front of house." Slots and video poker machines have nice bright colors and big numbers always showing how much someone could win if they play. Sometimes they have colorful placards hanging on the top of them that show off a compelling fantasy theme. There are linked slot machines with combined jackpots that can reach hundreds of thousands of dollars. People get paper slips and use poker chips as part of gaming and as a form of psychology that obscures the money involved. Bright lights and themes adorn machines, from slots themed after make-believe fantasy characters to game show and celebrity themes. Attractive servers approach customers in skimpy outfits, which work for male patrons as a fantasy landscape to accompany their gaming. Undercover security monitors observe for any untoward activities, enabling the business to continue uninterrupted. Casino design allows people to follow their gambling preferences in choosing what games to play and in what surroundings. They can make themselves more front and center by choosing a gaming activity where they play in front of others, such as poker or craps, or they can disappear into aisles to gamble.

High-end casino gambling was historically associated with elites who would dress up. Casinos like the Borgata Hotel and the Wynn offer opportunities for this high-end action of consumption. Erving Goffman (1967) coined the term "fancy milling" to describe where the action is for people in consumption, in people enjoying getting to be big shots by displaying an association with opulence to others. He wrote,

> Adults in our society can enjoy a taste of social mobility by consuming valued products, by enjoying costly and modish entertainment, by spending time in luxurious settings, and by mingling with prestigeful persons— all the more if these occur at the same time and in the presence of many witnesses. This is the action of consumption. (pp. 197–198)

Las Vegas offers plentiful opportunities for themed action of consumption with bottle service tables; fabulous, expensive "name" restaurants; and chances to drink expensive alcohol and show everyone what a rich and successful person you are. Casinos make an excellent show of calling attention to big spenders by segregating them visibly. There are special access entries with no waiting for people who receive comps, suites with perks, and VIP gambling rooms. Special lines and attendants signal an observable distinction as a customer. When checking into the hotel casino, right from the start, VIP members receive more of a "big shot" experience. For patrons who prefer to enter a fugue state on slot machines and disappear into their gambling, slots are located in rows, removed from overall public view so that people cannot crowd over and observe your play easily. Machines have seats where people can relax and lose themselves in the slot machine's action.

When people enter casino hotels in Las Vegas, they must go through the casino floor to get anywhere to eat, swim in the pool, or enter their rooms. They might not gamble on those walks, but they will have every opportunity to do so. The scale of casinos is immense. Consider the outside facades of casino hotels. The Excalibur is built as a giant medieval fantasy castle. The Treasure Island casino stages a pirate battle outside the casino to lure visitors. The Luxor is a giant pyramid-shaped building with inclined elevators. Circus Circus is a themed hotel with circus acts and an amusement park inside the hotel. The Paris Las Vegas hotel has reproduced the Eiffel Tower. New York, New York reproduces New York City landmarks throughout the hotel, and the Rio hotel stages an afternoon Mardi Gras parade through the casino.

People want to experience the productions that these spectacles offer. These imitations are pseudo-events of grand scale and also images that bear an approximation of the originals but in more appealing ways for tourists. New York City is reproduced without the crime and grime. Las Vegas brings all of these images together in one place in the same decontextualized way that pieces of art are placed in a museum. You do not have to speak Egyptian or risk encountering revolutionary upheavals to be inside a pseudo-pyramid. Excalibur's medieval castle has indoor plumbing. The pirates of Treasure Island are visible without a time machine and will not make landlubbers run the plank. Egyptian pyramids, New York landmarks, and the Eiffel Tower, all within short proximity, are a spectacle only available together in this imagined form.

There is also a democratic magic to casinos. People of all different social statuses and classes can be accommodated; people with different handicaps, of different ages, nationalities, and means (Goffman, 1967, p. 203). People can bet pennies in a slot machine or tremendous sums of money on special action tables. This cathedral of consumption welcomes all with no nuances as long as they can do business.

The Magic of Enchanted Products

Moving from casinos, many Americans now spend their time in a *chainscape* of retail chains with themed atmospheres that cumulate into a dominant consumer landscape where people buy. The brick-and-mortar *chainscape* comprises an image world as stores with themes and values that are planned out and staged by image makers. When people walk within them, their theme envelops the customers. Starbucks, for example, has a role as a "third place" destination between work and home, where people go to self-gift themselves with expensive coffee drinks and an atmosphere replete with progressive values, effete music, and pleas for ethical globalism (see Simon, 2011). Mini experiences are built into the process, such as having your name taken and announced in connection with your beverage.

Chick-fil-A serves God with a religious-inspired corporate mission, which though a sincere commitment, cannot speak for itself and must be staged for customers to identify. Plentiful plaques adorn the store speaking to Chick-fil-A's commitment to moral values, donating to charities, funding retreats to help improve family life and the institution of marriage, and being family-friendly dining. The chain closes for Sundays so everyone can worship, which puts their money where their mouth is, as closing that day carries some commercial cost. The chain encourages an "up with people" almost robotically cheerful attentiveness among employees. Here, as in other chainscape environments, commercial goals are achieved through creating the right atmospheric elements and experience for consumers.

Lifestyles that people can claim and partake in, to know the "good life" in whatever form, are part of the enchantment associated with consumption and overconsumption. For example, the idea of being able to buy your way into ideal lifestyles is easy to understand as a form of enchantment. Celebrity endorsement offers an illustration. Buy the sneaker to be "like Mike" and consumers will have a celebrity's magical talent because objects exposed to a celebrity can "magically" transfer their talent to the buyer. Wear the celebrity's perfume, cologne, clothes, and you capture some of that celebrity's aura. Is wearing Axe not similar to being given a magical spell to attract people? Today many people use products in a way that resembles our human ancestors who wore parts of animals to connect the characteristics of that animal to them, like wearing a cheetah's fur to acquire a cheetah's speed. Some animals are endangered precisely because consumers believe these animals have qualities that can transfer virility and youth to humans.

MTV ran a show called *Cribs* that focused on the lavish homes of wealthy actors, athletes, and celebrities, with the assumption that people aspire to live the charmed lives the show depicted. A similar show prior to that was called *Lifestyles of the Rich and Famous*. Celebrities grace products, advertising and promoting them, and lending their magic to urge consumption. People consume celebrities by spending money on items referencing them. Focusing on celebrities consumes people's time and thoughts. Further, by consuming celebrities, people are in an artificial dialogue with them that is on industry and image terms. For example, people read a celebrity's book that is influenced by the crafty hand of the public relations team. Celebrities go on talk shows or other interviews to promote a product involving them so the likelihood of seeing an authentic them is questionable.

When people sell a product, are they truly being themselves, or are they representatives of image life? Celebrities are vital to organizations in addition to being the sun around which many fans circle. Celebrities fulfill a need that media companies have to get page hits, sell advertising, and occupy people's interest. People also consume celebrities and entertainment products all day, in the television they watch, the magazines they read, the clothing they wear, and the posters on their walls. When people consume celebrities, they consume and speak a language of extravagant expectations in the restaurants of the stars, gowns worn at galas, expensive cars, and lavish homes. Celebrities are generally affordable to consume in magazines and consumer products. Celebrities can be made to order in whatever form people like. Celebrities spawn commercial clone celebrity look-alikes who perform as their namesakes at a discount. Salacious versions of these commodities can also be manufactured. For example, celebrity scandals are duplicated in pornography films. Movie and television stars have adult film doppelgangers, which allow people to see simulations of these stars in other ways. The celebrity commodity can be made to order even in extreme variations.

Trojan or stealth wholesomeness gains money under promoting prosocial values and sentimentality while obscuring acquisitiveness. Disney offers up sweet characters with beautiful values and songs and moral fiber, but they at heart are enchantments designed to get people to buy things. Right now readers are probably aghast at reading such sacrilege, but all the beloved characters like Cinderella, Mickey Mouse, Mulan, Buzz Lightyear ad infinitum are characters aimed to get consumers to buy the movie ticket and go to the amusement park wearing the t-shirt emblazoned with the character. Disney is about people spending money to live within a giant commercial, which may be great and sought after entertainment, but is also the enchantment argument at core. A character breakfast, which involves a child hanging out with a character in person, costs money. That is asking to live and make a brief home in the thicket of unreality.

With new means of consumption came consequences. The large scale of malls and superstores and the riches therein overwhelm. Disney characters are so wholesome, yet they are still a means to harness for the end of pitching burgers, soda, notebooks, and albums. Advertising can make us unhealthy. Images oriented to consumption can also impoverish us, as pursuing commodities is expensive.

How do people pay for new means of consumption? Companies encourage going into debt to enable people to keep up their end of relations of consumption. Many retailers allow buying on credit or issue credit cards for that purpose. Credit cards are a wonderful means to get people to spend money that they do not have. They can owe money, so people can pay and meet the demand need of companies, and then pay other companies again in high interest rates, after having already spent money to buy products. The ticket to the dream can come at a price many cannot afford.

In luxury retail, the sale of expensive items is accompanied by ceremonial features and staging (Dion & Arnould, 2011, p. 87). Think of examples associated with luxury, like experiencing an elite, top-notch restaurant meal or shopping at a name high-end clothing store. Ceremonial features exist such as rituals of entry, décor, and specialized accessories for the objects in question, whether food or jewelry. The waiters use scrapers, and there is more silverware at the table than you would expect. You may get asked for your choice of water from a water menu. There is a tablescape—a landscape for the table with flowers, candles, ornate chairs, and a beautiful presentation of the food items that transcends a typical dining experience. The high-end restaurant is also associated with the aura of the chef as a great artist responsible for making food transcend the mundane. These features do not speak for themselves but must be presented and performed so that patrons understand that they are consuming an experience as part of the meal.

A luxury retail clothing maker has a designer as great artist vibe and acolytes of fashion working inside, as the workers wear items designed to promote and affirm the creative designer's magic (Dion & Arnould, 2011). There are press or media materials that celebrate the creative genius involved in making the items you purchase, along with an origin story and laborious ceremonies associated with presenting the items. Here there is staging at hand. In the restaurant, the provenance of food items is clarified in an exalted manner, as "These peaches are sourced from Grand Junction, Colorado, and flown in," or "The cashmere comes from specially raised goats in Kashmir Province." There is a "ceremonial cadence" where language is composed carefully and actions with customers are choreographed. There are attendants for every need, because even though you do not actually require a serving staff of four to attend to you as you eat, the price tag is based in part on you wanting four attendants to wait on you. These performances bring people into a magical experience and, if done correctly, help participants cement an awe and reverence for their magical consumption experience. You do not just pay for the food or clothing or jewel but for the whole experience.

Borrowing an example from Mark Gottdiener's (2001) *Theming of America*, suppose a person buys mac and cheese for 80 cents for home consumption. Now, you go to Bubba Gump, a themed restaurant, and get mac and cheese with shrimp for $10.99. There has to be a small adjustment for adding shrimp, which sells as of writing at $5.45 per pound. You do not get served a pound of shrimp with your dish but probably five to eight pieces, so let's overestimate the shrimp cost at $1.00. Let's say that the restaurant is probably paying $1.80 for materials for the dish that you are eating, for which they charge you $11.00 dollars. Rent and labor cost money, but the restaurant can charge you over five times the cost because of the *experience* around the consumption. Suppose Bubba Gump is a themed restaurant based on the movie *Forrest Gump*. According the restaurant's press kit, you will want access to their merchandise (10% of their profits), for items like t-shirts stating "Run, Forrest, Run." You want to immerse yourself in, to quote them, the "charm and American spirit that made the film *Forrest Gump* a smash hit." You want to sit at the table with film quotes and statements there and pay more for that experience.

Aside from decorated interior themes, purchased objects are also enchanted and then placed for sale. For example, people like to eat sweet things, but they know that sugar is bad for them. Enter enchanted objects that appear to have lower sugar but actually taste sweet because their sugar content is hidden under different names than sugar. Low-fat foods have more calories in the form of undisclosed chemicals than advertised. Who doesn't want a food that tastes great to also be dietary? Unfortunately, the sodium, carbs, and sugar that make food taste good are not easily abandoned without sacrificing taste. So why not believe the magic that food can still taste like a snack and be good for you?

There is a snack food called Pirate's Booty, which many people, including me, enjoy. Unfortunately, this company was sued for false advertising. Why? The product was advertised as natural but is allegedly made using genetically modified crops. Further, there is so much processing, according to the legal complaint, that the food is considered man-made chemically rather than being a natural food. In a separate case, the company claimed to offer a product with 2.5 grams of fat and 128 calories. Testing by a lab found 8 grams of fat and 147 calories. The tested kale snack showed 10 grams of fat. After lawsuits, recent testing revealed 6 grams of fat; yet that content is still more than twice as much as was claimed. A product is enchanted if it tastes like a snack food but is miraculously identified as also being low fat, natural, and more dietetic.

Researchers have uncovered a variety of similar enchanting manipulations of food to increase demand (Raghunathan, Walker Naylor, & Hoyer, 2006). If you include a healthy item on a menu that can satisfy people's sense vicariously that they are being healthy, they will overeat more fattening options. There is a health-labeling effect in which researchers find that people eat more food when a low fat label is attached. Packages and portion sizes are manipulable. Restaurants move from a la carte pricing to setting all-you–can-eat fixed price buffet menus. These strategies encourage overconsumption, because as people see no further costs to their eating, they lose information about portion sizes of what they are eating, and they get easy access to the food rather than having to wait (Chandon & Wansink, 2011). Quantity discounts at big box stores lead to stockpiling, as "value" justifies purchase (p. 10), yet people purchase more than they need. The message of children's advertising is that "unhealthy eating . . . is normal, fun and socially rewarding" when the associations between tasty fattening food and entertainment are cemented in advertisements (p. 13).

Consider how these images, whether in advertising or packaging, can manipulate the senses. There are sensory and symbolic associations with consuming food that marketers exploit (Chandon & Wansink, 2011). In another example, water hydrates but is available on a tap inexpensively. Better for companies to sell energy drinks and soda as hydration miracles. Gatorade, for example, hired an ad agency to tackle the pernicious belief that drinking water during and after exercise is a good way to rehydrate (Huehnergarth, 2014):

> We came up with an entertaining and competitive way to reinforce to teens that consuming Gatorade would help them perform better on the field and that water was the enemy of performance. Working with a game developer (Rock Live, Inc.), we integrated Gatorade into Bolt!, a mobile game featuring Usain Bolt, Gatorade athlete and the fastest man in the world. The integration needed to position Gatorade as the hero helping drive better performance and higher scores with water as the enemy that hinders performance. See more at http://civileats.com/2014/01/07/water-is-the-enemy-gatorade-mobile-game-tells-youth/

Millions of teenagers played this game where the player guides runner Usain Bolt to a peak running time by avoiding water and drinking Gatorade to keep up speed. Not too subtle a way to associate water with curtailing performance and Gatorade with improved recovery and speed.

Not to be outdone, Coca-Cola offered a "Cap the Tap" program that provided strategies and dramaturgical instructions on how servers should encourage restaurant patrons to reject tap water in favor of Coca-Cola beverages (Bellatti, 2013).

> Capture Lost Revenue By Turning Off the Tap. Every time your business fills a cup or glass with tap water, it pours potential profits down the drain. The good news: Cap the Tap™—a program available through your Coca-Cola representative—changes these dynamics by teaching crew members or wait staff suggestive selling techniques to convert requests for tap water into orders for revenue-generating beverages. See more at http://civileats.com/2013/11/13/coca-colas-assault-on-tap-water/

Now restaurant servers become shills for Coca-Cola products by trying to sell consumers on Coke products (without telling them that they are doing these sales) through stating free refills, citing a range of products, and so forth. Servers become performers on Coca-Cola's behalf.

Advertising is a fuel supplying enchantment to everyday products. Of course, people do not believe that all advertising claims are true. If a teenage boy uses Axe cologne, he probably does understand that supermodels will not pursue him. If a woman uses a shampoo, she probably understands that her hair will not look exactly like that of a famous actress who has great hair and has benefited from highly skilled hair experts to perfect that hair. The point is that people want to believe these claims and do not mind a little nudge in that direction. People hope to attain a desire even when they know better. People can know images are false, but products promise hope, and doubting is painful. I want a diet food to taste as good as a snack food. It is not logic driving the purchase of Axe or a lottery ticket. It is hope and wanting to believe that a little magic can attain your ambitions. Rather than suspension of disbelief, the interesting question is how people work to sustain disbelief.

A constellation of forces brought together the unreality era, but in uncomplicated terms, a big factor is just that unreality fills voids. First, there is a void to fill to make the world accord to the extravagant expectations that people have. Second, there are limits to the amount of knowledge that people can have. People can't know everything, so fictions can handle the shortfall. Walter Lippman (2011) in *Public Opinion* wrote,

> The environment with which our public opinions deal is refracted in many ways, by censorship and privacy at the source, by physical and social barriers at the other end, by scanty attention, by the poverty of language, by distraction, by unconscious constellations of feeling, by wear and tear, violence, monotony. These limitations upon our access to that environment combine with the obscurity and complexity of the facts themselves to thwart clearness and justice of perception, to substitute misleading fictions for workable ideas, and to deprive us of adequate checks upon those who consciously strive to mislead. (p. 76)

Unreality also generates and satiates commercial demands.

Dramaturgy: The New Means of Consumption

The advent of enchantment, cathedrals of consumption, and unreality requires an updated application of dramaturgical theory. Among marketers, there is a keen focus on how dramaturgical activity shapes shopping experiences and service work.[9] An initial contribution in this regard was to examine retail atmospherics. Mary Jo Bitner (1992) then suggested examining the servicescape in retail. Grove, Fisk, and John (2000) have developed models of the use of front and backstage in retail environments. Robert Kozinets and John Sherry Jr. have worked with research teams to analyze the enchantment that

---

[9] Scholars of marketing who contribute work in this vein are Mary Jo Bitner, Walter Fisk, Stephen Grove, Russell Belk, Eric Arnould, Robert Kozinets, Kent Grayson, and John Sherry Jr. These scholars have updated dramaturgy in their analyses of contemporary marketing.

stores such as American Girl Place (Diamond et al., 2009) and ESPNzone (Sherry et al., 2004) provide. Their works connect dramaturgy and the retail environment in sophisticated ways.

Risto Moisio and Eric Arnould (2005) proposed extending the dramaturgical framework specifically in studying marketing. They believed in clarifying how "cultural resources, consumer agency, and formal components" impact shopping experiences. In their view, most applications of the dramaturgical perspective to marketing treat consumers as passive recipients of performance rather than as coperformers. They think that insufficient attention is paid to cultural components as part of performances. Moisio and Arnould advocate examining cultural resources that are brought to bear to make dramaturgical interactions more meaningful in service settings. For example, in their case study, a market selling goods imported from Europe had to manifest cultural displays of what being "European" is, to allow the consumers to become part of that story in service interactions. A person in the store could be invited to say why pressed olive oil is good and how they wanted to buy the foods there because of experiences in Europe. Employees can prompt such positively tinged reflections as part of furthering a customer's relationship and affinity with the store.

Moisio and Arnould (2005) suggest a three-part analytic focus for considering the dramaturgical framework in relation to marketing. The typical application of dramaturgy in marketing is to analyze the setting, actors, and performance during a service encounter between frontline employees and customers. Moisio and Arnould suggest that these aspects of setting, actors, and performance should be considered under the umbrella of *drama structure*. By performance they refer to actions presented to an audience but not the audience response. To add to the comprehensiveness of dramaturgical coverage, they suggest analyzing *drama interaction* separately, which refers to how consumers act in response to ongoing performances. What do consumers say and do in response to performances, and how do those responses shape subsequent actions?

They also suggest adding the component of *drama content* to the analytic mix. Drama content refers to cultural resources that frame performance—the cultural content that creates the particular "drama" or story associated with an experience. Moisio and Arnould (2005) suggest that marketing contexts requires more focus on how consumers interact during performances and what cultural ideas help craft performances that are suited to marketing particular products. They open the door to consider how consumers align or do not align themselves to the messaging that they receive and also how the cultural associations of images and extravagant expectations are inherent in the products that people are urged to consume.

An area where further background is helpful is in considering how brands engage in dramaturgy. Pine and Gilmore (2011) focus on this point in their work on the experience economy. Brands are repositories of social meaning. Companies produce objects under a name that conveys a distinct identity for a product. The kind of brand that someone uses or wishes to use or rejects is meaningful because brands express characteristics that communicate meanings back about the person and others using the brand's product. Put simply, using a brand makes a statement about what a person is like. A brand crystallizes an idealized set of attributes that constitute an identity for the brand and brand user. A man who drives a Harley Davidson has chosen a distinct brand-abetted identity. Someone is Ford Tough or about Subaru Love. Brands tell stories and have performances grafted onto them that extend their storytelling beyond the product onto the consumer. In this respect, brand relationships also urge people to enact dramaturgical relationships with a brand by acting in a manner consonant with the brand's narrative. You don't just have the Polo shirt; you proudly bear the logo and want people to know of your elite taste and that you can afford the product. Volkswagen just decided to remove the flower vase in their Beetle line because of perceptions that the Beetle was a "chick" car. Women who drive Beetles (a majority were female) did put a flower in the vase.

People do gender their cars and feel that Nike and Apple products are props that say something about them to others. Brands now become part of people's performances with other people. Like in all cases of anthropomorphism, to give these inanimate objects life and a story makes people a performance team with the object. My car doesn't come gendered; I need to refer to it using masculine or feminine pronouns, to decorate it in particular ways, and to use it as a symbol. Male teenagers used to see the *Fast and Furious* movies and to immediately want to race their "muscle" cars out of the parking lot in a masculine display. Storytelling and dramaturgy give the car a gender that consumers build upon. A branding is a refined narrative of cultural value that connects a product to a want that a consumer has. Products get idealized as brands and state something about the kind of person that uses them.

Brands offer products for purchase, and purchased objects become possessions. As Russell Belk (1988) observed, possessions constitute an extended sense of self that connects to an object. A meaningful social relation can form between the owner and a possession that is also a dramaturgical relationship. As an example, consider the loss of self that people feel when something they possess is stolen. Sometimes when people want to hurt someone, they hurt their stuff. When revolutions occur, the first thing done is to "kill" the objects of the previous regime, such as tearing down statues associated with previous rulers and regimes. Possessions are a medium of expression such as personal crafting and writing or gift giving. The possession as extended self extends to proclaimed psychics. Psychics will request an object owned by the subject under inquiry as if a person's essence is distilled onto an object and the object can trace that essence back to the person. The connection to dramaturgy is that possessions are a medium for stating meaningful messages about and to owners.

Consumers know, thanks to the clarity of images that advertisers offer, what message is associated with using a brand's suite of products. Advertisers and marketers are aware of dramaturgy to express messages about a product and brand's identity effectively. The dramaturgy here can occur at multiple levels. First, dramaturgical influences in store settings at points of purchase may drive purchasing behavior in ways that are not immediately obvious to customers but that are of tremendous interest to brands and their marketers. These influences include color schemes, olfactory elements, scripts, and visual design of the servicescape, props, and other elements.

Other uses of dramaturgy take place outside stores, such as in media advertisements that contain performances on behalf of products, like by anthropomorphic characters. The gecko is a small lizard that Geico animates in insurance ads. In this resulting scenario, people can take advice from a small lizard with a British accent on safeguarding risks to their possessions. Taking advice from a cartoon character on insurance or being tempted to consider buying a Kia car because animated hamsters get effective makeovers and ride in them should strike you as surreal. These campaigns cost large sums of money that companies would not pay unless they brought in sales, so there are great commercial strategies submerged in the surreal, which is kind of the new means of consumption point. If the content captures your attention, then you will pay attention to the logo, name, and message. In broadcast messages, there is not space typically for interaction to emerge between the audience and the brand representative as the audience views a previously recorded ad. Yet advertisers, on behalf of brands, still work hard to create possibilities for interaction by involving digital options for communication, such as going to a *Facebook* page, sending messages on *Twitter*, or playing a game on the website.

Marketing and the Dramaturgical Legibility of Themes

People consume and purchase products to fulfill wants and not just to fulfill survival needs. Even in the case of survival needs, marketing to wants emerges. For example, people need water to live, and they could take water from a tap or well or boil water from a river. Instead, they may purchase designer, sparkling, flavored, filtered, spring, or distilled water. Even the elemental need to drink water to live is up for grabs as a consumer issue of wants, as bottled and designer water come to promise more hydration than regular water or an origin source more pristine than a municipality's water plant.

Marketing to wants transcends buying items that are necessary to survive. A want that motivates purchases could be to look better through apparel or fitness products or to purchase for amusement or upward mobility, as in people who are "going places" wear product X. To appeal to wants requires marketers knowing what wants are attractive and what "personas" products must manifest to produce sales and form a relationship with a consumer. There are always wants at hand in products. For example, do people buy shampoo because they care about a particular chemical composition in the bottle? Or is a better marketing message one that emphasizes using this product to buy great-looking hair? When people buy shampoo, they want to buy great-looking hair. The messaging is great-looking hair happens as long as the consumer commits to the brand's product. Advertisers excel further in instructing us that we have wants that we did not even know we had. They are happy to manufacture new wants as needed.

The elements in relationships with consumers that must get into a brand's performance and identity are statements of what the brand "believes," why the brand exists, cultural forces that advance the brand's beliefs, some sort of demonstration of that culture so that there is interest among consumers, and evidence of connections between the brand and people that shows that the brand's products are convincing go-to objects that serve consumers well. For example, Nike is considered a brand with excellent marketing. "Just do it"; to pursue personal excellence through determination with a cultural connection to sports figures specifically and to human achievement more generally. There is evidence in lots of graphic images with accompanying music and voiceovers of sweating athletes persevering their way to success because of hard work and never giving up. At least the attitude is a reward in itself; because people can find comfort in being able to give their all if they cannot perform at a high level.

We can move from examples of brands to cathedrals of consumption built as extensions of the brand to sell the brands and their products. The use of images and symbols and the creation of engaging immersive experiences are not relegated to amusement parks and locations that are clearly just in the entertainment business. Remember the virtues of images as dramatic tools: They are simple to understand, vivid, engaging, and promise extravagant meaning. A cathedral of consumption has a straightforward drama structure, interaction, and content. The key principle across all of these aspects must be *legibility of theme*. The performers, set, and performance must tell the brand's story in such a way that the consumer gets the messaging and responds. The culture is framed to make the experience easy to grasp, like Disney is the Magic Kingdom or "what happens in Vegas stays in Vegas." The interaction must invite participation and contact within the cathedral of consumption or other site in a way that cements the connection and fulfills the consumer's extravagant expectations.

In Cabela's, a chain store selling hunting and outdoor supplies, there is an artificial mountainside inside that contains stuffed and mounted animals that people would want to hunt. There are chances to play hunting video games there, like *Cabela's Wild Hunt*. This tactic in cathedrals of consumption operates like playing pornographic videos at a strip club or parading fitness models in a plastic surgeon's office for potential patients. *Vicarious enticement* allows people to participate in a fantasy that people have by purchasing a product that lets them have some more limited relationship to the fantasy.

Erving Goffman (1967) in *Interaction Ritual* argued that one role of popular culture is to invigorate fantasy in patrons without their having to experience a significant cost. He mentions the example of James Bond movies where a person can participate in "fateful events without much serious cost." This feature is a key component of simulated images that attempt to give people a fantasy reward in association with a product, without the hassles involved in earning the real versions of the product. For example, you can wear a cowboy hat, have tattoos, and buy a Harley Davidson motorcycle to attach a sense of ruggedness to you without having to get into fights. Disney's Animal Kingdom invites patronage without having to deal with the hassles and costs of traveling to a real jungle location.

When a product helps a person imagine being the attractive man or woman wowing everyone, that fantasy helps motivate purchasing. The actor in ads is not a real person but a performer, so consumers are pursuing a fantasy of a fantasy—in other words, they want to be like the man in the Axe commercial with models clamoring for his attentions, which is a fantasy, performed by people who are doing make-believe. What people clamor for is not real but a simulation of an ideal real that is so overwhelming a vicarious enticement that we are happy to make its nonreality unproblematic and imagine it to be workable.

Products promise an engagement with fantasy at the low cost of buying the product with one's theatrical imagination doing the rest. You can buy Axe or a perfume or a car to become more attractive and make people take notice. These purchase options do not require anyone to get into better shape, to become a nicer or more charismatic person, or to work on any other aspect of their beings to help them achieve extravagant expectations in actuality. Instead, people can cheat that work and get the fantasy at the low, low price of whatever the product is. This illusion of getting to the fantasy is dangerous if people mistake the promise of the product as substituting for real effort. The illusions offered can also be corrosive.

Suppose a person goes to a club where men or women strip for patrons. The rules there usually forbid patrons touching performers. The performers are meant to be attractive physically and are dressed or not dressed in a manner to arouse patrons. A fantasy of engagement with these performers is invigorated in patrons, which cannot be fulfilled, as reality is that sexual contact is against the rules, and the performers are there as workers, not because of attraction or interest in the customers. The money customers have is what interests performers, not their sexual attractiveness.

Appreciate the irony here. The entire fantasy of the location is of access to arousal; the reality is that there is meant to be no sexual contact between the patrons and the objects of fantasy. A person is going there to feed their imaginations and be given glimpses of fantasy that they must pay to sustain. Patrons pay to ogle men and women who are unlikely to be interested and that likely view them with disdain and as ripe for the plucking. The financial exchange is for proximity and tolerating of ogling and sustaining of disbelief. The profits in this world are exploitative in multiple dimensions. Workers are hired and may be exploited to perpetuate the fantasies of patrons, and management and they seek to advantage themselves financially from patrons' imaginations. Perhaps exchanging money for access to semidressed men and women is a patriarchal high, yet it is also a statement of desperation as the fantasy is an empty promise in contrast to its vivid depiction. Mistaking the situation as one of real sexual promise is likely incorrect.

The more luminous the unreality, the more crushing its ultimate unattainability is. The hair model will always have better hair than you do. The Ray Bans that you wear will not make you as cool as Tom Cruise was in *Top Gun*, again a movie with makeup professionals and lighting experts who worked to make the magic happen. That a photoshopped body is so much better than the normal one is hard to take because unreality is so tempting and the shortfall between that and the real is so wide. But the photoshopped world and the real one do not overlap. For a price, we can enjoy vicarious enticement into that image world, and we are willing participants. We can reject the hardness of reality in favor of traipsing around mirages.

At an amusement park, a Dave and Buster's, a wax museum, or looking at a picture of a celebrity, people do not need to read paragraphs of details to make sense of the objects that they see or to understand the experience. When people go to a Vegas casino for a vacation, the selling point is letting loose in a hedonistic atmosphere. Whatever one's education, when you see a Disney character, you get the story. Fantasy is vivid and straightforward and more fun than reality. Details are an undesirable fine print. Your child sees Mickey Mouse, not an underpaid pimply teenager underneath who is steaming away and overheating in their costume.

Being a consumer is easy with some money. If you consume only as an audience member, then you can go and enjoy simply looking at Disney's castle without the experience requiring you to read about the era, an artist, or the reputation of the architects. Museums, for example, are moving away from complex detailing and verbiage to become more like themed amusement parks that attract audiences and compete with more entertaining alternatives. People are getting less depth and are less challenged.

David Mamet (2012), a well-known playwright, captured the distinction between connoisseur audiences that appreciate the culture of the theater to the theater "tourist" who just wants to see a hit revival with a celebrity star:

> The tourist has no memory of last year's play and actors, he does not come to see the new work of a director, of a playwright, or of a designer. He comes to see a spectacle, which will neither provoke nor disturb, whose worth cannot be questioned. He does not come with the theatrical curiosity of the native theatergoer but with the desire for amusement, and he comes as to an amusement park, for the thrill first of experiencing, and next, and perhaps more important, of being able to relate having experienced that particular thrill deprived to the stay-at-homes. He wants to brag of having seen star X or star Y. The tourist goes to the theatre much as I went, to London, to see the Crown Jewels. (p. 18)

Images hog the spotlight and in this regard also carry a cost of negating the appreciation of complexity in human achievements.

Dramaturgical Inequalities: Gender, Goffman, and Advertising

James Scott (1992) has observed that powerful and less powerful people perform according to their stereotyped public personas when they interact with each other in public. Both a public transcript and a hidden transcript are connected to those interactions. Public transcripts reflect the displayed status quo. In the hidden transcripts associated with those events, less powerful people reveal their resistance and disagreement with the inequalities that they experience, that they must suppress in the face of power. Scott's work illustrates an important application of dramaturgical thinking to situations of inequality. Hidden transcripts of the weak exist in the backstage of dramaturgical activities, and the public transcripts that images comprise hide this resistance. Public transcripts also exist in images that uphold the status quo and their representative power can lead people to form views that produce more unfair treatment.

A first inequality in the dramaturgical power of images is in the disadvantaging representations that images themselves provide. A second inequality comes from any unfavorable actions and attitudes that result from people being exposed to such images. In *Gender Advertisements*,

Erving Goffman (1979) addressed how pictorial advertisements offer hyper-ritualized displays of gender that disadvantage women. His ideas here also have a contemporary currency in considering how inequalities are incorporated into performances.

Pictures carry a component of self-worship where people can capture a best social self (well-dressed, winning an award, looking abnormally good, with a celebrity) that freezes an affirming status. People now have a captured moment of glory and triumph to hold against future routine failings or changes in body, mind, and status. Hence, people want staged pictures to "immortalize" themselves, typically in gloried moments. This self-worship may be for personal consumption or for other permanent display. Pictures can be trophies of "domestic propriety" or elevation from contact with a celebrity. They are definitely not the product of random samples.

Photos capture emblems and not just people. Goffman uses the example of boxers who pose with fists facing each other to promote an upcoming event. The photo is emblematic of the fight as part of capturing the individuals in frame. Similarly, a picture of a scientist at a college is usually pictured in promotional materials with some tool or emblem from that discipline—a microscope or set of ancient books or with a formula written on a blackboard in the background and dutiful-appearing students in frame. The goal is to provide an identifying emblem of the profession and of educational possibilities for students in an academic discipline. If there is a microscope there or an ancient book or formula, the student has something to do with such things and is progressing in accessing credentials of that profession to propel them forward.

How many emblem shows can you find in photographs of promotion to admissions in college and university publications? People used to pay commissions to artists to render them in grand stature. Details of piety or riches or beauty or bliss are denoted on canvas. Now the picture trophy of emblems replaces them. An audience of happy smiling multiracial students at all the schools seemingly broadcasting we are here, engaged, happy, and doing great things! The point is not to snapshot reality but to suggest an untroubling emblem, motif, or trope to be recognized in a positive way (hopefully for the producer) and which moves the audience in some way forward to the producer's ends. Look at the students abroad helping the exotic and troubled needy; the fans showing pride in place by cheering on the sports teams; students in a classroom looking at knowledge, entranced and fulfilled by the valuable wisdom being imparted by a generous, accomplished professor, who cares about teaching as the rapt audience and dignified pose attest. Look at the smiling exhilarated children grateful to parents for the trip to Disney. What a wonderful job you are doing as a parent in making your child happy and in being successful enough to pay for the trip! That look you put together with the clutch bag; how that timepiece (watch is too pedestrian a name) is a perfect accouterment to the new suit—you reek of sophistication and forward movement in life, just like movers and shakers who are rich and respected do. Heightening legibility and persuasive power is the point of combining tropes and dramaturgical presentation in pictorial depictions.[10] These images also sustain a public transcript.

Advertisements and other aspects of commercial realism are make-believe. These are not what Goffman called "caught" photographs of people in the midst of living out everyday life. Yet the hope is that make-believe can be taken for a portrait of the real and that the fantasy can cross borders into the real if the person only uses the product. We know better, but we don't want to know better because magical accomplishment is good. As when people put on a front stage of more perfection than they have, wearing Spanx or camouflaging grey hair, they know that this act perpetuates a fantasy. It is make-believe in the sense of a wish to negate the authentic. Just as a commercial producer advertises make-believe to sell, individuals do too, hoping that a toupee or Spanx or carefully layered makeup stands up to scrutiny. Practicing extravagant expectations makes dupes of us all; not completely foolish dupes but willing ones. I know going to the Animal Kingdom is not the same as being on safari in Kenya or Kruger National Park. However, I also know that I am more able to afford to go to the Animal Kingdom, that I will have my familiar Western comforts, and I do not have to encounter any of the rough things that could come with being outside in a real jungle, like danger, disease-carrying insects, overwhelming heat, the unpredictability of whether I will get to have sightings of any animals, and not being able to go to a well-stocked convenience store 10 minutes away. The fake may be an improved place to spend time because I can at least try to jury-rig that scene in ways that are difficult to do in undomesticated nature. Unreality represents a domestication of unpredictable elements that can otherwise frustrate or show an unpleasant side to events. Make-believe is great

---

[10] See TV Tropes for a great collection of tropes in media from which I am drawing on social tropes here.

because it removes the fine print. Why would I want misery when I can have guarantees that I will see what I want to see, and further be able to take what I have seen as what there really is to see? Hence troubles and inequalities do not exist in frame and are rendered invisible.

In *Gender Advertisements*, Goffman argues that relations of power exist in the visual representation of exchanges between men and women. Pictures carry arguments. If advertisements depict relations between men and women that are viewed to represent how men and women *should* relate to one another, these relations also act as instructional mannequins to guide behavior. They are public transcripts frozen in time. Just as a mannequin holds out a wardrobe that a person imagines trying on, advertisements display relations for people to try. In this regard, Goffman clarifies that advertisements are images and frame social ideas. Men and women become displays of masculinity and femininity; sexy images become images of what sexuality is, images of a city become images of what is urban, a picture of an athlete becomes an image of what athleticism is, images of a tourist site become emblematic of what travel means. Goffman's observation here is not original; the point of noting it here is to place that observation into a context when hyperreal images and their representativeness hold sway today.

Commercial realism is also not reality in an empirically accurate way. Ads are meant to be unambiguous to interpret where reality is harder to understand. That is the point of selling in commercial realms: to make sure that the choreography is clear enough to move sales. Scenes are altered physically and posed in ways that are not duplicated in everyday life, even though they influence real actions. I don't get to go to parties with celebrities or run as fast as an athlete, but through an advertisement, I enter that world vicariously however faux the nature of my entry is.

Gender displays show what some of the conventions around gender are. According to Goffman, categories to read gender relations through as dramaturgical inequalities include the following:

A: Relative size in images where men have greater height and weight than women, who are also placed lower than them physically.

B: Subordination through posing and leveraging of relative size difference. Women and men have different body posture and posings: men and women have their bodies contorted in different ways, bend their knees differently, cross their legs differently, lower head or don't in connection to deference to another, cross arms defensively or open arms up.

C: Feminine touch versus a man's grasp. Goffman argued that there is an implication of dominance versus gentility in terms of who has power in situations as a man grabs things while a woman touches them gently.

D: Hierarchy of function: When a man and woman are pictured together in a work situation, who appears in charge? Who instructs or leads? There are "work" situations such as conducting business or instruction. If the setting is "women's work" in the domestic sphere, who is depicted as leading? Is the male portrayed as childlike under the protective wise gaze of the woman who leads in this domain? Or is the role reversed?

E: Who is clowning more or taken in a less serious childlike pose?

F: Sexualized posing: A person is depicted with a finger or physical object near their mouth, lips open, or different body parts are accentuated that have a traditional sexual association, or the posing of bodies is in a loose way as a faux sexual positioning.

G: Delirious or withdrawn posings: One is being taken care of in a task or one is delirious with joy at a particular task being accomplished in one's domain, like an ecstatic response to a washing load or a man's happy shock that his cologne has attracted the attentions of multiple models. There are exaggerated reactions to gifts or people who just can't accomplish some task without a guiding hand steadied in purpose.

H: Nuzzling or snuggling poses reaffirm role and domain of gender.

Goffman argues that artificial representations of "natural" expressions of gender relations, in advertisements, are taken to the nth degree. When a person buys shampoo to buy great-looking hair, a person may look to ads to see what form of masculinity and femininity is being framed and to purchase the item depicted to buy a desirable version of masculinity or femininity. Advertisers and companies also create gender differences in products to sell more of them. They will make a version of the brand for men and another for women. The same ingredients may be in both bottles; just one package is pink with a floral pattern, and the other is blue. A gender ideology is present as well as implicit instructions that constitute strategies for doing gender appropriate to that ideology.

What can characterize people in performance of a gender is the "competence and willingness" to put forth appropriate displays of gender on the right schedule for performance. The question raised in depictions is what is the appropriate display of gender? If people take their cues from gender advertisements, the appropriate gender display is one that disadvantages women. Given the tendency to seek images to guide living life by, gender advertisements promote an illusion that people then act to make real.

Conclusion

The upshot of the thicket of unreality argument is that because people demand more than is realistic, they immerse themselves in fabrications to make up for shortfalls between preferences and realities. Sustaining this thicket is a dense amount of dramaturgical activity by large commercial organizations and a vast audience of consumers. Dramaturgical performances have a visceral power today as life increasingly is influenced by show business techniques.

SIX

Dramaturgical Involvements in Popular Culture

Tonight, the arena is sold out. A dozen shades of gray will square off in a pageantry of war. The opponents are unlikely in the real world, but in the amphitheater of our imagination, they're well matched. The punk rockers will battle the mountain men. The black separatists will fight the post-apocalyptic warriors. The gang-banger will rumble with the aristocrat. . . . In the end, just like a good Soap Opera, no issues will be resolved; the story is "To Be Continued." The combatants will live to fight another night, in another town. Is wrestling fake? Absolutely. It's as fake as your imagination, as phony as your daydreams.

—Steve Allen

Who wouldn't want to have perfect boobs and kill s**t and be born again?

—Female *World of Warcraft* player

Let's face it, a lot of us wish we could live in video games/TV shows/movies/ comic books/animes, because it's so interesting. And it's nice to devote a part of yourself to something.

—Sabrina Ranelluci, cosplayer

Introduction: Dramaturgical Involvement in Popular Culture

Have you dreamed of taking themed cruises with Paula Deen, Kiss, or New Kids on the Block as guests of honor? Are you one of 67 million North Americans who play *League of Legends* online? Were you one of 140,000 people that attended the last San Diego Comic-Con? Will you be visiting the "Wizarding World of Harry Potter Diagon Alley" attraction at Universal Studios? Have you tried to get on a reality television show? Do you write fan fiction and/or know what the characters you follow on your favorite shows would do in any situation? Are you interested in touring the filming sites for *Game of Thrones* or *Lord of the Rings*? Do you costume play (cosplay), for example, as Batman, a zombie, a Manga character, or dress up as a Wisconsin cheese head for Packer football games? Even if you do not answer yes to any of these questions, millions of people do.

Henry Jenkins is a leading scholar of fandom and *participatory culture*, a term that describes today's audiences as active participants and partners in culture creation and the popular culture industry. The participatory culture idea suggests that people's contemporary involvement in arts and culture is more interactive and that this transformation is changing what culture means and how cultural products are made. Instead of people just being passive viewers, more people want to involve themselves in helping create and enact characters within the cultural forms that appeal to them. Ethan Gilsdorf (2009) observed,

> Others in pop culture and fantasy fandom want to participate and extend the experience of what they find to be so engrossing. They want to design new settings, write new plots, and add new characters. So they sketch pictures, write short stories, perform songs, and shoot movies. (p. 141)

When participatory culture involves people sharing and participating jointly in a particular cultural form, that shared involvement can create a joint engrossment in a fantasy world, whether in a role-playing game or in cosplaying as the Avengers or in conducting a draft for your fantasy sports team. Participating, as opposed to just watching, takes work. Many people have an active "crafting" relationship to their pastimes that requires dedication and hard work. A cosplayer makes a detailed costume by herself or himself; a person writes a story based on her or his favorite TV show characters; a historical reenactor acquires or duplicates authentic regalia; a fantasy sports manager builds a team and masters statistics; a person posts a *YouTube* parody of their favorite show; and a dungeon master creates an adventure world—all are doing cultural work as a serious "craft" activity. There is sometimes money to be made in these endeavors. For example, a former student of mine earned money building up characters for sale in *World of Warcraft*. These people all share a commitment to enacting imaginary phenomena; they are participating dramaturgically in joint fantasy.

Forms of participation differ. Sports fantasy leagues simulate reality using real empirical data of players on their teams, yet they are not "real" in terms of actually owning these actual players. In *World of Warcraft*, the actual reproduction is impossible. Other "craft" activities like cosplay are also based in fantasy "unreal" characters, even though they use concrete physical products like costumes and props. The commonality across these activities is people working to make something real out of a world that engrosses them. To do this work, participants develop special knowledge and skills to engage their cultural pastime more fruitfully, which transcends mere passive involvement. Cosplayers may learn fabrication and sewing skills; fantasy role-players learn detailed minutiae of their gaming worlds.

In his essay, "Fun in Games," Erving Goffman (1961) argues,

> Something in which the individual can become unselfconsciously engrossed is something that can become real to him. . . . *Joint* engrossment in something with others reinforces the reality carved out by the individual's attention, even while subjecting this entrancement to the destructive distractions that the others are now in a position to cause. The process of mutually sustaining a definition of the situation in face-to-face interaction is socially organized through rules of relevance and irrelevance. (p. 80)

This quote identifies some points to consider in understanding people's contemporary engagement with popular culture. First, in participatory cultures, people work with others to sustain a fantasy reality and that joint involvement helps reinforce that definition of the situation. Second, joint engrossment in aspects of popular culture requires distinguishing between participatory versus marginal involvement. Where passive participation might be limited to watching a screen or wearing a t-shirt with a character's image, more extreme participation occurs through actions like dressing up to reproduce a character, reinventing characters and disputing their creative arc, supporting the moral codes of a fictional popular culture universe, forming fan communities, pursuing memorabilia, writing fictional adventures, or battling fellow players (Gilsdorf, 2009). Further required is ignoring attempts to disrupt one's fantasy pursuits. Goffman contends that an order of "rules of relevance and irrelevance" help to sustain definitions of the situation. To explore the operations of participatory culture, we must examine how that engrossment involves impression management and an underlying order.

LARPs: Live Action Role-Playing

Take live action role-play (LARP) as an example. The popular movie *Role Models* used LARP events as a plot device, which brought LARPing more attention. LARPs involve enacting characters in a fantasy world through engaging in events like battles as if one actually resided in that fantasy world. People organize battle campaigns; they create systems to judge combat between players, form alliances and antagonistic groups, and divide up a state park or other area into geographically divided realms to stage conflicts (see Tychsen, Hitchens, Brolund, & Kavakli, 2006, for a more detailed presentation of LARP characteristics). A group of planners organize the event, develop challenges and scenarios, and put "monsters" into place for players to battle.

LARPs differ in intensity level and genre. Fantasy LARPs receive publicity, but there are other kinds of LARPs that exist. There are horror-themed LARPs, including the popular zombie genre, where people can do zombie walks or participate in horror survival events such as fighting one's way out of a zombie-infested mall where paid actors and willing fans play zombies. Some paintball games come close to being LARPs, in having employees play zombies and crazed survivors for patrons to shoot. There are LARPs where people play vampires or that have Steampunk and Victorian themes. LARPs can involve

> 24/7 immersive role-play. They take the fantasy a step beyond. You create a character, invent a backstory, put on makeup, dress the part, and physically wander around a real setting, interacting with other players and making up the banter as you go along. And occasionally you beat the crap out of them. (Gilsdorf, 2009, p. 87)

The grandparents of LARPs are military games and war simulations. Some use LARPs to bring "history" to life; an argument that could also apply to renaissance fairs (sort of), serious historical reenacting, and tourist sites such as Colonial Williamsburg. There is also a commercial aspect as some LARPs are for-profit commodities rather than labors of love that organizers put together for like-minded aficionados.

In addition to currently popular zombie experiences that companies bring to life, new commercial horror survival experiences are out there, which provide LARP-like experiences, often along the line of "you are the brave monster hunter that. . . ." One such example is *The Great Horror Campout: Only the Dawn Will Save You.*[1] According to the promotional materials, the Great Horror Campout is a "choose your own adventure, overnight, interactive camping experience." Onsite campers will experience overnight attacks by monsters of different kinds (demented hillbilly cannibals with axes) during a night of "organized" terror. The companies that put on these kinds of events do open casting calls for actors, makeup professionals, and design experts, and are serious businesses. These kinds of commercial horror experiences are increasing in number, as traditional commercial haunted house attractions staged during Halloween are spreading across the calendar year. In-depth participation is the attraction of these events. Sleeping in a tent in a creepy location with actual simulated horrors that can touch you is a deeper involvement than watching a horror movie at home. There are versions that ratchet up the experience's intensity, where you can be bound, carried, insulted, fed unsavory items, and otherwise brutally engrossed in an experience you paid for, such as in the "Basement" attraction or New York City's extreme attraction "Blackout: Haunted House."

Engrossment in Popular Culture Experiences

Forms of participatory popular culture represent investments in commercial imagination products created and developed further by for-profit companies. In the last chapter, I discussed the ideas of image life and imagination products. Image life involves performing and playacting a more exciting and vivid identity or image than available in countervailing reality. Imagination products are products that encourage fantasizing to consume them as fictional characters, RPGs (role-playing games), and toys. Companies have the interesting task of creating and designing

---

[1] See http://greathorrorcampout.com/#/about.

appealing themes. In this chapter, I do not criticize corporate rapacity in the imagination business.[2] I just point out that imagination businesses exist as a domain for further analysis, which is often overlooked through choosing to focus more on a product's "fun" nature rather than on how the product represents commercial strategies.

Cultural objects represent shared significance embodied in a distinct form (Griswold, 2012), meaning that popular culture refers to socially meaningful features of broad appeal. Some characteristics of popular culture include having large audiences, appealing values that most everyone can understand, and being treated with less repute than high culture forms like art, ballet, classical music, and opera. Goffman (1974) observed that modern cultural forms might increasingly work to get fans more involved: "One can appreciate, then, how modern cinema and theater might work many changes and in each case manage to generate a calculus of action and reaction in which audiences could involve themselves" (p. 241). Today participatory culture has expanded with grand momentum, in part because of forces associated with enchantment and unreality discussed in the previous chapter.

Here are some cases in point: There are themed cruise ship experiences where people can take cruises with adult film stars, country musicians, professional wrestlers, Paula Deen, and stand-up comedians. There are massively multiplayer online (MMO) games where people participate with others by leveling up and playing together; 27 million people play *League of Legends* every day (Sherr, 2014). Male fans of *My Little Pony: Friendship Is Magic* (called Bronies) meet up online and at conventions. The advent of *YouTube* channels provides aspiring celebrities and fans with a vast forum for participating in cultural pastimes. People can pay for participation experiences with celebrities, like playing golf, having dinner, getting a video message, or attending a sporting event with a celebrity from that sport.[3]

Reality TV programs are an example of a recently thriving popular culture genre. In reality television, producers use "non-actors in marginally scripted interactions" (Ouellette & Murray, 2004, as cited in Montemurro 2008, p. 8). The array of reality program genres seems limitless, including

---

[2] Such criticism is rampant among some academics and social critics. They excoriate companies for using amusements as a venue to exploit children, get money from parents, and encourage self-hatred, sloth, patriarchy, and a slew of other sins. The idea of "Trojan wholesomeness" applies here.

[3] For example, see the Thuzio website at www.thuzio.com.

makeover shows; documentaries; fairy godmother type shows where people, through a staged intervention by the program, get to live out a dream; survival shows; competitions for cash prizes or professional opportunities shows; practical joke shows; romance themes; unusual job themes; "days in the lives of dysfunctional celebrities" themes; "fish out of water" filmed together shows; and contemporary "freak" shows of people with unusual characteristics. Steven Johnson observed that "Monday-morning quarterbacking" was coined to describe the engaged feeling spectators have in relation to games as opposed to stories. We absorb stories, but we second-guess games. Reality programming has brought that second-guessing to prime time, only the game in question revolves around social dexterity rather than the physical kind (Johnson, 2005).

The current intense participation in popular culture includes greater involvement in second-guessing show arcs, characters, and "universes." An apex here in getting viewers invested is the reality TV show innovation of viewers voting on show outcomes. This enhanced participation helps enliven the show's content and enables fans to connect directly to events as an intervention tied to second-guessing them. Rather than mumble to themselves at home, viewers can now try to intervene directly. Would their contestant on *American Idol* have won without them?

Innumerable commentary forums exist where people write about what characters and people are really like, as if the fans "know" them like the showrunners do, or as if they were real people. In some reality shows, the goal is to pair and ply everyone with alcohol, which does not encourage the peaceful resolution of disputes. From dozens of hours of filming, editors choose the most outrageous reactions where a person who could be a paragon for 23 hours and 58 minutes in a day acts like a jerk for 2 minutes. Showing only those 2 minutes allows fans to involve themselves in criticizing the characters and their choices. In general, the more obnoxious the behavior, the more intense the reaction generated. The protagonists on the *Jersey Shore* TV show provided another example of people cast as fodder for audiences to jeer. The actors get to "laugh all the way to the bank" in performing unlikable roles.

The sense of entitlement that fans have in second-guessing programs even bleeds into thinking they know more about the characters than their creators do. A producer of the show *Supernatural* comments on a fan that thought that show's creator didn't "get" the character he created (unlike the fan who "gets" the character better):

Sera Gamble: I read something once, to the effect of "Eric Kripke doesn't get Dean." I was like, okay, everyone is entitled to an opinion or three, and it's great that fans are so possessive of the show, but that's officially ridiculous. He created the character. (Zubernis & Larsen, 2012, p. 181)

Some participatory fans enjoy hijacking preestablished content creations in subversive ways. Maybe they write slash fiction about the imagined sex lives of superheroes or science fiction characters, or make established bad guys into heroes or established heroes into villains. Fans transgress fantasy boundaries in creative ways that demonstrate how they find freedom and engrossment in participatory culture. These commercial interests in fantasy are important to study as sources of values, attempts to own properties in the contemporary imagination, and for how they attempt to structure the relations that fans have to fantasy products. How people respond matters, both in what those responses reveal and in how audiences can reject content.

Engrossment requires work. This point splits into two aspects. Part A requires understanding what engrossment involves and how people find meaning in that investment. Consider the rewards articulated, for example, in this analysis of cosplay:

Adult cosplay dress-up activity is not an end in itself, but an important social process. . . . It is the creation of an imagined and imaginative world whose passport for entry is the wearing of fantastic costumes derived from a commodity culture, forming the basis of shared relationships that are dynamic and which shift over time within the structured setting of cosplay conventions, competitions, and meetings. At the same time, this dress-up activity affords the individual player a way of celebrating individuality, irrespective of gender boundaries, whilst also expressing and performing the secret self publicly, albeit within the safe confines of the collective. This is all achieved by mimicking fantastic and divergent guises in the entertaining and empowering process of dressing up. (Peirson-Smith, 2013, p. 104)

Part B involves examining how people who are engrossed are vulnerable to other people's sabotage, criticism, or unwillingness to support imagination activities. This problem connects to issues of stigma management in terms of appreciating Goffman's applicability to analyzing popular culture. Outside threats imperil the sanctity of an engrossed state. Maybe someone must return to work, or a player's significant other is tired of how much time a partner spends in fantasy realms. Maybe someone wants to mock the activity. Triumph the Insult Comic dog, a *Conan O'Brien* show character, once was assigned to cover a *Star Wars* series film premiere. He kept teasing people dressed as *Star Wars* characters who were waiting in line. The humor's premise is that all audience members enjoy making fun of sci-fi "geeks." Triumph saw a person dressed in a Darth Vader costume and asked, pointing to colored buttons on the chest part of the costume: "So this is to help you breathe, yes? And which of these buttons calls your parents to pick you up?"[4] The frame of being "in character" is disrupted by Triumph pointedly "breaking the fourth wall" by bringing the character back to earth through denigrating his role-playing as a form of pathetic juvenility. This "bringing back to earth" threat must be avoided to remain engrossed.

Goffman (1961) argues that an *interaction membrane* forms to protect activity, referring to a boundary around an encounter, game, or situated activity system that protects the integrity of game events from rupture and the participants from being "unengrossed." A more strict definition of an interaction membrane is "as a protective filtering boundary metaphorically cutting off the encounter from the wider world, protecting its integrity and rewards" (Goffman, 1961, p. 65).

Goffman viewed playing games as a situation where people set up social worlds through minute face-to-face interactions. He analyzed games to derive principles of how face-to-face interactions work in constructing social worlds. As a child, perhaps you engaged in the activity in which you or a partner drew a line in the ground and dared the other to cross the line, implying that if that person crosses, they initiate a fight. Somehow, the situation gets framed such that a foot drawing the line is more than a division of the ground, but is now a territory of the self. That line has a shared social meaning that one is "invading" a newly artificial "territory of the self" of the person or parties whose line is crossed. This performance enacts a joint fantasy into reality, because if people start hitting each other (instead of doing the comedy routine of continually crossing additional lines in lost territory while jokingly daring the other to cross, which keys the event as a game), a fight occurs. The line is real enough in consequence, even if someone is outside in a park they don't own when drawing a line in

---

[4] Triumph the Insult Comic Dog, "Come Poop With Me," DVD.

the grass. The space becomes concrete territory in fantasy that becomes real in its consequences. An arbitrary line creates a sudden border. That moment's willing shared belief is a dramaturgical accomplishment, and its nature also helps explain how today's engrossment in popular culture can exist.

Playing a warrior in a dungeon, duplicating the historical circumstances of a real battle as if present there, and cosplay all involve creating and inhabiting a temporary situation of fantasy as real, taking actions that make engrossment seem transcendent and "real" over being jarred out of this temporary state. When Goffman (1961, p. 80) writes, "Sustaining a definition of the situation in face-to-face interaction is socially organized through rules of relevance and irrelevance," he is commenting on how people must act in interactions in order to maintain engagements within the scene. They must attend and disattend to information carefully to keep the line that they are taking on temporarily.

Dramaturgical Residency

To understand how participatory culture works means considering how face-to-face interaction applies to creating what Goffman called role embracement. *Role embracement* occurs when people are attached to and identify with a role, they have the quality or capacity to play that role, and they are engaged in the role (Goffman, 1961, p. 106). Engrossment in an activity and escaping the stressing toll of the real world leads to successful role embracement; being engrossed is transcendent. In role embracement, someone takes up a temporary *dramaturgical residency* in an existing character that is not technically able to exist with its powers intact. They see themselves in some sort of active relation to the fictional character, an expert in staging a fantasy world, or a meaningful audience for engaging in the real world with fantasy characters. Participation in popular culture means people take temporary dramaturgical residences in their cultural pastimes. The previous chapter examined dramaturgy and enchantment in commercial enterprises such as cathedrals of consumption. The idea of enchantment is also a self-service phenomenon where people contribute their own capacity to be enchanted and engrossed to participate in popular culture, aided by the commercial support of imagination products. Dramaturgical residences reference situations in which people "reside" in fictional characters and enterprises in a participatory vein, in addition to, or other than, living primarily in a nonfictional identity. These residences are a home away from home. A dramaturgical residence is acting a part, yet there are distinctions of this part being expressly fictional and also being chosen as a residency of affinity for actors. This part is a residency because the actor has a self-identification with the fictional part. A residence is a comfortable, temporary voluntary habitation in a fictional character and participation in popular culture that one enacts with others. People invest themselves and serious dramaturgical effort to enact fictional characters, whether in LARP, fan fiction, or *World of Warcraft*, in their leisure time or perhaps as work. These dramaturgical residences require intense discipline to maintain engrossment in their fictional identities and to preserve the atmosphere from jarring disruptions. To explore these dramaturgical residences requires understanding some of the meanings that they generate and their contexts. Comic conventions, for example, offer both a commercial community and subsequent rewarding experiences. Henry Jenkins (2008) writes,

> Comic-Con is a field of dreams, and wearing costumes transforms those "dreams" from something personal and private to something shared and public. Showing a pudgy midriff or pasty white skin amidst fur and feathers allows nerds (typically defined by their brains and not their bodies) to feel sexy. Donning cape and cowl allows children and adults to play together, strangers to find others with the same values, and fans to become micro-celebrities posing for pictures with other guests. (p. 30)

This chapter will connect the increased availability of engrossment in participatory popular culture to Goffman's useful ideas about face-to-face interaction and roles. A participatory audience wants to be in or part of the shows, which is a newer wrinkle on the traditional integrity of bounded cultural performances that are just to be watched. Audiences engage more readily now, rather than sit in thrall to performances. The large appeal of contemporary popular forms is almost as a common language that people speak and communicate to one another as "real." How people act to make these available fantasies more "real" comprises an important contemporary application of Goffman's ideas. After examining the basics of interaction, I turn to how ideas from *Frame Analysis* apply to explaining people's contemporary capacity to manage fantasy elements as "real."

Face-to-Face Interaction

When two individuals interact, a miniature version of society emerges. Face-to-face interactions represent small-scale moorings of social influence. Individuals adjust their behaviors in anticipation of being observed, and behaviors follow social conventions. Those sequences of actions are concessions to social order and other individuals, which eventually (more broadly) collectively help establish a society. What could be more vital for people's capacity to live together and establish large-scale social systems of expected behaviors and reciprocity than individuals anticipating actions and judgments and responding to them consistently and predictably? A productive coexistence then bears many fruits, including developing the cultural institutions that people share.

Large-scale society begins in face-to-face encounters. Goffman's ideas on this subject, particularly in his books *Behavior in Public Places*, *Interaction Ritual*, and *Relations in Public*, offer analytic concepts to understand how face-to-face interactions work. I cover these concepts briefly here. I then argue that limits in how people can interact help generate an increased participatory involvement in contemporary institutions of popular culture.

Face-to-face interaction starts in participation units of "singles" and "withs."[5] A "single" is an individual, and a "with" is a plus one or more group. These units, in individual or "with" form, encounter and participate with other units. To communicate, these units use props, sign vehicles, sets, identity badges, tie-signs, and game-like tactics. Exploring how communications between interactants work led Goffman to set up a "traffic" analogy for the organization of face-to-face interaction.[6] Just like road traffic flows in an organized system of roads, traffic lights, and signs, the traffic of human communications, interactions, and encounters between people uses an underlying organizational structure. These "traffic" rules offer an organizing scheme through which interaction can flow.

Consider some examples. People must abide by unstated nonverbal physiological idioms, like cover your mouth when you cough or

---

[5] This discussion draws on the terminology Goffman (1971) uses in *Relations in Public*.

[6] Goffman used analogies like games, rituals, theatrical performance, and animals sensing threats as occasional motifs in his work. An interdisciplinary scholar, he cites ideas from numerous fields, including dramaturgy, ethology (study of animal behavior), anthropology, literary theory, game theory, psychology, sociology, symbolic interaction, literature, and nonfiction books.

sneeze and avoid embarrassing (what he called) "creature releases" like flatulence. People who are interacting work to respect a bubble of personal space that individuals travel with and to honor "territories of the self" that belong to others like people's possessions (a wallet or purse). Noncompliance in honoring those territories is seen as disrespectful. Individuals also work to make and protect their own territories of the self. For example, you sometimes see people suddenly create new temporary "private" property in public places by laying an object down at a table or on an adjacent chair or draping a coat in an adjacent movie theater seat, which claims a "territory" for themselves.

The flow of interaction uses *supportive interchanges* to establish and help maintain relations between people. For example, there are established ways to greet people and ceremonies that constitute accepted forms of everyday diplomacy, ranging from stating "how are you" to proffering a hand. People use "tie-signs" like pictures in a wallet or an engagement ring to demonstrate connected and anchored relationships with others. Traffic also requires that interaction not halt because of people becoming offended. Avoiding situational impropriety and sustaining normal appearances is important as a pillar of social order. Sets of *remedial interchanges* between people consist of apologies and excuses for violations that acknowledge a breach and which request permission to repair and continue interaction. Public order requires a regulating system to govern interactions among many who do not know each other who meet in public. Private contact is more bounded and familiar, but both private and public interactions involve abiding by social norms. Apologies and excuses, for example, must hit some legitimate default reasoning in people's knowledge of what conditions make a particular apology reasonable to accept. The steps people take, the rules they follow, how moves in social interaction proceed in turns and sequences that organize them; these are all products of a social world over and above the individual.

To Goffman, a social gathering is the initial level of "society" writ large that merits more attention from scholars. Uncovering the rules of social conduct that govern interaction means obtaining a foothold in identifying potential bases of larger institutional-level bonds. The lines and faces that people pursue do not belong to the individual, but to the social body. Lines and faces involve esteemed attributes and goals. Goffman (1961) again emphasizes the importance of "not men and their moments, but moments and their men," in writing,

Universal human nature is not a very human thing. By acquiring it, the person becomes a kind of construct, built up not from inner psychic propensities but from moral rules that are impressed upon him from without. These rules, when followed, determine the evaluation he will make of himself and of his fellow-participants in the encounter, the distribution of his feelings, and the kinds of practices he will employ to maintain a specified and obligatory kind of ritual equilibrium. The general capacity to be bound by moral rules may well belong to the individual, but the particular set of rules which transforms him into a human being derives from requirements established in the ritual organization of social encounters. (p. 45)

Interactions have stakes involved. People must coexist. They can gain or lose from their interactions with one another. As interactions between people occur, basic issues emerge. What lines should people follow to save face before others? What are different communication styles? Who has more or less rights in interactions between individuals? Individuals want to avoid losing face, they have lines of interaction to pursue, and they may feel a need to remedy misalignment with social norms or pay proper deference to honor someone.

Surpassing Performance Limits in Fantasy or Killing S**t in Made-Up Worlds

A consequence of these requirements is that the social world imposes limits on people's discretionary behavior and choices. Goffman (1967, p. 10) notes, "Approved attributes and their relation to face make of every man his own jailer; this is a fundamental social constraint even though each man may like his cell." Even though some can "like their cells," others can chafe at their restrictions, both in what attributes others approve and in an inability to manifest those attributes. People might prefer to have a different face and to be judged on criteria that they choose. Real limitations contribute to individuals simulating, in fantasies in their heads, the "daydreams" and actions that they want to achieve despite real social constraints. Goffman (1974) viewed people's inner daydreaming of social actions as deserving focus:

The individual spends a considerable amount of time bathing his wounds in fantasy, imagining the worst things that might befall him, daydreaming about matters sexual, monetary, and so forth. He also rehearses what he will say when the time comes and privately formulates what he should have said after it has come and gone. Not being able to get others to speak the lines he wanted to hear from them, he scripts and commands these performances on the small stage located in his head. A point to be made here is that this traditional balance between doings and dreamings leans much too far, I think, in the direction of doings. (pp. 551–552)

The dramas in people's heads respond to and seek some transformation into "real" lives. Yet limits on what people can actually do forestall individuals from living out their dramas as they would want, particularly ones associated with extravagant expectations. Some alternate paths to fulfilling this dramatic impulse can come from today's participatory popular culture. The contemporary world's popular culture offerings enable people to enact aspects of inner fantasy lives increasingly in their "outer" external lives. Participation in popular culture allows people an increasing opportunity to invest time and personal energy into fantasy worlds, where restrictions are more malleable and entry is possible.

Many people spend time in fantasy worlds, in complement or opposition to, or in substitution of, the non-fantasy worlds around them. Technological developments and social acceptance increase how people can pursue fantasy offerings in their available leisure time. Yet a popular canard emerges. Perhaps people retreat to fantasy participation in things like *Star Trek* fandom or writing slash fiction or costume play or *World of Warcraft* because they are alienated and too beleaguered by bullies to have a comfortable place in the "real world." This generalization is a limited and weak one. Many participants may *not need* but rather *enjoy* a diversion from reality's disappointments and obligations; they seek a good time and fun in escapist pleasures. They do so despite shaming and a reasonable fear of being humiliated for their interest in living a more intense fan experience. An explanation appropriate to the large numbers of people who put their attention, time, and money into some form of popular culture, whether being a historical reenactor, being involved in online gaming, collecting Disney artifacts, or being one of the 140,000 who attended San Diego Comic-Con in 2014, is that those worlds are fun and empowering alternatives to inevitable reality.

To build on and paraphrase an observation from Gary Alan Fine's (1983, p. 60) research on playing fantasy role-playing games, people can overcome mundane characteristics, inhibitions, shame, or shyness by role-playing fantasy personas and participating in the roles and collective engrossment that fantasy characters offer. Fine argues that a motivation to play games is to seek fun and an occasional distance from the world. Fun in the game is a worthwhile pursuit in itself. This point is important in qualifying the idea that immersion in fantasy is only to find "haven in a heartless world"[7] and that only socially incompetent people play these games. Fine identifies four reasons why people play fantasy games: educational aspects of learning through gaming; escape from social pressures; increasing a sense of personal control; using games to help in dealing with people, specifically using the games as a means to transcend shyness and build relationships through game participation providing a focus (Fine, 1983, pp. 53–62). These strands thread into a theme of participation overcoming constraints in people's lives.

An additional point to consider now is the contemporary context. The fantasy worlds that people escape into and the social worlds they escape from and into do not remain frozen in time. Today, the "real" world can be harsher and prompt more escapes into an "elsewhere," just as new popular culture options to immerse oneself within may now offer deeper and plusher oases. Are contemporary "real" roles more boring or full of ennui? Certainly, most conventional role performances seem less fun to play than the ones available in fantasy worlds, where instead of being a retiree or a worker, you can cast spells, topple kingdoms, fight monsters, and engage in great adventures. Who wants to be ordinary? Similarly, online virtual identities can bring to fruition more fantasy elements than exist in the conventional world. For example, creating virtual fantasies of better looking and more socially successful online profiles to enact virtually also represents an escape from conventional reality. Investing oneself in being a mage or paladin in fantasy RPGs and men and women faking good looks on deceptive Internet profiles seem kindred spirits of the escapism variety. Both involve a temporary disappearance into a fantasy role that popular culture offers. To acknowledge and build on Fine's observation of role-playing fantasy groups, people can overcome mundane (for them) characteristics, inhibitions, shame, or shyness by playing fantasy personas and invest attention and life into the positive attributes that desirable fantasy characters offer. People do not forgo reality completely and get lost in the game. They do get to add playing a character and participating as player to reality and can switch between

---

[7] This phrasing comes from part of a book title by Christopher Lasch, 1976, *Haven in a Heartless World: The Family Besieged.*

all of these frames. A fantasy element adds another layering to reality and can make a meaningful and pleasant addition to one's life.

Before examining the prefabricated and organized fantasy realms that people enjoy, be they Second Life or LARPs, a brief return to the topics of daydreams and escapism is helpful. Important differences exist between individual-level daydreams and the empowerment available in participatory culture. First, there are no limits in the simulations that can exist within an individual's imagination. Fantasies of revenge, desired sexual acts, and wishing to be more powerful than one is are all unlimited possibilities in a person's head. Second, an individual alone is the ultimate guarantor of privacy here. People may only open up the visibility of their fantasies depending on their own discretion and if they make their Internet history impregnable. People can hope to defy whatever conventional morals they wish in their imagination with no one the wiser.

However, fantasies have an individual private existence and a collective, shared public level. People can revisit private fantasies in their own heads, seedy or otherwise, and they can also participate in prefabricated fantasy realms that can capture some of their own ambitions and desires or trigger ones that they did not know that they had. There are benefits to moving away from a private quarantined fantasy world to a shared one, albeit one with less stigma. Activity now brings benefits from being collective. Avoiding lonely isolation is significant. Having a prefabricated world ready to go is also a pleasure. Whole fantasy realms like *Star Trek* and *World of Warcraft* preexist, with all kinds of themes to enjoy, and they are better fleshed out than a single person could do on their own. One can remove oneself from their own cares and perhaps also from their own dark imaginings in those worlds. Or they may seek them there.

For example, if you wish, you can avail yourself of rampant possibilities for aggressive violence. That may not be the motive that makes participation relevant for you, but those aspects exist and matter to at least some. *Grand Theft Auto* enables you to run over people and shoot them; other games also allow you similar sadistic privileges of being a murderer with unlimited capacities to engage in what I call "designer" killing. Designer killing refers to many games being designed purposively to include spectacular ways to murder in the game world. Designers plan a variety of murderous abilities and weapons as an incentive to interest players in the game. A first noteworthy example of designer killing is the range of "fatalities" the *Mortal Kombat* game series offers. Joining a fantasy realm may also allow you to be a much bigger jerk in anonymity, engaging in bullying that may be more satisfying than ranting in your own imagination or in typed-out screeds. Whether motives are dark, light, or both, people may need an escape from the frustrations of real life and also from being too trapped in their own daydreaming, which has limits (they cannot be actualized in one's heads), though also rewards (lack of external judgment and privacy).

Engaging in a shared fantasy world brings in sociation. In this regard, fantasy subcultures are popular beyond just the disaffected or socially awkward. People want to imagine possibilities and share them with others. People form idiocultures and shared social worlds in fantasy. Some joy in participating in these worlds comes from sociation in playing fantasy roles together and in enjoying friendship in working collectively to bridge real and fantasy worlds. For example, people enjoy competing against others in countless college dorm room video game contests and in collaborating together to play popular team shooter video games. There are also unexpected rewards for participation. The informant quoted as saying, "Who wouldn't want to have perfect boobs and kill s**t and be born again?" did not know that she would find these fantasy aspects fulfilling, as she was a feminist, a PhD, and liberal. She just started playing *World of Warcraft* to spend time with her child and discovered the fantasy thrill of "killing s**t," regeneration, and "having perfect boobs" (Gilsdorf, 2009).

Participatory popular culture provides venues that allow people to take up dramaturgical residences and enact aspects of these worlds. There is now a blurring of worlds, for example, in the amusement parks offering *Harry Potter* worlds, conventions for cosplayers, and live-action role-playing worlds like the *Realms of Dargarth*. Someone can write fan fiction for a television series they love with a community of like-minded others. Further, in a world where people are more locked into McDonaldization, a greater embeddedness in personal fantasy can make sense. People may be driven to seek distractions by forces of routinization and McDonaldization, which organize work life in alienating ways.

Role Distance and the Actualization Gap

Role distance addresses the distance individuals want to put between how they or others think of that person's "self" and a putative role that carries a discrediting depiction of the kind of self that occupies that role.

People may have to play a role, but that is not to be taken for "whom" they are. People can attempt to split their selves to stand at a distance from some roles, which demonstrates some disparagement of whatever is contemptible about the role. In role distance, the claim is that I may have to play this part, but this part should not be interpreted as who I am. For example, a boss may act chummier with subordinates to show that he or she is really "just one of the guys." A fantasy character that is evil would do things like this, but as a person, I am not that character; or a risqué appearing cosplayer is dressing like that for the role but also clarifies not being a prurient person.

A reverse of role distance is *role embrace*. Here, instead of people distancing a self from a stigmatizing role, people now wish to embrace the role as representing the "self." The role does match a person's self. A man in an authoritative role may not want to relinquish control associated with that persona as he considers himself as being the kind of decisive person that befits the role. They prefer to live more in the role rather than state how distant their real self is from the role. As an extreme example, a subculture called *otherkin* exists, whose adherents believe that an aspect of their self is authentically supernatural in origin, as in being, for example, part fairy or extra-dimensional. In that sense, a human self is what they seek distance from, as they see themselves more in this role of "other" and wish any sense of self that implies differently to be diminished. Certainly, many might wish to be more like the online profile of perfection that they build rather than a self that disproves that characterization. There are people who do not want to acknowledge the "IRL" (a slang reference meaning In Real Life) when they play such roles, as to them, their "selves" were always really supposed to be like the role.

The distance between fantasy and reality connects to an *actualization gap*. A person can fantasize in their heads about leaving a job while knowing that they cannot for economic reasons. Someone else can dream of how successful they would be if they had just not run into so many unfair people. Another person might want mind-controlling superpowers to bend others to their will. The degree to which these examples all count as fantasy is debatable, but the important key across them all is that a distance exists from being able to actualize them. The desire to overcome such gaps is so palpable that self-help books will always be best sellers. If people could buy magic spells or use voodoo dolls to traverse those gaps, they would, and they certainly buy advertised products that make such promises. So why not take up a temporary residency in a fantasy realm where a person can have actuality be reality? In real life, I cannot play perfect soccer, but as Ronaldo in *FIFA*, I can. Why not enjoy making the impossible a possibility?

As an illustration of this wish fulfillment, the humorist Dave Barry (2010) wrote a scathing parody of *Twilight*, titled *Fangs of Endearment*, which captures this fantasy appeal. Barry's parody begins with the female character parking at the high school:

> I glanced into the rear view mirror and scrunched my forehead in dismay as I realized for the millionth time that I do not consider myself at all attractive although roughly 85% of all the male characters I encounter fall in love with me. . . . Before I could speak I was struck dumb by the perfection of his chiseled cheekbones and the realization out of all the girls in the world, I was the one he found irresistibly attractive, as so many males do. (p. 215)

Barry proceeds to question the logic of powerful, centuries-old creatures of great intelligence, vampires, who have looks, wealth, and power, choosing (a) to return to society as high school students, coincidentally enabling the gorgeous male vampire to (b) fall madly in love with the teenage girl protagonist as the only object of attention among all competing mortal women in the world. Further, these desirable men are full of love and desire to wed her, keep her safe, and fulfill her every wish. These are appealing themes to readers.

Some male interests in fantasy themes seem disproportionately catered to being great fighters who conquer every opponent with physical brawn and weapons in combat, who become rulers of all against overwhelming odds and involve every woman being beautiful, objectified, and attracted to the male's character. These themes, however gendered, (a) are unlikely to be actualized in everyday life and (b) provide immensely enjoyable dramaturgical residencies for sojourns from reality, beckoning people to participate through imagining new stories set in those universes or in role-play.

The theory of *interaction ritual chains* (IR chains) argues that, over time, participating in rituals and the emotional energy emanating from them "chains" people into greater social integration and a "society." Randall Collins (2004) argues that conditions for IR chains to succeed include that two or more people are together in a significant exchange; they see themselves as bonded insiders; they "focus their attention upon a common object or activity, and by communicating this focus to each other become mutually aware of each other's focus of attention"; and they share "a common mood or emotional experience" (p. 49). IR chains produce increased solidarity and common cause; infused emotional energy, which is motivational and generates enthusiasm; new symbols; an empowering of old symbols as sacred that can store "social" energy; and a moral code that punishes people who violate the sanctity of rituals.

Consider these criteria in connection to people's participation in popular culture rituals, such as live-action role-play, costume play (cosplay), and massive online multiplayer games. Include the growth of increased participation in convention culture, where people attend conventions with multiple others celebrating and or dressed as their favorite characters. You can meet celebrities and purchase memorabilia and photos as commemoration. You can indulge in a temporary manifestation of a popular culture community. Such events are immensely popular.

Do *Harry Potter* fans, as an example, appear chained together in community? Do people involved in LARPs seem bonded in significant exchanges in a bound universe that has emotional meaning to them, for which they are enthusiastic and that proffers them some kind of moral concepts? Fantasy examples are not in the typical oeuvre of IR chains, but today's fantasy worlds do constitute IR chains. They offer people dramaturgical instructions to guide them in social interaction, enchanted roles, and fantasies in which to participate, and they are empowering substitutes as needed for potentially weakened social positions elsewhere.

Frames: A Social Phoropter

Diegesis refers to treating a fantasy world on its own terms and acting as though one is living in a "truth" or "reality" as considered valid by the rules that apply to that interior world. Goffman's ideas help us understand how people can transform a fantasy into an experience that is shared and more real. How do people accomplish *diegesis*?

If you have visited an optometrist, you have looked through a phoropter. A Snelling chart (the one with the letters in decreasing size) is on a wall in front of you, facing you in the examining chair. You look through the lenses in the phoropter machine while the optometrist turns different lenses to change your view of the chart. The optometrist then asks if you see better or worse depending on the lens prescription that he or she adjusts. Taking a step back, a phoropter machine always operates with the same Snelling chart in front, but the chart changes in the patient's perspective, to be seen in better relief, or blurrier, or in different shading.

The base is materially the same before all lenses, but for practical purposes, each frame changes how you view and understand the information. The lens prescription changes your interpretation of what is before you.

Now imagine if you had a "social" phoropter. You view social information, such as a person striking another person. As the phoropter lenses change, you could imagine overlaying different interpretive frames that can exist over the base information you just saw. Depending on the overlay frame, you might see the action as an attack meant to injure. You might see the strike as "play." The frame might be that the strike is a "person teaching someone a lesson" but is not violent in the character of wanting to harm or play, but rather is an effort to "educate" through punishment. Depending on how the scene is "keyed," the meaning is transformed. Each transformation changes the scene's meaning and adds another layer of meaning. So what was once a harmful blow could be brushed off as play and then transformed again into education and then possibly into a case of physical abuse. The act can take on several different laminations as people try to settle on "what is really going on here."

Considering what the phoropter does as an analogy will help to understand Goffman's arguments in *Frame Analysis*, which is a densely written and hard-to-follow book. In his introduction to *Frame Analysis*, Goffman argues that frames "render what would otherwise be a meaningless aspect of the scene into something that is meaningful." In other words, people use frames to interpret their experiences of events. Frames answer the question, "What is going on here?" and Goffman examines how what we take as "what is really going on here" is organized.

A frame organizes experiences by providing a perceptual handle on the situation before a person, just like the phoropter lens. Once a frame exists, people "actively project those frames of reference to know the world immediately" (Goffman, 1974, p. 39). What is going on here is nothing less than Goffman trying to theorize how establishing a social context works. "What is going on here?" is a question people ask all the time. If you consider the phoropter example, a "strip of activity," to use Goffman's terminology, can take on different frames. People perceive "what is going on" in the scene based on the frame. As the phoropter example can clarify, the frames of the scene originate outside us in socially available "lenses" that are typically applied or can be applied to such scenes. Part of a person's social acuity, then, depends on how much knowledge and access he or she has to a range of different framings and understandings of events and how much he or she can persuade others to adopt those frames.

For example, in *fabrications*, others lead people to have a false belief about what is going on (Goffman, 1974). Fabrications can be benign, like in hosting a surprise party, or exploitative, like in creating an illusory storefront to facilitate a con job. People use frames to organize a subjective meaning of experience that is then treated as more or less objective in nature until someone changes the frame another time. For example, people can play-fight, but then someone "goes too far," and the frame now becomes a fight. The point of view and understanding that an individual participant adopts within a particular frame is called the *footing*. Footing describes how people associate themselves within a particular frame of reference. When people transform from one governing frame to another, they use *keys*.

To adopt and explain the usefulness of the *frame* model for examining popular culture, there is a great example available in how Gary Alan Fine used frame analysis to analyze the construction of reality in tabletop fantasy role-playing games.[8] The primary framework of people playing a role-playing game consists of a group of persons sitting around a table together involved in game activity, with the game paraphernalia scattered on a mutually adjacent table. There are probably some chips and drinks around the table; players twirl pencils and sit close to one another. This real setting is a primary framework of understanding "what is going on here"—one look and people know the activity fits "playing a game." A second frame is that those same people are there with the purpose of being *players*. They now operate by the rules of that game world and not by what someone could actually do in real life. In other words, they integrate two realities here: The first is the real one, and the second is the game one. In the game world, a player can roll dice to apply a +3 Vorpal sword of flaming righteousness to battle a monster, which they can't do in reality; while in empirical reality, they chow on snacks.

A third frame of meaning construction also exists. People must play characters; they are not just players. They assume and enact an identity in the game. Hence participants in this game negotiate the boundaries of being persons, personas in the form of their characters and players abiding by the game's orienting guidelines (Waskul & Lust, 2004). Fine

---

[8] Fine's analysis in *Shared Fantasy* (1983) is considered an important contribution to analyzing meaning construction in game studies and in studying Internet gaming. Statements of that importance can be found also in Linderoth (2012) and Rettie (2004).

points out that playing a character is different and more layered than being just a game player who moves pieces according to game rules. If someone plays chess, for example, they move the pieces but they do not personify the chess pieces, say, playing the role of a bishop or a rook, as if these pieces had associated personalities to embody. But personality and roles associated with characters and role-playing are intrinsic rewards of playing games like *Dungeons and Dragons* (D&D). People flip between these realities. You roll the dice to see if your sword strike is effective, while eating Cheetos, while telling the dungeon master in character of your character's intent to attack as befits a Paladin, maybe in your imagined Shakespearean English accent for a "Paladin," which is the fantasy frame where people act the roles. In D&D, people roll for personal attributes to embody, like intelligence and charisma.

People shift around these different frames. *Keyings* transform one frame meaning into another, perhaps making them more or less real. Goffman lists the categories of make-believe, contests, ceremonials, technical redoings (such as simulations), and regroupings as types of keyings. Once an activity is "keyed," the activity can be rekeyed (Linderoth, 2012). When you move between these framings, you can move closer to the base reality or further away. In the example of fantasy role-playing, an upkey moves you further away from reality. Treating the Dungeon Master as an omniscient deity is an upkeying of the fantasy. A downkey moves you closer to reality, as in complaining about the game's quality as a real player and not a character. In bullying, an upkeying attempt is that bullying is "really teasing taken the wrong way" by an oversensitive person. The intent might be harmful but the person is trying to key that harm as less real because of overreaction. A downkeying is that teasing is actually bullying. The acts of teasing retain a flexible meaning until assigned a frame and potentially a keying to interpret them.

An Extended Case of Frames and Dramaturgy: The World of Professional Wrestling

Professional wrestling is a popular culture dynamo. In its heyday in the late 1990s and early 2000s, World Wrestling Entertainment (WWE) could count on 50 million viewers a week, and this form of sports entertainment retains worldwide appeal, selling out arenas from Abu

Dhabi to Tokyo. The WWE Company is traded publicly and had a value of over a billion dollars in early 2014. The WWE is a big and popular business.

A burgeoning academic literature on pro wrestling exists (see Barthes, 2005; Craven & Moseley, 1972; Mazer, 1988; Smith, 2008). Some scholars focus on performativity, such as the emotional work required to perform "bad guys" (heels) and "good guys" (baby faces) storylines. Others focus on gendered and racial aspects, such as how masculinity and certain body types are emphasized through characters and violence. Some examine how stereotypes galvanize people's relationships to pro wrestling, for example, by playing on nationalistic sentiments such as those evoked by characters with names like "Mr. Fuji," "Iron Sheikh," and the "Russian Nightmare." This stereotyping practice extends to other countries. For example, the top heels in Mexican wrestling used to be a team called "Los Gringos Locos" who were American villains, and wrestlers playing anti-immigration American characters have been raising the hackles of Mexican fans.

At its core, professional wrestling is a theatrical production combining expert acting, athleticism, acrobatics, role-playing, and stunt work. Erving Goffman (1974, pp. 416–418) compared pro wrestling to amateur wrestling to illustrate aspects of frame analysis. He stated that pro wrestling's aim is to involve audiences rather than organize an objectively determined athletic competition. From a commercial standpoint, involving fans is meant to get them engaged enough to consume the product and associated merchandise. The more involved the fans, the more the characters "draw money."

For anyone unfamiliar with professional wrestling, the idea is that athletes enact characters that fight in an apparently improvised but also orchestrated battle. The moves in the fight require athleticism, and the protagonists are athletes, but the fight's winner is predetermined. The fight's purpose is to entertain, not establish who the authentic better combatant is, as a boxing match would do. The match here is between good and bad *personas*, not actual people. A "good" American character fights an "evil" Russian character; the two individuals playing these characters are not fighting each other as persons. To that end, some features unique to pro wrestling come into play.

First, the people who wrestle play characters as antagonists who are supposed to settle their accounts in the ring. The individuals playing the characters might be friends in real life and occupy one frame as coworkers who actually must be on the same page to generate fan interest in their conflict. Similar to Fine's analysis of frames in playing D&D, the wrestlers must inhabit different frames. There is a primary framework, and then there is the frame of role-playing that the characters do, such as have a particular tone or verbiage to play their characters so as to engage the crowd. Although playing antagonists, the people, not the characters who wrestle, actually have to work to make each other look good in their characters. Once in the character frame of the WWE "universe," the characters stage a "story" for the audience and enact the feud according to the tropes that are appropriate for the characters, such as the heel being villainous and the good guy being heroic and attacking the bad guy on the fans' behalf.

An example of a successful feud involved a wrestling character named Stone Cold Steve Austin, who played a rebellious employee of WWE owner, Vincent McMahon. The WWE's actual owner at that time, Vincent McMahon, played a character called "Mr. McMahon," who was the caricature of an egotistical and tyrannical boss, who threatened employee jobs, fired good guys (and fans), and berated everyone who "didn't worship me." One typical sketch was requiring employees to prove their loyalty by joining the Mr. McMahon "kiss my ass" club, which could be joined only by actually kissing the Mr. McMahon character's ass. At the character level, Stone Cold Steve Austin would beat up Mr. McMahon in the character frame, after overcoming Mr. McMahon's henchmen. In the game frame, he reported to work for his real boss, Vincent McMahon, and received scripts and orders from Vincent McMahon about how to entertainingly beat him up as the Mr. McMahon character in the character frame during the wrestling show.

The character frames and game frames overlap into a state that was called *kayfabe* in the wrestling world, which describes situations when wrestlers are to treat the performed characters and actions as "real." For example, if a wrestler is supposed to be injured from a match, he will act injured, even if the injury is a "work" to cover a wrestler taking a few weeks off work, while providing storyline motivation for the wrestler to revenge himself upon his return. Claiming the fake as real means enacting kayfabe or a "work" and always being in performance mode. When wrestlers say and do something real, in lieu of as kayfabe, their behavior is called "shooting." If a wrestler actually hits the other wrestler with intent to hurt him or reveals information that discloses that kayfabe exists, he is "shooting."

Pro wrestling is so in touch with impression management that a well-developed vocabulary exists to describe features of real and unreal performances. For example, the players are to "sell" pain in what Tyson Smith (2008) called a "theatrics of pain" as they respond to holds and strikes from other wrestlers, who hold back to avoid actually hurting the opponent. Conflicts are organized with "psychology" in mind, to wring drama from the proceedings by "selling" the pain, intensity, and retribution the characters enact for the audience. Kayfabe requires acting as if the staged events in the wrestling ring are real, as in the characters are real, the performed violence by those athlete acting stuntmen is real, and the stakes are real. Kayfabe is a term of great salience to dramaturgy, as representing an effort to create a fabrication: to put on a reality that is not real, but to act as if the portrayed reality is actual reality to promote fan engrossment. The history of professional wrestlers stating that the sport is not "fake" illustrates the kayfabe's hold. Kayfabe is an important idea for considering engrossment in participatory culture.

Wrestling storylines are "angles" that are meant to get "over" with fans. The wrestlers whose feuds are promoted are being "pushed." The nonverbal acting by wrestlers is consistent with evoking the characteristics of faces and heels, as are the identity tags evident in props. A bad guy sneers and glowers at crowds. When winning he taunts, but when the good guy is winning, the heel falls to his knees to beg for undeserved mercy. The good guy enters the ring with a brave and determined face to confront the bad guy. The bad guy will sometimes have a "valet," usually an attractive female character, whose job is to distract the good guy wrestler or referee with her looks long enough for the bad guy to attack the good guy from behind and steal a victory. The postapocalyptic warriors appear dressed with face paint and football shoulder pads with spikes. The effeminate wrestler appears in an ornate pink robe with ruffles. The Hillbilly wrestler appears in overalls, a dirty t-shirt and a straw hat, and in one case, carried around old animal bones.

Professional wrestling has a consistent cycle of storytelling. Bad guys cannot beat the popular good guys fairly, so they cheat, usually without being caught by the pointedly unobservant referee. The good guy suffers from doing the right thing by not cheating, and then after suffering more treachery, comes back against all odds, usually to the audience's screaming support, and beats up the bad guy. The feud, or angle, between the "heel" and the "baby face" usually continues over time in arenas and on TV, until an ultimate match is arranged to settle matters, such as a "gimmick" match contested in a steel cage. The penultimate match will see the bad guy winning or doing a final dirty deed that calls for the extreme of the steel cage, usually sold to fans as a necessary stipulation to keep the heel from running out of the ring to avoid the good guy's overdue retribution.

The tropes of feuds reflect matters that in reality anger people, although sometimes feuds are based in nonsense disputes, like who is a better dancer, or who really has the right to call himself a wrestling catchphrase name like "the nature boy," or paying for interrupting the British wrestler's tea party. Nationalistic tensions influence feuds between wrestling characters who represent nations; there are employee-employer tensions; good ole boys versus arrogant types; effeminate versus macho characters; good, virtuous, poor people against the cheating snobby rich; authority figures versus brave rebels; underdogs versus the advantaged. Wrestling companies milk feuds so audiences can purge venom on characters that portray disliked traits, and they especially enjoy that bad guys can lose in the kayfabe world, if not so much in the real one. For example, the good guy beats up the IRS character that threatens to audit all the fans, including those watching at home, but good luck to the average person who confronts a real IRS audit. The bad guys are aware of the joy the fans get from insulting them and goad them into more and more interaction, which whets the appetite for them to pay to eventually see the show where the bad guy "gets what's coming to him."

There are moments of pure antagonistic genius here. A wrestler who plays a lothario character goes up to women in the stands who are with men and tosses fake hotel key cards at them as he invites them up to his room and insults their male companions. Another character, the "Million Dollar Man," offered to pay a child five hundred dollars to dribble a basketball 15 times, and then he kicked the ball away after the 14th dribble to cheat the child out of the money and victory. Some quotes from him include, "Do you know there are still some people out there who think that their morals and pride are more important than money?" He urges fans to "stop dressing like paupers!" In a holiday vignette, he sent a Thanksgiving message of thanks that he is rich, unlike the fans.

The wrestling show's essence is good and bad in a violent showdown. Fan interest is much more important as a commercial consideration than whether a given performer could win or lose an honest contest of abilities. If there is more interest in an underdog five-foot-four

140-pound wrestler's character beating up a six-foot-ten 350-pound bad guy's character, then the smaller performer wins because the goal is to "draw" money. The money emerges from cultivating emotional reactions to the action. Before a match, much of the programming involves promoting the upcoming match, with an exchange of insults and threats that galvanize interest and build up hype. That exchange includes insulting the fans or fawning over them. Sometimes the insults are more specialized. The wrestler called "IRS," who represented the "tax man," screamed things to fans like "Move out of the way before I audit you!" A trope is a common narrative device, like evoking an expected norm. Professional wrestling excels at identifying tropes that garner "heat" from the crowd. Surprise, surprise: Getting someone to boo paying taxes (not known for their popularity) works.

A key aspect of the staged drama is ensuring that character names connect to gimmicks and tropes. The names for characters are unmistakable in generating identification with a type of social identity that is well known, sometimes in ethnic and racial groups, types of occupations and characteristics that people dislike, and foreign identities. The goal is generating interest in the characters, and making sure that fans understand the social trope the character evokes. As a popular culture activity, appealing to the easiest image is useful. There is some character in the list in Figure 6.1 that will generate heat, whether an "evil foreigner" who threatens Americans; smarmy guys like the Spirit Squad (male cheerleaders); the rich street gang of the "Mean Street Posse" from Greenwich, Connecticut; or Senator No who doesn't want to help citizens.

During bellicose times, dominant heel wrestlers are from enemy countries. In an economic downturn, the villain is a wealthy snotty character or a boss who threatens to fire people, especially telling the crowd that they all deserve to be fired and are poor losers. Physically, wrestlers fulfill extravagant expectations for physiques. Many men look like serious weightlifters and are larger sized than average people. There are also sometimes people treated as freakish characters who are morbidly obese, exceptionally large and tall, or "little people" who fight. Women are also viewed as embodying a physical ideal and their matches can center on appearances, consisting of themed matches like "bikini matches." The wrestlers are all typically serious athletes and have gone to wrestling schools, both men and women, but what people consume is not purely the athleticism but the athleticism in service to a story written on their bodies and nonverbal actions.

Figure 6.1	
Professional Wrestler Characters	
Male Characters	Hillbilly Jim
Big Boss Man	Honky Tonk Man
Irwin R. Shyster (IRS)	The All-American All American
Isaac Yankem, DDS	Senator No
Gorgeous George (played a feminine	Superbarrio
male and had his valet spray	Kamala the Ugandan Giant
perfume at the crowd because they	Yokozuna
"smelled")	Boogeyman
Mr. Ass	The Shah
Mr. McMahon (an evil boss)	Spirit Squad (male cheerleaders)
Nikolai Volkoff	Sheamus the Celtic Warrior
Iron Sheikh	The Alpha Male
Mohammed Hassan	Mr. Perfect
The Sheikh	Kwan Chang the Asian Nightmare
Sabu	Trailer Park Gangstas
Wild Samoans Afu and Sika	Joey Soprano
Abdullah the Butcher	Red-Blooded Italians
Baron Von Raschke	Los Gringos Locos
The American Dream Dusty Rhodes	
British Bulldog	**Female Characters**
Hollywood Blondes	The Billion Dollar Princess
Rick the Model	Raisha Saeed
Adrian Adonis	So Cal Val
The Undertaker	Debbie Debutante
Ravishing Rick Rude	Sunny Beach
"Sparkplug" Bob Holly	The Beautiful People
Papa Shango (Voodoo Priest)	Glamazon
Sexual Chocolate Mark Henry	Dirty White Girl
The Million Dollar Man Ted DiBiase	Miss Congeniality
The Matador Tito Santana	Miss Kitty
Rene Dupree	Prodigette
Uncle Elmer	Cheerleader Melissa
Kung Fu Naki	Trudy the Farmer's Daughter
Mean Street Posse (from Greenwich,	Lady Justice
who wrestled in sweater vests and	The Blonde Bombshell
dress pants)	
Faarooq	
Fatu the Headshrinker	

With this background on heels (bad guys) and baby faces (good guys)
and getting "heat," we can return to some microdynamics of performance

in the "game frame." Goffman used ideas from frame analysis to identify some ways that wrestlers work to involve audiences and distinguish professional wrestling from legitimate sports.[9] First, wrestlers ignore temporal brackets by fighting before the "fight" starts and by continuing to fight after fights are decided, or after injuries take place that should have ended hostilities. These bracket violations do not occur in amateur wrestling or boxing. The bad guy may "sneak" attack the good guy from behind as he walks to the ring. A more elaborate maneuver is when a good guy fakes an injury and then actors playing EMTs place him on a stretcher. The bad guy then attacks the stretcher and throws the "injured" wrestler to the ground because heels are that despicable. Heels will continue to apply a submission hold once the good guy taps out and won't let go until "officials" can pull the bad guy off or a good guy's friend (another wrestler) runs to the ring to "make the save." Wrestlers also antagonize the crowd or look for crowd approval during the match, which is normally when athletes focus only on the athletic contest and not on the audience. A boxer is not supposed to stare at the crowd when the fight starts, but playing to the crowd is exactly what a wrestler is to do when the match starts, or even before, such as by walking through the aisle to the ring and yelling things at the crowd, who wholeheartedly yell back.

The referee's involvement in professional versus amateur wrestling is completely different, as the referee in pro wrestling is a performer, not a judge who observantly and objectively administers rules and otherwise stays out of the way. The professional wrestling referee's job is to be *consciously* unobservant so as to miss all of the bad guy's cheating. He must angle himself perfectly to miss the heel taking a club out of his trunks. He must also get out of the way so that fans and the television cameras can see the cheating. He must be observant secretly to make sure not to get in the middle of the action and, at the right time, to get into position to be attacked (always by an accident that renders him incapacitated just long enough for the heel to cheat), to remember who should win, and to ensure that the match goes for the right time.

In amateur wrestling, the mat forms a border, and once people are over that boundary, the action stops and the competitors return to the area designated for competition. In pro wrestling, the ring and ropes are still boundaries, but they enhance the action when the boundaries are breached, which leads to meaningful action. For example, a bad guy

---

[9] See also Ford (2007).

draws hisses when he escapes a good guy by running away outside the ropes. When both of them are outside the ropes, they can also interact more with the audience, pick up a weapon "out of the referee's sight," or threaten the opponent's "girlfriend" or "manager." Allies of the bad guy can attack the good guy "out" of the referee's view. Bad guys also "bribe" referees. "Corrupt" wrestling "official" figureheads also conspire with bad guys to ensure that fan favorites lose. The referee, as a character, is a shill for the performance, doing whatever is needed to attract interest. His incompetency is purposeful and aggravates fans by illustrating how people who are supposed to ensure that life is fair never do.

Goffman (1974) captures the strategic calculation of wrestling perfectly:

> As already suggested, the story line itself depends on issues of frame. . . . Foretold by the differential reputation and appearance of the two men, the differentiation begins to be established through the heavy-to-be's beginning to break the rules. He starts to make moves that are illegal, persists in these so that more than verbal admonishment is required by the referee, and when he finally desists he sneaks in a post-terminal dollop. He threatens the audience, haggles with the referee, and shamelessly pleads for mercy when he is disadvantaged. He slaps the hero and steps on him in imperial acts of contempt that radically reframe fighting moves into purely ritual ones. The hero, weakened by punishing illegal attacks, inflamed by insulting gestures, abused by countless infractions of the rules, falters. His righteous indignation boils over, releasing new strength, and now, having earned the moral right to take the laws of wrestling into his own hands, he becomes downkeyed into a wild beast who roars for the kill, strikes back illegally, and wins the match. And what has been faked is not a demonstration of wrestling skill (there is very little attempt to do that) but, sometimes magnificently and sometimes cathartically, the violation of a traditional frame. (p. 418)

The violation of a traditional frame integrates "being pushed beyond all decency" to take matters into your hands and have good reign by force over evil. The character differentiation work and the artistry of the making of reputation and storyline warrant analysis for how they carry out framing and keying. For any person interested in concepts of face, line, and face-to-face interaction, pro wrestling offers a veritable clinic of imposture that shows these concepts in stark relief. The construction of this world is also scripted, as excerpts from a recent WWE script for a 3-hour telecast demonstrates.

In this first excerpt, a new wrestling character is being introduced. The character, Alexander Rusev, is being pushed as an agent of Russia. A manager, "Lana," accompanies him to the ring and does the promotional speaking for the "Rusev" character. A trained actress, she impersonates a Russian accent and glowers out every word in the script. The script makes clear that the intent is to frame an easy villain for fans to hate.

> Promo: Ladies and gentleman, greetings from Russia. It is your honor to bask in his presence. You are fortunate to be living during his time. And now, people of America, it is futile to resist. His greatness unfolds before your eyes. Superiority is what drives him. Monuments will be erected bearing his name. . . . And all of you will be the ones who build them. Now rise in appreciation, for the Bulgarian Brute, the Super-Athlete Alexander Rusev![10]

The fans are asked to applaud an opposing country's hero (he dedicates his victories to President Putin) and to glorify a person who insults them. A display of nativism is also called for, including showering down insults about Russia, the actress, the wrestler, and chanting "U.S.A., U.S.A." The cartoonish quality of the speech is the invitation extended to get into the game frame where diplomacy and international understanding are not the point, but insulting the stereotype of other countries is. In this regard, fans are asked to role-play characters themselves as the vicariously avenged offended victims of the heels. The fans are actors themselves in the show, which is the privilege they paid for.

A thorough checklist appears in the WWE script in which writers clarify important themes, encourage rehearsal, and tell performers to stay on theme. Prior to the checklist are the lists of stories to be told, such as who is to win and what themes require emphasis. Here are some items from the checklists excerpts:

- Does this pretape make sense?
- Have a big finish.
- Grab the audience's attention.
- Tell a story/make it entertaining.
- Talk to talent: (a) Provide approved verbiage—if talent has verbiage changes, present changes to VKM or Paul.
- Make sure talent knows what not to do: (a) Don't look directly at camera.
- Character Motivation: Make sure talent understands their motivation.

---

[10] Script quoted from posted WWE Raw script on http://deadspin.com/this-is-what-a-wwe-raw-script-looks-like-1570327862.

- Bring stories forward: (a) What happened in the last segment? Should the interviewer reference something that just happened? (b) Make sure the talent looks sweaty if they just competed. (c) Make sure talent is selling if they sold in the match.
- Make it real. Make sure people are filling the hallways. Make sure characters have the proper tone in conversation.
- ****If you're unsure with what the talent's tone or delivery should be (angry, frustrated, happy, etc.), use (named person) or (named person) as resources, and if needed confirm with VKM or****[11]

These performers make every effort to encourage fans to kayfabe belief, and fans are complicit because they seek involvement, to root for heroes and to see villains lose. As the examples demonstrated, wrestling shows demonstrate crystal clear instructions in labeling people, or put differently, in keying. Arrogance, for example is a concept that people can embody, but gifted scriptwriters create compelling characters to enact this trait as the performer's master status. Upon recognizing the trait in the performance, the audience can engage in public judgment and condemnation of that character. As an example, a group of female wrestling characters identify themselves as very attractive and call themselves the "Beautiful People." They enter the ring and bring paper bags to cover audience members' faces so that "ugly" fans don't "offend" them and distract them from winning their matches. Given how many people hate snobby and mean cliques, these antics generate heat.

The outcomes of professional wrestling events are predetermined, unlike most athletic contests, but that predetermination is *exactly the point* of staging the contest. Staging the contest allows people to script comeuppances, the villains to attract hisses, and the hero to garner support. Scripting allows for the most desired elements of staged fights to be inserted so that all the aspects of the "contest" have highlights. There are no 45-second knockouts in the headline match of a wrestling pay-per-view show as there might be in a legitimate boxing match, which might disappoint patrons hoping for a long fight. Professional wrestling is a theatrical production with popular acts and scenes always guaranteed to appear—there will be a wrestler in character playing out the expected tropes. The predetermination of getting skilled athlete-actors to portray annoying tropes, so as to stage the comeuppance of those who are

---

[11] Excerpt from WWE script posted on http://deadspin.com/this-is-what-a-wwe-raw-script-looks-like-1570327862.

difficult to retaliate against in real life, is exactly the offering that people pay to see. Fans pay to see frames they recognize and can relate to for abominable characters and larger-than-life heroes.

In discussions of professional wrestling and dramaturgy during a class, many students understand that the sport relies on performances, scripts, and enacting characters. Yet many also stated that professional wrestling is "stupid" and the idea that anyone who could like it is unfathomable. After hearing this view, I asked these cynics to consider what might engage people in being fans other than being too stupid to know better—what could make someone enjoy something so "fake," "stupid," and "unreal"? I asked students to create a wrestling character that they would want to boo or cheer and, most importantly, who could hold their attention. One student suggested creating a character based on a campus parking enforcement agent who regularly tickets students' cars. Suddenly, students in the class all chimed in and started talking about how much they would want to insult that character and see him "fake" assaulted. Soon people contributed ideas about how to build up the "Officer's" villainy. During his ring entrance, he would hand parking tickets to fans, lecturing them and saying, "You're welcome." They would do promotional films of him handing out unreasonable fake parking tickets outside to a bunch of fans' cars. He would bring a fake parking meter prop to the stage. He would use this meter in the films to arbitrarily give tickets out by placing a violated meter in front of anyone he would want to ticket. He would hit his opponent with the meter. He would have matches to revoke tickets. When he defeated an opponent, he would scream, "Tow him away!"

Every single student, including ones who disdained professional wrestling, said that they would pay money to see the parking enforcement character beaten up in a fake wrestling match. Seeing him get his "just" deserts would get them to the show. Although parking tickets cause a lot of bad feelings, the larger point is that the cultural frames here can engage people. The students came up with other great characters in this regard. A red-headed student came up with "Ginger Justice," who stood up for the rights of beleaguered red-headed kids. A woman came up with the character of "Miss Priss, who is that annoying, superficial beauty queen that every girl has always wanted to punch in the face." Whether people disliked professional wrestling at the onset or not, they all generated characters based in the frame-speak of cultural tropes that comprise this venue of popular culture.

Fan involvement in consuming this dramaturgy takes on active forms other than watching at home. Sam Ford (2007) conducted ethnographies of fans and identified seven means of engagement. Fans acted as spectators, critics, participants, members of a fan community, and theorists. These frames of engagement overlapped. People who are spectators can also be critical of performances (Ford, 2007, p. 7). Fans can participate by bringing signs and engaging in their "U.S.A., U.S.A." chants with other fan regulars at shows, which integrates them into a temporary community of fans. Ford also suggests that fans are involved as proselytizers and archivists. Ford also argues that fans can be fans of other fans, as they sometimes watch how other fans react to the show as if those fans are performers too.

The fakeness of seeing "punk rockers battling mountain men, black separatists fighting postapocalyptic warriors, gang-bangers rumbling with aristocrats and dandies tackling macho men" is keyed as make-believe. But within that fictional frame, the conflict is acted as if real, with effort expended to make fake battles seem authentic and as engaging as possible. The effect is meant to be cathartic, and as participatory culture, it allows fans to enjoy triumphs over adversaries that are unlikely in real life.

Stigma, Horror Genre, and Frame Traps

Framings and keyings direct people about how to embed themselves in different realities of "what is going on here." For example, encountering a broken-down car on the road with helpless-looking people around the vehicle can be interpreted as people who need assistance or as an exploitative fabrication, an ambush, designed to rob good Samaritans. Frames and keys lead people to interpret and then act on these different potential realities and then to either avoid or help the vehicle's apparent occupants. While people interpret, they also receive messages that are nested within frames. So in the broken-down car example, helping other people in need is an appropriate social value associated with altruism; or you cannot trust people's treachery in a dangerous and down-on-its-heels world.

Framings have social values nesting in them, and keyings are like knobs that adjust their direction and intensity. In a technical sense, frames, keys, and front stages are mediums through which people communicate. Much of Goffman's work encourages readers to appreciate how these communications work and not to take them for granted. The mechanics of social interaction must be appreciated at a microlevel; for example, being able to see a teammate wink at another teammate and understand what has been observed is a private communication layered over and commenting upon ongoing group interaction.

An important distinction exists in scaling between private interactions in public and the communications that are built into larger, prefabricated, mass cultural entities like movies. Spontaneous or planned performances in interactions between individuals and group members are not scripted, directed, and perfected to the level that "stand-alone" popular cultural offerings are, where teams of professionals ensure that every aspect of a visible performance is organized for dramatic best effect, whether in an advertisement, TV show, or movie. Performances scale up when more is involved in crafting the image.

A theatrical analogy helps people understand that everyday individuals put on acts for each other. However, the resources going into how people act vary by scale. An individual can perform by feigning interest in an acquaintance's story. Alternatively, acting in a play involves performances based on actors having a director, costumer, stage manager, and playwright to impact performance. Both levels involve actors performing, but a play is a *production*. A production is an organizationally developed dramaturgical presentation informed by resources and intended to have a calculated, typically commercial effect. Productions are scaled-up versions of individual dramaturgy. Values nest inside productions just as they do within face-to-face individual-level dramaturgy.

Communications from mass culture phenomena have meanings designed to generate commercial appeal. Cathedrals of consumption attract consumers by offering them enchantments. Professional wrestling allows for the communal expression of joy at seeing social villains *able* to be punished in that make-believe world. Fantasy role-playing enables people to educate themselves, escape social pressures, transcend limitations, and engage with others in amenable and controlled circumstances. These meanings and messages are nested in frames and are products of them, but they are not the frames themselves. A game frame involves abiding by and knowing the rules of a game and acting accordingly. A character frame involves role-playing what the character would decide to do in the game as a function of the character's nature. The rewards of playing *Dungeons and Dragons*, of escaping social pressure, or of engaging with others are cumulative products of the two different frames here, but they are not the frames themselves. These are values nested and built up from frames; they are the *cumulative social products* of dramaturgy discussed in an earlier chapter.

Participatory culture offers frames that people can interact within and treat as real on a temporary basis. Within those frames, whether a game or character frame, people are immersing themselves within an idioculture associated with that frame that comes with its general contours prefabricated (like a *Dungeons and Dragons* rule book or a video game character illustration or cosplay), but the resulting characters must be enacted through participants' dramaturgical activities. The idioculture that forms there links to larger social entities that the idioculture represents. A single group of *Dungeons and Dragons* players have their own idioculture that may be like a different dialect of the general culture of D&D players, but they still speak the same language as the general group. The small group is a sample of the larger cultural group even if the small group differs in some ways.

A book, movie, TV show, or picture is a finished, self-contained product with nested values. A group can build upon that content and do fan fiction or role-play or meet to debate the genre, and they build up an idioculture from that activity. However, the dramaturgical product that the commercial popular culture book or movie comprises is a baseline. The *Harry Potter* books have to exist before people can freelance new meanings from them, such as a fan starting a school newspaper for Hogwarts. Participatory culture emerges in the responses people have to cultural stimuli.

A source of worry is that people fear some negative values are imparted in the baseline cultural display that represent the "nature" of the cultural genre and fans unfairly. Cathedrals of consumption breed overconsumption and debt. Professional wrestling celebrates violence, sexism, and crude stereotypes. Fantasy role-playing is thought to embed people in that preferred unreal world because players cannot easily transition to function in the "real" world.

Fans become aggravated that people might cherry-pick certain negative depictions of the culture (as I did above) and then use those criticisms to stigmatize the adherents. These criticisms can then threaten the legitimacy of frames for participatory culture and disrupt activities. Erving Goffman (1963) describes stigmas as deeply discrediting characteristics. A stigma can be comprised of a physical imperfection, a moral flaw, or a tribal stigma. Discrediting stigmas are physically visible, like being morbidly obese or disfigured. Discreditable stigmas also exist, like mental illness or a criminal record. Unlike discrediting stigmas, discreditable ones can be hidden and remain undetected. Both discrediting and discreditable stigmas present different problems for audiences and stigmatized people to manage. The presence of a stigma injects tensions into interactions, which Goffman referred to as *strained interaction*. If a person has a visible stigma, that aspect of the person usually unsettles audiences or angers them, and that person must manage interaction to avoid poor treatment of some kind. A discrediting stigma has a problem of concealment, in which people must manage their actions to not reveal that they have a mental illness, are carrying on an affair, or have a hidden deformity.

Goffman's work on stigma management covers the control moves that people use to anticipate and manage reactions to their stigmas. These actions center on the visibility of information and control over expressions. Some stigmatized people reject negative treatment and embrace their deviance as a source of pride rather than shame. Others accept such stereotypes. Some exploit stereotypes, such as beggars who exaggerate the stigma they suffer in order to yield more panhandling returns. Stigmas are labels that people fight to attach to or remove from others. In the scholarly literature on deviance, addressed in a different chapter, sociologists focus on how moral entrepreneurs of different kinds generate labels and use them to oppress specific types of people and occupations. When a social group is to be scorned, they are stigmatized, and a door opens to punish that group for a variety of reasons, often opportunistic and political ones. More powerful groups often battle to contain vulnerable groups by attaching stigmas to them, like castigating "illegal" immigrants who steal jobs and welfare queens, stating all conservatives are bigoted rednecks and that such people are religious fanatics, and so forth. Want to ban marijuana? Then marijuana is a gateway drug that makes kids miscreants and killers. Oppose decriminalizing prostitution? Then people who exchange sex for money are prostitutes, not "sex workers" (because *workers* only do *legitimate* types of work), and they all engage in trafficking, ruin neighborhoods, and exploit people.

The importance of the stigma concept lies in how social power is harnessed to harm others through labels that typecast people into less powerful roles and that key adverse treatment. Homosexuals are the "enemy" of all religious faith. Pro-life movement advocates "hate" women and want to restrict their rights. When a powerful group stigmatizes others, they can place them into a "frame trap" that gives them restricted social powers and greater vulnerability if others act on and honor the frame. If I pigeonhole the status of someone to a denigrated role, I set the stage for how others should react and treat that person. If I succeed in that stigmatizing effort, I diminish the social power of the other and increase my own power in return, as the other person or group is placed on their heels.

When an individual treats a stigmatized person poorly, a small level of power is used against them. If an organization or government agency places a frame trap and label to act against that group, the situation is graver and more power is loosed against them. This is an issue of *scaling* in which the consequences of impressions are more significant when supported by an organizational-level actor. If a bank, for example, as a blanket proposition, frames poorer people as risky bets for loans, even though some are good bets, the applied stigma results in more than hurt feelings; a group is denied the financial capital to advance economically. The stigmatized group is trapped within a frame that views them poorly that has rationalizations for that status, ideas in the frame, and people working to cement a reality in that frame that acts to make the world reflect that the assumptions of that frame are true. The stigmatized people can fight against that trap, but they fight uphill trying to counter a frame trap from within the very frame that speaks against them (Hancock & Garner, 2011).

Frame traps also disrupt one's engrossment in participatory culture and work to deny people their escapist rewards from that immersion or, conversely, unite fans in solidarity to resist the frame. Professional wrestling fans are thought to be crass imbeciles who cannot understand how fake and stupid that activity is. The trap in liking pro wrestling is then set as one who likes pro wrestling then advertises himself or herself within that frame as stupid. William Shatner famously told *Star Trek* fans in a *Saturday Night Live* skit to "get a life." To embrace that fandom in that frame means being synonymous with being pathetic socially. In response, fans battle efforts to stigmatize them, and they assert their right to a participatory culture "self" that is above ground, is unembarrassed, and should not be insulted (Kozinets, 2001).

Many participatory culture fans cite embarrassment and a fear of how others will react to them and their interests. No one wants to be mocked, so many participatory fans treat the degree of their interests here as a discreditable stigma, and they keep their involvement quiet, except among like participants or others who are sympathetic and "wise" to the subculture. At a cosplay contest I observed, a well-known cosplayer, Riki Le Cotey, stated that cosplayers have "a lot of balls" to go out there and "own" their costumes. She said that cosplayers have to be brave enough to risk embarrassment and shame by putting the costumes on, which then tells judgmental people off as long as the cosplayer has fun and reaps joy out of participating.

The fight for many who participate in participatory culture is being vulnerable to frame traps laid out for them. People who engage in dramaturgy understand that stigma and embarrassment are visible like landmines in interaction. As aware dramaturgical performers, we act on the front stage to avoid stepping on a mine and getting "blown up" through being embarrassed and shamed socially. Participants in stigmatized popular culture *decide* to step onto social landmines on purpose. Pause for a moment to consider how hard this action is. If you are an adept interactant, you work to avoid being stigmatized in interaction. Imagine now choosing to breach norms and embarrass yourself, and as you do, you will feel forces of situational propriety urging you back to "proper" noncontroversial behavior. In norm-breaching studies, doing the socially unexpected, such as suddenly negotiating in a supermarket line for an item to have a lower price or bursting into song in an elevator, is difficult to do. Even accidental norm breaches like creature releases are shamed. So imagine dressing up as a superhero and walking in public on a day other than Halloween. Walk around with your World Heavyweight Championship Wrestling replica belt on your waist. Wear your elf ears. Be a 45-year-old man who advertises liking *My Little Pony: Friendship Is Magic*. Engrossment has rewards, but it also has risks in stepping on social landmines by daring to participate outside private spaces.

The attempt to shame others for their cultural choices is a means of control and garnering power, because if you have someone locked in a frame trap that benefits you and lowers them, you have an advantage. When someone says, "Look how she is dressed," that person is aiming and firing a social weapon of judgment intended to wound the target socially. If you say that those people are weirdos or outcasts, you, by implicit omission, are not. The fun aspect of analyzing dramaturgy is that you can see many such expression games occurring. When people start the name calling, they are throwing little grenades of potential embarrassment at people that they hope blow them up. People can toss the grenades because they are insecure or because they are right or because they are nasty people or for a myriad of combined reasons.

A person who wants to embarrass someone is not a sweetheart, but there is a sociological point that is higher in scale. Embarrassment grenades represent usable social power. In dramaturgical terms, one might as well yell, after tossing the embarrassment grenade, "You can't act your way out of this," as if to note, "I'm making you lower than me and now have some leverage over you." A discreditable person has an important choice to make in response. Is the person going to acknowledge the grenade and react? Or can the person have the latitude to ignore the grenade as a response, asserting that the grenade has no power over them? Here is the minidrama encapsulated in these scenarios.

If people fret about how others judge them based on the cultural forms they enjoy, then fans of horror genres should be worried. Here even conservatives and liberals find common ground in critique. Liberals disapprove of "dead teenager" movies that can make heroes out of monsters and sexism. Conservatives see a veneration of disorder and celebration of dark values in these films. Ironically, horror movies often have values nested in them that support conservative perspectives. The "horror is actually conservative" argument appears counterintuitive as people often think of horror movies as low culture and antiauthority, and hate them. Yet consider even the basic takeaways from horror movies that you have watched. Teenagers take their clothes off and sneak away to make out . . . and get killed. A person messes with dark beliefs and the supernatural . . . and gets killed. A person messes with science and creates disastrous monsters . . . and gets killed. A person doesn't listen to mom and picks up a hitchhiker . . . and gets killed. A person is tempted and sins . . . and suffers eternal punishment. People ignore the advice of wise elders who tell them to stay out of the woods, haunted house, abandoned camp, cave, old factory, mine, and spaceship . . . and get killed. People hang out with the wrong crowd . . . and get killed. See a theme yet?

On the plus side, people use crosses to survive vampires. The power of prayer expels demons. Religious figures aid in the incipient troubles. Love and traditional family connections comprise virtues that enable people to bond together to vanquish perils. Harry Potter was to defeat the horror villain Voldemort using the underestimated power of love. Conservatives may decry horror films, but from a functionalist viewpoint, the horror genre venerates traditional social bonds.

Evangelicals have certainly taken the horror tropes that monsters represent and the suffering they inflict, by running what are called "Hell Houses" that depict sinners going to hell (Herman, 2013).

Based on haunted house attractions, churches offer tours with sinners defined as people who have abortions, are homosexual, use drugs, and commit the seven deadly sins, and as a consequence, suffer taunts and tortures by demons. The last room in these houses often depicts heaven and proselytizes evangelism by advocating getting saved. Horror movies may not depict these sins as being punished, but they definitely argue for a belief in traditional social bonds as how to be saved.

Horror films identify plenty of social dangers. Why highlight them? One argument available in the case of the hell houses is that frightening people about threats to them is a means of gaining compliance and control. Separately, teaching people to avoid dark and abandoned places and not to taunt venomous creatures or take shortcuts through dangerous areas is also probably good advice. People also like a world in which, like in role-playing games and professional wrestling, monsters can be overcome. Though not always, mortals usually win, even though their victory is implausible against the odds facing them.

In Stephen King's (1980) analysis of the horror genre, he identifies some key themes. People cannot trust science, authorities, technology, nature, or people's appearances. Horror offers cautionary tales and warnings. The capacity of personal control has limits, as people have dangerous beasts lurking within them just under the surface. In a nice turn of phrase, King wrote that humans "wear their fur on the inside." Presenting collective nightmares in the form of monsters can create some functional solidarity in opposition to them.

Conclusion: Conflating Reality and Fantasy

Many fear that consuming imagination products like popular culture leads to a downward spiral in behavior and thinking. Sexist images emphasize looks over brains and teach both genders to value that distinction. Movies celebrating anarchy or drug use are thought to act almost like a contagion that comes to affect teenagers upon exposure. Like creating more zombies, one bite of the media virus is enough to transform otherwise potentially promising youth into whatever form of cultural degenerate raises alarms among elders. If this model sounds paranoid, then pause to remember that this model is meant to represent the effectiveness of advertising. Expose someone to a message promoting an idea or physical product through advertisement, and the person is meant to be "infected" enough to want to consume those items. Since advertising works, there is no shortage of reasonable concern that media message by-products, the stuff other than the product, which sells the product, like attractive models having a nested value of emphasizing looks, also infect consumers.

The array of popular culture before us allows us to improvise a participatory cultural form. Want to be like a hippie, martial artist, surfer, or punk rocker? You take a baseline on what you need to wear and say from the media depictions of these phenomena, and you go from there. A college friend saw *Top Gun* and knew he should be a naval aviator. Countless numbers of young men and women ask hairstylists to give them a look just like a particular celebrity. These scripts come from the media, but then the individual can improvise their takes on that cultural form. Henry Jenkins (2008) describes a convergence culture forming in which the mass producers of cultural products look to converge with "grassroots" participatory culture fans regarding appealing new products and support. There is a cycle here in mass culture generating subcultures, followed by participants spinning off resulting idiocultures and performative manifestations based on that initial baseline.

Some concluding points to consider are the bracketings from disruption that participatory culture involves and resulting forms of dramaturgy and framings of reality. Goffman's frames and keys concepts help dissect the context creation that allows for immersion into fantasy as temporary reality. There are other necessary brackets and frames to sustain disbelief and disruptive forces. This book is oversimplifying the discussion of this topic here, which is a cornerstone issue in cultural studies where plenty of thinkers theorize the constituent elements of creating cultural phenomena. There are different kinds of fans, and conflicts among them and producers, and all sorts of power issues in terms of discrimination that occur in what kinds of cultures get valued. The particular salient point here is, what type of social construction of reality must be manifest to maintain a culture activity *at a participatory level*? The social phoroptor frames that people sustain that allow them escapism are delicate and require more reinforcement when the attachment to the popular culture form is stronger, as stigmatizing is always a present threat and a more damaging one the more someone cares.

As an example, Robert Kozinets (2001) examined how some *Star Trek* fans view their relationship to *Star Trek* canon in a quasireligious manner. They find a utopian set of beliefs worth embodying in *Star Trek's* creation myths.

Arrayed against them are different cynical and skeptical forces to bracket off with an interaction membrane so as to avoid their throttling the fan's meaningful joy in participating. Some people who are too out there in their adherence are threatening, like the overly invested person who wore a Starfleet uniform as a member of the jury of the Whitewater case or who have beliefs that anyone who likes that culture is a misfit. These threats are clear to see, but there are also more subtle ones to bracket. The point again is what must be disattended in order to keep a performative venue open for immersion.

The commerciality of the *Star Trek* franchise is considered as one such threat. This threat is two-pronged. First, commercialism is seen to cheapen the sacred quality of the belief systems of humanitarianism and tolerance that people value in *Star Trek*. Basing a belief system on a "franchise" movie series, for example, may lead to doubting of the commitment's value. Second, the commercial power has creative control over the content of the popular culture type involved, here *Star Trek*. As Kozinets (2001, p. 82) puts it, "Their comments indicate that certain modalities of marketing and monetizing a culture of consumption's content commoditize and defile it."

The response fans have to this threat attempts to wrest away "creative control." According to Kozinets (2001),

> This ethnography found that producers and subcultures rearticulated entertainment texts, images, and objects with legitimating meanings of moral community in order to bracket them from the unavoidable reality that they are commercial creations—and thereby to enhance consumers' consumption experiences. (p. 85)

Though Kozinets (2001) does not use the following term, he seems to argue that "moralwashing" is required in order to frame the popular culture activity from being disrupted by the stigma of commercialism. This issue is in play for many forms of participatory popular culture where people may not necessarily see a quasireligious element to their investment, yet they do perceive a deeply meaningful value that is tainted or "taintable," if not bracketed off through making one's own variations in the culture or reinterpreting meanings. This issue requires some performance of morality and solemnity to avoid disrupting the pastime.

Media form a backdrop on and against which notions of reality are framed and used. Though I have not discussed popular music in this chapter, one can often see hip hop or rap discussed as "giving voice" to what some extant social conditions are like and how people should appear to "respect" them. Musical artists spur costuming and lifestyle choices, ranging from being nonracist skinheads, to emo and goth, to influencing hipsters. A variation on this kind of influence is thinking about how people feel a certain kind of cognitive coaching by taking media input from popular culture as a lifestyle guide. There was Jennifer Aniston's hair bob from the TV show *Friends* that become a widespread phenomenon. The television show *Jersey Shore* led many men to start weightlifting to cultivate a certain body type and phrases like "GTL" (gym, tan, and laundry) became a behavioral code for valuing a certain kind of looking good.

There are different dramaturgical points here. One is that participatory popular culture can mean integrating the affectations you draw from popular culture forms into your own acting without thinking you want to play the character. You can "get big" like the *Jersey Shore* characters without wanting to act as if you are playing one of them. You can buy Ray Bans to look cool like Tom Cruise did in *Top Gun* without thinking you are playing him. As an example, think of how many times people use comic phrases from movies, music, or television shows in everyday front stage speech.

The second is that you may construct reality falsely by committing the depiction fallacy of thinking that the media product, which is actually a funhouse mirror of reality, is actual reality. *Urban Dictionary.com's* website lists the term "Hollywood Historian" as someone who takes the depictions of facts in movies as if they are accurate historical information. In the "War of the Worlds" broadcast by Orson Welles, people heard the teleplay and thought Earth was being invaded. Today, people may believe that dinosaurs coexisted with people, that it is possible for people to have the proportions of action figures, and that certain moments of history that were embellished for storytelling purposes reflect fact. As a teenager, I remember people from Europe asking me if everyone in the United States lived as depicted on the *Dallas* TV show. A student of mine from Panama said that the media images of Latin America in the United States made everyone think that in between guerilla warfare, he lived in huts and trees when he was home. Here people may not see fiction and nonfiction blurring and flooding over, but they do.

A third issue is that people now share tropes of popular culture as a common language. When millions of people see the same movie, TV show, or video and can binge watch Netflix, the largest audiences in history observe the same stimuli in terms of content. We create shared trope images of the world, some of which perpetuate sexism and other ills. To see examples, try reading *TV Tropes.org* to see tropes that everyone immediately recognizes from media examples. Below is an example of some tropes regarding Native Americans.

> All Native Americans speak Tonto Talk in a deep voice, while mentioning words and phrases like "How," "Ugh," "Um," "white men," "pale face," "brother," "ancestors," "many moons ago," "Big Chief," "pale face speak double talk" . . . at least once a sentence. They all have names where a state of character is combined with the name of an animal, plant, or something other nature-related. For instance: Sitting Bull, Crazy Horse. . . . The only tribes that seem to exist in popular culture are Apache, Cherokee, Arapaho, Cheyenne, Comanche, Blackfoot and Sioux.

a. A more positive depiction of Native Americans that became the norm since the 1960s is the Noble Savage or Magical Nativeamerican, all of them badass. They will be Perfect Pacifist People who prefer smoking the Peace Pipe and signing peace treaties with white men. Unfortunately, they are usually the victim of the white man's greed and colonialism. Often they live in such harmony with nature that they only kill as many buffaloes they need and not a single one more. Usually will provide the foolish white man with a Green Aesop about nature and the danger of destroying the environment. This image has become so strong that they are often used in environmental messages, like the Crying Indian.

b. Other stereotypical images are Indian women carrying their papoose (child) in a bag on their back and Indian maidens and The Chief's Daughter falling in love with a white prisoner thus saving his life. When Native Americans make friends, they perform a Blood Brothers act. All communication is done by sending smoke signals to one another. When they travel, it's usually by horse or by canoe.

c. In popular culture, Native Americans are virtually a historical artifact. Stories set in the modern age hardly show them, except as proprietors of Native American Casinos. Those who aren't are poor, live in reservations, and are either alcoholics, diabetics, or both. In horror movies, the Twist Ending explanation why the house was haunted is usually because it was built on an ancient Indian Burial Ground.[12]

A vocabulary of tropes is a resource for understanding culture but also does so in clichéd terms. The advantage of speaking tropes are familiarity

---

[12] Quoted from the TV Tropes website at http://tvtropes.org/pmwiki/pmwiki.php/ NationalStereoTypes/NorthAmerica

with iconic cultural norms, and the downside is that taking these tropes as real involves people acting like morons or, at best, unrealistically. As a concluding test, see if you recognize some of these other popular staged tropes from *TV Tropes.org*. Leadership conflict is settled by "chief by combat" rules among "warrior race" tribes and in "badass versus badass" matches. The trope—"asskicking equals authority." Or how about romantic comedies where the girl dates the "boy the parents don't want her to date" after they "meet cute" in an unexpected way, and eventually their "romantic rivals" show themselves to not be the nice people they claimed to be. Or where the "one true love" can subsequently only be realized after carrying out a "last-ditch and last-minute grand love gesture." If you recognize these tropes, then media have gotten you to speak trope too.

SEVEN

The Internet

Society's Newest Stage

Online you have friends, lovers, enemies, and intense moments of truth without a thought for who's watching, because ostensibly nobody is—except, of course, the computers recording it all.

—Christian Rudder

One of the problems the Internet has introduced is that in this electronic village, all the village idiots have Internet access.

—Peter Nelson

I was raised on the Internet.

—Lena Dunham

Introduction: The Internet, Disembodiment, and Networked Audiences

Recent technological advances have produced a "triple revolution" in communications that have led to the Internet, mobile devices, and web 2.0 social media networks like *Facebook* and *Twitter*. Widespread adoption of these technologies has had profound consequences. Among them are

- A digital divide of inequality where some populations have greater access to the advantages of these technologies than others
- New forms of social connectedness and online communities
- Disrupted industries and new labor markets
- Online marketplaces like *Amazon* and *Ebay* and the emergence of peer-to-peer and sharing economies populated by companies like Airbnb and Uber
- New crimes committed online, such as stealing credit and identity information and pirating movies and music
- Commercial and state surveillance and erosion of privacy
- Cyberwarfare such as the Sony hacking as well as international espionage and sabotage of civil and military infrastructure
- New generations growing up as "digital natives"
- Online political activity
- An unprecedented ability to distribute information, whether antisocial, advocacy, medical, religious, repair guides, pornographic, scientific, or stigmatizing

This chapter offers an examination of how computer, mobile, and tablet-mediated communications (CMC) differ from the face-to-face communications (FtF) associated with dramaturgical ideas. I focus on how Internet technologies transform impression management and social interaction. These interests form the lens through which we explore some of the consequences of society's newest stage: the Internet.

Online Impression Management: Disembodiment and Networked Audiences

Goffman's work on face-to-face impression management centers on the physical copresence of actors and observing audiences. Performances occur in real time. Audiences observe and judge performances on the spot. Actors adjust their performances in response to audience reactions. Observable nonverbal movements help or spoil an actor's performance. For example, if a person claims to be calm under pressure, but visibly sweats and trembles, those physical cues constitute expressions given off that undermine a performance. In Goffman's model, people can see and judge each other based on their physical colocation.

Now impression management can occur on an online stage without physical copresence. Technologically infused means of communication make simultaneous two-way "disembodied" interaction possible. People use computers, mobile phones, and tablets to input and receive expressions, from sending e-mails and text messages to using *Snapchat* and posting images. Current technology also enables people to use applications like Photoshop easily that have no equally rich equivalent to enhance presentations of self off-line. Shanyang Zhao (2005) argues that a person's self-presentation via the Internet is different enough from off-line interaction to warrant introducing the concept of a "digital" self. Bernie Hogan (2010) notes, rather than a person interacting face to face with another person, performance of self is now akin to an exhibition site online. With an e-mail, text, or website, "people submit reproducible artifacts—read: data." Personal displays on the Internet can be selectively composed, searchable, and self-interested mini databases.

Disembodied online presentations create new dramaturgical dilemmas and possibilities. First, people can make false claims about their identities online that audiences cannot double-check just by looking at the actors off-line. Someone online can masquerade as having a different age, body, and gender, and post virtual artifacts like the misleading photographs that "catfishers" use. Photoshop, voice alterations, aliases, a soundtrack—there are a bevy of technical options for augmenting online impressions. Danah boyd (2014), among others, refers to these possibilities as *affordances* that technology now can "afford" users. Their availability does not mean that every individual uses them deceptively to make blatantly false claims about themselves, like claiming to be female when they are male. The point is more that opportunities to employ technological means to embellish presentations have never been easier to access and possibly more tempting to use. Bullingham and Vasconcelos (2013) use the term *identity tourism* to describe people who want to experience inhabiting a different gender or racial persona than their own online. To combat such pretences, some online groups require new individuals to "cam up" and turn their cameras on to accompany any interactions with group members. Those efforts hope to bring in the off-line advantage of personal observation.

However, Gottschalk (2010) and Bullingham and Vasconcelos (2013) both argue that most individuals prefer to edit their off-line selves for online presentation rather than choosing to devise completely new personas and identities for their online interactions. People want to go online as themselves, but as more idealized versions of themselves. As Gottschalk (2010) notes regarding Second Life avatars: "Although one can represent oneself in an infinity of ways, most avatars look like their 'real' self—only more attractive, more athletic, and typically better endowed" (p. 511). Integrating technically available adornments into expressing one's identity enriches the staging of this self-expression. People can use multiple virtual props to enhance self-portrayals and essentially build museums of their "identity" in profiles and websites that they populate with self-selected items that communicate their "selves" to others. People want the power to be their own curators in making self-presentational choices, and the technology available today is close to fulfilling that goal. Someone can choose the best picture ever taken of them, cut and paste witty gifs and text into communications, and pick representative avatars. Consider how many people use images to construct their own "highlight" reels on *Instagram* and *Snapchat*. People work to take the right photo with the right people to post on their social media profiles. People take digital pictures that offer idealized depictions. There they are in the right group shot and selfie, wearing the right clothes at the right party. There is constant image control that is more customizable to the poster's wants.

In a symbolic interactionist sense, people can go online and have an unprecedented ability to build and test freestanding "looking glass selves" for an audience and see what "me" appears back. People can operate almost in a third person and interpret their "me" as an external object, right alongside the intended generalized other and audience from which they seek feedback. We can use a mirror for this purpose, but now the online profile provides a much more complex surface to review (Gottschalk, 2010). Audiences, in turn, can also use technology in sophisticated ways to affect someone else's communications and identity. For example, individuals can tag pictures, write snarky messages, forward e-mails without permission, and work to spoil identity.

Online audiences exist in intended, unintended, imaginary, and invisible forms, and include designated recipients, lurkers, snoopers, and unknown parties on blind carbon copy (BCC) e-mails (boyd, 2014). Danah boyd (2014) notes that teens posting online, for example, have an imagined community audience in mind for their communications in addition to their teenage friends. That audience is constituted of kindred spirits, such as fellow fans of a music group or other members of a particular subculture. However, there are audiences that were never in mind for communications that can end up as malevolent party crashers, who follow their postings, including adversaries who might seek to use the content maliciously.

Individuals can reroute stigmatizing content about a person to audiences without that person's permission. "Revenge porn" is a particularly noxious example of this stigmatizing tactic. In "revenge porn," the adversary, typically a he, punishes someone by sharing private content like nude and/or sexual images of the person, typically a her, with her employers, family, and friends, without her consent. This vindictive act is an increasingly legally actionable form of revenge. *Doxxing* is another form of unexpected airing of private information. Doxxing describes when someone gathers someone else's personal details (addresses, family members' names, places of employment) through online scavenging and then posts that information publicly, "documenting" those persons against their will.

Audiences are also disembodied and exist often in the form of *networked publics*. Danah boyd describes networked publics as communities shaped around common interests that people establish over social media. A networked public is a place online where people assemble, but unlike physical publics, network publics are in a noncorporeal space, and technology mediates them. Networked publics have the qualities of being persistent and durable, they are visible online, so there is a vast potential audience; they are spreadable, such that content transfers are a click away, and they are searchable in that people can find them (boyd, 2014). Technical mediation results in performances now being more "public, permanent, internationally shareable, and immune to time and place" (boyd, 2014).

The Collapsing of Front and Backstage Contexts

The concepts of front and backstages provide sociologists with diagnostic frames to help them understand the impact that distinct social contexts and situations have. A front stage always can demonstrate what norms and values are considered appropriate in a situation such that they demand display. This feature has sociological importance in that the front stages expose norms to analyze. A backstage cordons off a distance between the demands that social expectations place on people and the reality that one may not naturally meet those expectations easily or without work, or conversely that they disavow those expectations but cannot demonstrate that disagreement and must accede to them. In some cases, front and backstages reveal social contradictions between authenticity and fabrication. In other cases, these stages illuminate functional social spheres, where people practice how to perform, and then they perform successfully. For example, people rehearse in workplaces, and the goal is that this practice leads to an excellent performance onstage for customers.

The concept of back and front stages offers a consistent analytic contribution. Yet the specifics involved in performances transform over time, and tracking changes in the situations that people must perform within, and the new partners and tools they integrate to carry out those performances, is exciting. The social values that people want to show can change over time. People used to hide tattoos; now they may not worry about displaying them. People might have once dressed formally to go to dinner, shows, and other social events; now norms about dress are more relaxed. Audiences and performers must be mindful of keeping their shows current. Yesterday's cultural fashions will not always suit today's expectations.

How people perform also takes in technological innovation, as people can now augment their front stage displays, in terms of resources they can draw on from backstage preparation. More options also exist to look up how to perform. People can take more time reflecting on their image and then build that image online. Possibilities like plastic surgery innovations and the availability of new consumer products alter the displays that they can offer off-line.

However, the availability and spreadability of data across the Internet has now made traditional boundaries around front and backstages more porous. Danah boyd (2002) coined the term *collapsed contexts* to describe how previously separate contexts and stages for performing can now converge. People hide discrediting information by segregating audiences (Goffman, 1959). Some audiences are never meant to see information designated for another audience. For example, the way college students act with each other at a Halloween party is different than how they manage their impressions in front of coaches, parents, and professors. In some circumstances, however, restrictive barriers fall, and an unintended audience sees a persona that the performer wanted to avoid that particular audience seeing. Context collapse is a routine trope of romantic comedies and farces. An example is when a character's two boyfriends, or two girlfriends, whose existence the protagonist hides from one an other, learn about one another simultaneously and unexpectedly. When context collapse occurs, the caught out person may not know how to act given a now contradictory situation where audience segregation is no longer possible.

Hiding discrediting information in a searchable environment is difficult and leads to more context collapse. As boyd (2002, p. 33) points out, now just "by searching for an individual's name, a user can acquire a glimpse at the individual's digital presentation across many different situations without seeing any of this in context." In dramaturgical terms, collapsed contexts raise a problem of *stage breach*, as backstage information is more available than before, and as people are tempted to vent backstage data through social media. Bernie Hogan (2010, p. 381) notes, "curators mediate our experience of social information" through search engines and their algorithms. Searching through an unprecedented archive of recorded impressions can yield a virtual library of details. With the Internet era in full swing, backstages are increasingly vulnerable. Meyrowitz (1986, p. 135) notes, "Through electronic media, groups lose exclusive access to aspects of their own back region, and they gain views of the back regions of other groups." As an example, Bernie Hogan observed that children are exposed to adult worlds sooner, as they can access conversations, interactions, and knowledge that might otherwise be off-limits to them.

Self-expression is all the rage in the triple revolution era, even in situations when discretion is wiser. As an example, Conner Riley made national headlines when a message she tweeted, "Cisco just offered me a job! Now I have to weigh the utility of a fatty paycheck against the daily commute to San Jose and hating the work," backfired. Cisco employees could access and read her tweet and decided to rescind their hiring someone who revealed that she would actually hate her work. People now must exercise more restraint in terms of what, to whom, and where they say or write things in an era of instantaneous distribution, despite the temptation to always express their personal views and report on their moment to moment state of mind. People can set up some communications and personal sites as private, but many are public, and even private sites can be breached. Some default settings online allow for information to be open to all users. Further, what was designated private at one point in time on a site may later go public. Old Usenet information that was never meant to be public can also end up archived in search engines.

For some, accessing backstage information is a sought-after lucrative opportunity, in seeking money or attention by publicizing secrets that others hide. A married male politician posts nude "selfies" to women other than his wife. A celebrity preaching monogamy gets caught with her adulterous partner. A crusading antihomosexual congressman searches for male prostitutes online. The antidrug celebrity has a drunken, drugged-up binge posted on the web. Justin Bieber is photographed leaving a Brazilian brothel. Members of One Direction are filmed smoking marijuana in Uruguay. Capturing these images brings in money and views. Means to film people without their knowledge and catch them *in flagrante delicto* have existed for decades. Today, filming devices are smaller, portable, carried everywhere on mobile phones, and spreadable at the push of a button. The present ability to film and spread information about people's backstages is unprecedented and exposures are ubiquitous.[1]

Beyond seeking to reveal secrets, accessing the backstage has educational, marketing, and research returns. As Christian Rudder (2014) notes, computers can record everything. In addition to a record-keeping function that delivers organizational and storage benefits, the research world of big data is a positive flip side to computers storing back and front stage data. Rudder, a cofounder of *OkCupid*, gathers research data from users of that site. Amazon, Facebook, Google, and Microsoft all employ researchers to analyze information from people using their sites. Advertising and marketing agencies pore over these data to attract consumers and discern their purchasing dispositions and preferences. This work may concern consumer advocates as being too invasive, but that activity also has economic benefits in personalizing advertisements and products for potential buyers.

For social scientists, user data reveal what people do and search for online, not just what they say on the surface about their actions and preferences. What they retweet or how they connect and pass on information yields insights about how mass communications work (Watts, 2012). For example, Duncan Watts (2012) used big data to test theories of social influence because the huge number of cases available online enabled implementing a research design that was cost-prohibitive and untenable prior to the Internet. Such information informs social scientists about actual behaviors among populations. Further, people sometimes hide "dirty data" to avoid being shamed for "untoward" activities.

---

[1] Elizabeth Butler Breese (2010) examines the modern growth in media coverage of celebrities, particularly in exposing their backstage.

People seeking affairs, having racist sentiments, or wanting to promote controversial belief systems and express secrets; they all exist online, and information on their searches is available. Off-line, people may lie and engage in dramaturgical efforts to camouflage those actions, which produce blind spots in social science knowledge of peoples' actual behaviors. To avoid being stigmatized, behaviors that imperil a person's status can go underground to thrive on the Internet. Large datasets gathered from backstage information can identify peoples' actual actions and "dirty data" (Rudder, 2014). Like a double-edged sword, the Internet can enable deviant activities while also exposing them through their leftover online traces.

Performance Online Versus Off-Line

In face-to-face interaction, reaction time is quick. When an individual speaks to someone off-line, he or she expects to receive a response within an appropriate amount of time. Online, response time is now more flexible. People ignore, reflect, or respond immediately to an e-mail, posting, or text. A person is now presumably locatable at all times, which changes people's relation to work. For example, with e-mail and mobile phones, people can be on call 24/7. Family and friends expect quick responses to their messages because they believe that their messages are received right away. People prefer rapid responses to texts and can be offended by delayed responses. In copresent interaction off-line, people usually watch each other during conversations. Online, no pressure usually exists in terms of a respondent watching the e-mail get sent. Being observed off-line can influence people to respond too quickly or mistakenly; people feel under pressure when others watch them. Alternatively, people who might faint from speaking visibly in public can become fervent and passionate communicators online.

Switching from physically copresent speaking to texting carries other interactional costs. For example, conversation through texts limits the qualitative complexity of interpersonal interactions. If people improve their conversational abilities and competence with practice, then the prevalence of texting does the conversational arts no favors. Texting limits conversational opportunities and may be changing language use. Textual language involves many abbreviations and emoticons that oversimplify and transform communications and the flow of language into staccato written outputs of short length. A *Twitter* communication of 140 characters or less may get the job done and be a boon in getting to the point. But communications of 140 characters or less are not conducive to description and the poetry that some people can create in conversation. Being extroverted in online interaction can substitute for being extroverted in verbal interaction and encounters with people. The Internet improves people's range of communicative forums, and outreach to others is enhanced, but that does not mean that a quality of communication improves.

Some interactions traditionally conducted off-line, like dating, are now moving to online venues. The dramaturgical activities associated with those interactions change when moving online. As an example, looks play a role in dating, and evaluating people at the superficial level of appearance occurred before the Internet appeared. Yet a smartphone app like *Tinder* accelerates the superficial quality of dating to a new level. A person posts pictures from their *Facebook* profile onto *Tinder*. People go online and swipe right if they find the pictured person attractive and want to connect with them. If the pictured person finds the picture of the person who swiped them attractive, they also swipe to the right, and contact may occur. If either person swipes left on a picture, then that person is eliminated from further consideration. Dating possibilities are premised initially and, in a binding way, on physical appearance. Image takes on the utmost importance here in determining even a chance to discover compatibility with a person. The importance of having a good front stage is heightened. Physical attraction is relevant in dating selection, yet the Internet and programs like *Tinder* make that feature a priority. To whatever degree looks mattered in previous dating options, they matter tremendously in the online era.

The move to online interaction has also introduced a new dependence on technology. The cell phone is now an irreplaceable possession for most people, especially digital natives. People use mobiles to stay engaged with their networks and to allay their "fear of missing out." People sleep with their cell phones under their pillows or by their beds. They check constantly to see if they received messages, even when there is no indication of a message arriving. Many people find being away from the cell phone to be traumatizing.

Norms of civility are also held to be on the wane because of incessant cell phone use. Many individuals call and text others no matter where they are at the time or what other people around them are doing. Ling (2012) conceptualized the occasions when people sometimes text or speak in social circumstances where others have the right to their full attention. When people do not devote their full attention to others, people feel insulted, as if that action demonstrates their having less importance or feelings to take into account. These "side involvements" do carry a message that an audience member or teammate is not investing full attention in the ongoing proceedings. Texting during classes, concerts, meetings, and theatrical productions annoys many people who also do not want to be distracted by these side interactions. People performing are especially aggrieved when audience members text. The message communicated is that others' "social rights" do not matter compared to continuing engagement with the phone. This action physically manifests disrespect for the integrity of the unfolding proceedings.

Dramaturgical circumspection and discipline require individuals and teams to attend to performance. When a person considers texting a suitable accompaniment to any activity, performances are affected in two ways. First, the person is not focused fully on the performance because their attention is split between the cell phone and the action. Researchers from the Massachusetts Institute of Technology have shown that people who text and simultaneously perform tasks like driving or studying do so less effectively than when not texting. People also may judge a person more harshly when they observe that person pays less attention to them and more to their phone.

Other than offending people, ceaseless texting, regardless of context, is rewriting social norms and causing new social control efforts to emerge. People text while they are cooking, driving, dining at restaurants, in meetings, churches, and attending funerals, and even while exercising. Managers at entertainment venues often request that people not text to avoid interrupting performances and to preserve the show's sanctity. Texting during lectures and plays is annoying but not necessarily a dangerous form of disrespect. Texting while driving is actually dangerous to others because less than full attention when driving a vehicle imperils everyone on the road. Pedestrians, who ignore their surroundings by focusing on phones and not traffic, are also neglecting the obligation to act safely.

Altering Performance Content

The virtual world offers us new stages to consider, as people now have multiple front stages for their performances, and more locations exist where backstage information is hidden. People can offer impressions in virtual settings, on *Facebook* profiles, and in text messaging. They can manufacture multiple profiles of themselves, each having different degrees of accuracy and modeling a different variation on self. People can attempt to mobilize team performances, forming teams of performers online who become partners that they need not know personally. For example, people have a capacity to organize large teams like flash mobs or to participate in actions with online hate mobs.

The Internet also brings in the capacity to see infinite performance content. In terms of the entertainment economy, people are now exposed to even more large-scale marketing efforts through a glut of digital campaigns. There is more surveillance of people's online interactions and more subterfuge to avoid that surveillance. The new opportunity to observe how others perform in whatever activities, unobtrusively, is also unprecedented. The Internet beckons to people in "gated" and publically accessible worlds. While some forms of connection are open to everyone, other sites are limited to an enclosed community of people who have formed private groups. Whether content is stored in private or public sites, much content is vulnerable to being copied elsewhere and forming an unexpected virtual exhibit. The gated and open dichotomy represents an important attempt to control information. The private domain and connections that comprise these groups are backstage communities where people are free to be themselves in some ways that they do not want strangers to observe. Forming a gated community online also creates a new front stage for participants, although those borders are penetrable.

For example, sometimes information that people think will remain private does not, as people will distribute secret information that they receive more widely. In revenge porn, the premise of sending the shaming image is to punish a specific person. Teammates are supposed to protect the secrets entrusted to them, but the web's capacity to transmit secrets entices, offering an increased temptation to release a secret widely and beyond a given network. For example, teenage boys may send a sext or lascivious image around the school to show that the sender received a sexualized token. They also get the bonus of humiliating the person in question. The capacity to widen a revelatory circle is particularly noteworthy when the information at hand involves deviant behavior or shameful actions. People sharing their favorite movies or distributing helpful suggestions is a peaceful and positive form of pooling information.

Where teens and trolls maintain anonymity, they intentionally avoid providing the same protection to the people that they post about, as the point is hassling those people by name. In smaller circles, the dynamics of humiliation may be meant just for the local crowd, but the temptation still exists to keep the information going, fueled by more and more acquaintance-linked recipients who have fewer ties to the original groups until a sense of obligation to the group dissipates. Eventually, the content becomes general entertainment rather than private information that was supposed to circulate to limited number of recipients. A "small" stigma that began as an inside joke can grow into a showcased stigma.

As an example, consider an infamous Duke student PowerPoint presentation that went viral (see http://jezebel.com/5652114/college-girls-power-point-fuck-list-goes-viral). In this case, a PowerPoint presentation evaluating the personalities and sexual prowess of male athletes that the author slept with ended up being distributed virally, beyond the small circle of Ms. Owen's friends, causing controversy. Ms. Owen used people's real names in her post. Her PowerPoint was decried for raw descriptions of superficial sexual activity and disparaging characterizations of her sexual partners, their bodies, and their personalities. Despite an initial intent to limit the audience to just friends, the post ended up in wide distribution, as with each forward, the possibility increased of someone sending the post to others, until the post went viral through sites that archived the material and increased promotion by advertising the information as content to attract clicks. Today, the choice to create and send any post or e-mail involves some risk of sacrificing control over information, because even with trusted recipients, content can still leak out publicly. Once the information is out, people cannot put that genie back into the bottle, as the cloud and countless individual computers now offer permanent archives.

Deceiving Others Online and Strategic Interaction

As noted earlier, Internet technologies offer new means to carry out impression management, and they make new content available to people to communicate. Whether Internet claims and images are honest is an important issue for both personal safety and economic trust. Hany Farid (2009) coined the term *digital forgery* to describe some of the exaggerated features in photography that are now possible using Photoshop and other software programs. People are awash in virtual photographs, claims, and images that are easily falsified and intentionally misleading. People also increasingly want to be consumers and perpetrators of deceptions on the Internet, so the phenomenon involves more than just avoiding victimization—people want to become a part of the deceptions, through actively producing and taking advantage of deceptions over the Internet. People use websites like *Ashley Madison* and *Seeking Arrangements* to locate partners for affairs while covering up those infidelities. Students use the web to access essays to pass off as their own work. The Internet is a treasure trove of available opportunities for lying and, in impression management terms, can be studied with that orientation in mind.

Charles Seife (2014) highlighted an important form of online deception: the use of sockpuppets. A sockpuppet is a fake persona created online to perform and pose as an online person. A sockpuppet takes advantage of the disembodied nature of online interaction. In off-line life, we cannot easily create fake people at a whim to support our views.[2] Seife (2014, pp. 49–53) identifies what he calls type 1 and type 2 sockpuppets. A type 1 sockpuppet is a created online persona that has a quality that the poster lacks in real life, but fakes online, to give him or her an important advantage or to gain sympathy. Sample type 1 sockpuppets could be people posing as veterans or victims of diseases or people "who were there" or as men or women to enter into a charged debate over gender.

A type 2 sockpuppet is a fake persona whose characteristics are unimportant except for meeting the one key criteria of appearing to be an individual other than the poster—for example, acting as a "random" stranger who inserts himself or herself into a debate on the inventor's side. Seife (2014) argues that the main role of the type 2 sockpuppet is to enter into a feud or fray to reinforce whatever view the sockpuppet's creator favors. He cites examples such as writing favorable book reviews of your own work under the sockpuppet's identity or criticizing a rival's writings. He also argues that sockpuppets are increasingly employed for more nefarious ends, such as to entrap rival politicians, trash commercial competitors, and rip people off in dating and financial scams.

A variation on the sockpuppet theme is the use of various bots on Internet sites. The bot, in the sense that is relevant to this chapter, is a software program designed to pass for a kind of real person of some interest to the poster who can give automated responses to inquiries. For example, Seife

---

[2] Off-line people can hire actors to portray characters that act in the employer's interests, but this step is more complicated than setting up sockpuppets.

(2014, pp. 140, 147) describes how, on some adult or dating sites, bots impersonate a sultry woman who repeats salacious pick-up lines to try to get someone to pick up on the bot bait and send a payment for further contact, or to believe that he might actually meet a "real perfect" woman on the dating site (Seife, 2014, pp. 140, 147). The bot carries out a minimal form of discourse with canned responses to posted questions. Bots are shills for sites.

The Internet may tempt people to act deceptively at more minimal levels than putting bots in place. As an example, Judith Donath (1999) notes that some of the conventional "signals" that people send about their identities in virtual communities are deceptive. At a basic level, consider all the possible descriptors that people can use to identify themselves. In the smallest example, a man might use an online user name like "mr. deadlift" to convey strength but not actually be strong (Donath, 1999). Employing misleading usernames is a minor but frequent online deception.

A concern about online deception is warranted in an interactive world rife with new people to lie to and more technology available to structure those lies. In *Strategic Interaction* (1969), Goffman adopted a game analogy to analyze how people attempt to win *expression games* that is useful for exploring online deceptions. *Expression games* refer to how individuals scheme to gain information from others while concealing their own information from external prying. Goffman described types of moves that people play in expression games. They include *naive* moves in which people are unaware of being observed and *unwitting* moves that refer to actions that a person does not care that others observe. People also use *control* moves such as *covering, uncovering, and counter-uncovering* ones, which refer to sequenced efforts to hide personal information while extricating information from others.

In *Strategic Interaction*, Goffman (1969) focuses on the "calculation" that people exhibit in thinking through their moves in expression games. As an example, Goffman (1969, p. 12) sees control moves as representing "the intentional efforts of an informant to produce expressions that he thinks will improve his situation if they are gleaned by the observer." The control move is meant for others to observe and is self-interested. Goffman describes an *information preserve* as "the set of facts about himself or herself to which an individual expects to control access while before others." Controlling one's own informational preserve is one side of the story; the other half involves gaining access to someone else's information preserve. Given these goals, people playing expression games will create false versions of their own information preserves.

Goffman argued that people learn to anticipate another's point of view in planning their information moves. These efforts to understand the other's view can have malevolent, benevolent, or neutral intents. A platitude people repeat is to walk a mile in someone else's shoes before you criticize them. The expression game version is to understand that person's perspective, how they feel, think, and experience the world, so that you can exploit them or foil their efforts to exploit you. People detach their interests as distinct from the "other's" interest even when attempting to understand the other's viewpoint. From an impression management standpoint, empathy is optional (Goffman, 1969, p. 16). Thinking like the target thinks enables you to take better advantage of them and choreograph their reactions. Goffman uses many examples from espionage to illustrate these expression games, in which people make conversation and seduce and waylay each other to extract and protect secrets.

Today, the Internet is rife with occasions where people conceal their private information and have no compunctions about trying to acquire other people's data, whether invoking false pretenses or not. Consider the old "419" scams in which people receive e-mails claiming to be from a person connected to a rich African family or other notable who offers to give the e-mail recipient millions of dollars for their assistance in spiriting funds out of a country. Here is the catch: The e-mail recipient must send money first as a show of good faith and collateral as they will be trusted with "millions." Similar scams exist in which people construct fake e-mails from banks or credit card companies or the "IRS Criminal Investigations" division to fool people into providing account data or money that belongs within a person's information preserve.

Online deceptions attracting current interest beyond criminal activities include catfishing, lying in online dating profiles, and subtweeting. In catfishing, a person adopts a persona to fool another person and seduce them into a platonic or romantic relationship. The term came into vogue from a documentary movie by Nev Schulman describing his experience discovering that "Megan," a woman he was in an online relationship with, was actually not who she claimed to be, but instead was an older married housewife living in Michigan. She faked an identity to keep the relationship and ruse going, and the documentary is powered by the suspense of awaiting the unveiling of "Megan." This poster developed the "Megan" character by using a different computer and *Facebook* account than the one used under her actual name in daily life. Schulman eventually become host of an MTV show called *Catfish*, in which he helps people investigate whether someone they are in an online relationship with is actually who he or she claims to be, in appearance, situation in life, and intent toward the partner. So far, this show has unveiled multiple masquerades.

As a form of deception, the control moves here involve understanding the relationship need of the partner to have a confidant, the expectations for appearance, and appropriate excuses to cite to avoid having to meet in person or otherwise "prove" that the person really is as he or she states. The technical tools of the imposture involve finding someone else's picture and biographical details and posting them as one's own. A common trend is for people to post a picture of a more conventionally attractive person, thinner, handsomer, prettier, and younger. The depicted appearance demonstrates more success in life (whether in looks, occupation, wealth) than actually exists.

A sad aspect is that the show's deceptive protagonists could want a real relationship with the person that they are lying to, but they feel that their actual appearance or shyness over their looks immediately disqualifies them from any real shot at happiness with that prospective partner. When exposed, the catfisher usually apologizes for stringing along the other person, claiming remorse over pushing a relationship that the lying partner knew would never be actualized off-line. Donath (1999) suggests that lying is less risky in the Internet context because online relationships are more disposable presumably than off-line ones, as people can just detach themselves and disappear from the persona's interactions in the virtual world. Seife (2014) uses the term "pseucide" to refer to the idea of people killing off their fake online identities. People also can be incompetent liars online, as a broad range of new things to lie about also presents new opportunities to get something wrong that exposes lying. Deceptive performances can fail when performances are too out of character from the expected category to fool people. A person who wants to pose must present signs competently to maintain the ruse. If you want to pretend to be a doctor, stockbroker, model, and so forth, there is an expectation to post content that makes sense for those standings in life.

People give and receive expressions from each other. From a communications perspective, communications involve using conventional and understandable signals. *Signaling theory* is the idea that people send signals to inform an audience about what qualities to expect in that person (Donath, 2007). The Internet can create a *signal flood*, in which the sheer amount of information that is available can overwhelm people. Now signals can occur in different paths and be channeled. You can channel the flood into filter bubbles through feeds. You can search and get a flood of information. Among that information, you require some mechanism of judgment to decide what information you value.

A conventional sign is wearing a university t-shirt that someone could think meant you went to that place versus flaunting a graduation ring, which is harder to get and use for masquerading. A conventional sign is easier to fake than an assessment sign. I can post a fake profile, but proving that I was a Navy SEAL who modeled professionally while getting rich from my start-up tech company is harder. Off-line, people typically perform for a designated audience at a particular time, with a particular purpose in mind. However, once presentations become storable and transferable, they can be loosed from their original context. A different audience and purpose can exist for recorded off-line performances because of the portability of accessing the performance beyond the original contextual frame. If being quoted out of context was a nightmare worry for people *before*, an online world now places that concern on steroids. Recorded performances still are presentations of self, but without being bounded to the specific audience and purpose that existed when the performance first took place. Limits on performance are lifted. The upshot is that signal strength can be weaker online than off-line. There may also be greater possibilities for surveillance to investigate claims. The goal here is to point out that these issues are larger and more pervasive because the amount of signals is much higher than in the off-line world. Technology has made a flowing stream of impression management to bathe in where before there was a creek.

Deception in Online Dating and Romance

Nicole Ellison, Jeffrey Hancock, and Catalina Toma have conducted several studies on deception in online dating (Ellison & Hancock, 2013; Ellison, Hancock, & Toma, 2011; Toma & Hancock, 2010a, 2010b; Toma, Hancock, & Ellison, 2008). According to Toma and Hancock's (2010b) research, 8 out of 10 online dating profiles contain a lie about age, height, or weight. Researchers investigated online profile information about age, weight, and height by actually weighing, measuring, and looking at birthdays on the drivers' licenses of the real individuals. The lies they found were minor, like adding an inch to height or shaving a few pounds off. According to these researchers, although online lying is easy, not everyone takes advantage of that opportunity because there are still countervailing costs that create disincentives to lie. Relational and psychological costs minimize serious lying on online dating profiles.

As an example, one motivation to lie is that the more attractive people can portray themselves as being, the more they may be rewarded with suitors. Yet when people want to meet later in the physical world, lying now problematizes that encounter because certain expectations are set. Liars can try to postpone any reckoning that would give a lie away, but that avoidance works against the goal of people who actually want to be with someone off-line. In addition, some people want to see themselves as honest people.

An additional variable emerged of people finding "wiggle room" to justify their deceptions. For example, people thought that during the time between posting to and actually meeting someone, they could transform a currently deceptive inaccuracy about themselves into a truthful, genuine aspect of themselves. As an example, if they listed themselves as being 10 pounds lighter than they actually are, they expected to lose that weight by the time a meeting was set. So if a person thought that they could change some feature of themselves by a later point in time (lose weight, quit smoking), they would identify themselves as being in that future state despite being in a different current state. People thought the falsehood would turn true over time, so they were not necessarily lying; they were just in some way telling a story to be made true later. As an informant in a different study told me once, he was just telling people the "most optimistic version of the truth." This assertion connects with what Ellison et al. (2011) and Ellison and Hancock (2013) refer to as the "promise as profile" idea, in which the shared understanding is that the profile is not the exact person the profile promises but is approximate. People can make a more attractive promise for themselves than their current condition, but importantly, the person cannot over-promise, which is considered to cross a line. You can lose 10 pounds before meeting but claiming to be 80 pounds lighter than you are is too much.

Online self-presentation has all kinds of manifestations, from idealized to mundane. A person can have an avatar, a *Facebook* profile, a dating profile, a series of photographs and comments. Ellison et al. (2011) point out that these presentations can contain discrepancies from the "corporeal self as experienced through face to face (FtF) communication" (p. 2). In their research, they were interested in how people made strategic decisions about misrepresentations in making online dating profiles. As more social activities move from off-line to online realms, presentations of self adjust and change. Researchers need to explore how self-presentations change given the stages and social activities that are now available in a new technically mediated realm. The basic goals of coming across in socially favorable ways remains, but the means available to enhance interaction are prompting important research into the new self-presentations that are emerging online.

Ellison et al. (2011) write, "Telling the truth entails appearing less attractive but telling a lie invites negative repercussions" (p. 3). Interestingly, in communications like with catfishing, the goal may be to have interaction without a deceiver's goal being to meet physically. A person who falsifies their appearance and socioeconomic success may find a reward for being taken as that ideal person they prefer to be, and they might prefer to play at that fake existence rather than have the illusion falter. So the goal is key in understanding the stakes in misrepresentation, which can be to live through a lie, as its own reward, or to exaggerate a little, but with the goal of being relatively truthful to actually get and keep a date.

In the off-line world, we have always worried about being accurate judges of the credibility of information so that we are not taken in by deceptions. Online, this problem remains, except in greater magnification. There are more people who can reach you now from all over the world or that you can seek out. That heightens your exposure to erroneous signals, intentional or not.

Virtual Role Engulfment

There is a concern about the role engulfment people embrace in choosing to absorb themselves in virtual worlds, whether in addiction to games, not wanting to leave a powerful avatar, staying glued to *World of Warcraft*, a *Second Life* identity, or being obsessed with pornography. In these personas, one lives out dreams virtually, as a powerful figure, object of desire, engaged in activities that are either not in the cards off-line or impossible practically, like being an elf or being a foot taller. J. K. Rowling (1998) wrote in *Harry Potter and the Sorcerer's Stone* about a mirror that shows people's greatest desire. Rowling writes that people have a difficult time stopping staring in that mirror and cautioned a main character against falling prey to that virtual imagery. She wrote, "It does not do well to dwell on dreams and forget to live, remember that" (p. 214), and "Men have wasted away before it, entranced by what they have seen" (p. 213). Her quotes offer a reasonable warning to be wary of too much role engulfment online in a virtual mirror of fantasy.

Off- and online lives can interact in interesting ways. Consider the case of Dave Pollard and Amy Taylor (graphics for this case are at http://www.dailymail.co.uk/news/article-1085412/Revealed-The-woman-Second-Life-divorce--whos-engaged-web-cheat-shes-met.html). In addition to changing themselves to reflect a more ideal height, weight, and facial appearance, deception also occurred in the temptations that the online world of *Second Life* offers. Pollard's *Second Life* alter ego Dave Barmy was interacting with a virtual online call girl when his real-life wife, Amy Pollard, caught them together on the computer. She claimed that Pollard was an adulterer in "real" life because he was adulterous in *Second Life*. Pollard and his wife were also married in *Second Life*. Pollard later began another virtual affair that he hid from Amy. Pollard and his real-life wife divorced in *Second Life*, and in real life, Pollard became engaged to the real person behind the virtual persona of "Modesty McConnell," with whom he was cheating in *Second Life*. Virtual role engulfment led to new roles.

Today's virtual worlds do enable "living" in fantasy, which makes "dwelling in dreams" possible, but not usually physically so. There is a sense that people can "waste away" before the pull of the eloquent fantasies on offer, and there can be a sense of self-deception about how "real" they are as expressions of who a person "really" is. Given a choice between power in an imaginary world and less power in an off-line one, the decision some people make to spend time in what feels like a more empowering context makes sense. In a BBC documentary addressing virtual relationships in *Second Life*, a protagonist states that online she becomes whom she felt she was always supposed to be, a gorgeous and slim woman with a happy, perfect life.

There is also an existential despair involved in confronting the painful truths that are inherent in facing one's imperfections. For some, a new identity online is a salve, however temporary, from resenting what one actually is, compared to what one thinks they deserve to be. Is going online a salve, placebo, or barrier to off-line efforts that might enhance someone's happiness and potential? Open to debate is the impact of neglecting reality to stay online, in an off-line world that demands employment, familial obligations, and a certain level of engagement with the mundane.

People can enter into virtual worlds as a temporary form of escapist pleasure and as a form of work. Why not enjoy entering the fantasy lands that science has made possible to visit, as a distraction, or for any other reason? The point is not to condemn all who are absorbed in online worlds as being maladjusted people who are limited in their off-line lives. People who love virtual worlds may also be masters in the off-line world. The point instead is that if someone escapes to an off-line world as their preferred primary address, for whatever reasons, the Internet now gives them an alternative form of virtual role engulfment in which to dwell, perhaps a more powerful one than has existed prior.

Exploring Online Deviance

The web also offers many additional opportunities to learn about actions that people label deviant behavior. The Internet supplies the world's largest "adults-only" store, from pornographic clips to the "deep web," where people can ostensibly hire assassins and buy illegal drugs. The idea that access to adults-only sites or to the deep web is limited to adults is wishful thinking. There are end runs available to any determined youth who want to access that content. The irony here, to paraphrase one of Todd's (2014) informants from her study of cyberbullying, is that parents tell kids not to hang out with the wrong crowd at school, yet kids can find infinite wrong crowds online to become potential bad influences on them.

Should someone want to acquire drugs or worse, they can use the *Tor* browser and similar programs to access the deep web. The *Tor* browser is an anonymizing browser that people use when they are worried about having their online activities traced. Others use *Tor* to access the deep web and the criminal activities and products available at *Darknet* markets. People may set up private browsing modes, but those steps are insufficient to access the deep web. Applications like *Tor* can thwart law enforcement scrutiny, enabling people to pursue deviant preferences or contraband that are available for purchase in the *Darknet* marketplace. The most well-known *Darknet* market was called "Silk Road" until the FBI arrested a man operating the site under the name the "dread pirate Roberts." More "casual" browsing of legal but controversial phenomena is rampant using general commercial browsers, but for those seeking the utmost secure privacy and most controversial and illegal materials, *Tor* is the go-to option for making users anonymous.

Anonymity is valuable commercially and personally. Undisturbed browsing is considered a "right" as long as one is not breaking the law. Anonymity, in both off-line and online forms, impacts how people present themselves in general. Privacy is an important component in one's online decision-making, viewing habits, and purchasing choices. Anonymity also produces more honesty in evaluations of performance, so people can abandon tact and not worry about retaliation for harsh criticisms. If people want to watch pornography, confess to personal troubles, enjoy guilty pleasures, or complain about other people and politics, they may want to protect their identity from discovery. Anonymity is also absolutely vital when connected to online political activity, whether to protect dissidents in states with repressive policies, to protect antistate commentary, or to permit access to information. Anonymity in those contexts can mean staying out of court or worse.

Anonymity is also problematic for contributing to the abundance and corrosiveness of negative commentary online. People make hostile comments online without fearing accountability for any vicious mean-spiritedness. When people believe they are unidentifiable, rules of conduct may no longer constrain them, so they can "get online anonymously and beat people up because they think no one will be able to track them down" (Todd, 2014). Anonymity has multiple functions, from supplying bridges to hide trolls to helping whistle-blowers expose problems. Analytically, anonymity constitutes a dramaturgical cloak of invisibility that conceals backstage information, protecting someone from judgment and punishment. That cloak constitutes a significant performance tool people use for varied purposes, such as to get away with controversial, illegal, or uncivil behaviors and to protect the curious and dissidents. The very title of Anonymous, the group that hacks regimes and people whom they deem as harmful, demonstrates this use.

User-Generated Content: Everyone's a Star, Everyone's a Critic, and I'm Into Documenting My Life Onstage

The spreadable nature of video content makes anyone with a cell phone or tablet a potential cameraperson and broadcaster. Random individuals are infiltrating traditional news media territories as on-the-spot documentarians capturing crises, human interest stories, international conflagrations, and appealing whimsy. A smorgasbord of user-generated entertainment content is available. *YouTube* stars like the Fine Brothers, Jenna Marbles, and the Screen Junkies have millions of fans who consume their *YouTube* content. Tay Zonday's "Chocolate Rain" song has logged over 98 million views since 2006, and recent marketing sensation Grumpy Cat inspired a movie and a coffee brand called Grumppucino. Besides becoming film-makers, people write countless blogs populated with their opinions on all things. This technological democratization of opinion is empowering for self-expression and also noteworthy for upending filters of quality, as everything on the blog gets published because the author is the decision-making publisher. There is no peer review to gatekeep content, just access and popularity as a determination for why a work should be read. This point is key: Everyone can put on a show; they just need to have an audience find them and be interested. User-generated content competing with, and/or integrating with traditional media content, is another example of Internet-related business transformation, as entertainment content is rewoven with new user-generated content.

Internet technology allows for do-it-yourself (DIY) participatory culture. People post their own artistic performances on *YouTube* without confronting the entrance barriers of getting talent agents, record labels, or broadcast venues to post their offerings. The very name "YouTube" is a narcissistic call to arms. A huge audience is available for online performances, although acquiring and getting that potential audience to watch is another story. Appeal for "views" is the dilemma, not whether consumers can access content. The web is a stage that reaches millions, but getting that number of views is infrequent. For every Psy and Rebecca Black, countless self-promoting aspirants exist who remain unseen by masses. But should the stars align, technology makes the "many millions viewed" performance possible.

When gatekeepers disappear, the result is a double-edged sword. In entertainment and writing realms, when anybody has the capacity to showcase their talents, the field is democratized. In other contexts, the new unhindered ability to express DIY culture is harmful. In medical and scientific realms, people can make factually incorrect claims and have a mass-distributed pulpit available on the nearest computer. Peer review in science is meant to provide a quality assurance mechanism from which the best research findings are put forward for attention, but there is no guarantee that persons will access that information. Now individuals can go on blogs and websites, which act as virtual printing presses and distribute erroneous or harmful junk information. They can tell people not to vaccinate their children or spread misinformation about how Ebola spreads.

Science is methodical for a reason, which is to discover accurate conclusions about cause and effect and other phenomena. Now anybody's version of science competes for eyeballs, and while quacks are new to no one, having them be able to reach anybody with a connection is new. No doubt valuable innovations also exist to publicize online and widely distributed information is a boon. For example, online classes may end up bringing science to people around the world at discount prices. Yet such positives come accompanied by people who spread dangerous nonsense like wildfire.

In Charles Seife's (2014) recent book, *Virtual Unreality: Just Because the Internet Told You, How Do You Know It's True*, he describes many examples of people who plant false information online. Seife identifies a plethora of cases, including conspiracy theories and erroneous scientific information about medical drugs. He discusses examples of people who take advantage of Wikipedia's open policies to make inaccurate entries on that site, whether for their own laughs or in their employer's or their individual self-interests. Seife cites Stephen Colbert's coining of the term "wikiality" to describe the flexible standards for what is real on Wikipedia, and Colbert's exhorting of his fans to understand that "together we can create a reality that we all agree on—the reality we just agreed on" (p. 25). People want to sprout "reality offshoots" that are untrue, which is an important development for audiences to understand about impression management online. In the online world, lies are more ornate and plentiful and possibly easier to take as true if people decide that fact checking and verification isn't necessary, because, as Seife implies, if the Internet says so, the information must be true.

The phrase "everybody's a star" refers here to the self-worshipping archives that people build on the Internet. The phrase speaks to how hard people work to be a center of attention through constant autobiographical chronicling online. As Gottschalk (2010, p. 508) notes in regard to people on *Second Life*, "Here they can be the stars of every encounter in which they participate and reinvent themselves every time they log on." *YouTube's* slogan was "broadcast yourself" and *Myspace* was self-evidently about "me" (Twenge & Campbell, 2010). Posting messages on *Twitter* or *Facebook* about getting coffee, sunny weather, or heavy traffic is not momentous but reflects public exhibitions of self-absorption, as if audiences eagerly await such musings. People document their home renovation projects, hobbies, vacations, and favorite walks. Animals and children are must "post-abouts." These displays are captured perfectly by the word "selfie" becoming accepted vernacular. People manufacture digital museums of self-expression to commemorate themselves, and they curate those exhibits. The mantra here is not objectivity but to offer subjective expression of personal actions, affiliations, dispositions, and identities. Dramaturgy and impression management operate 24/7 in this noncorporeal plane. What a person posts is a proxy for what he or she considers impressions for others to know about him or her in light of current applicable values, norms, and roles. Impression management is a well-suited approach to examine the social construction of these self-images, of the constantly evolving "me" put out for public consumption.

According to Twenge and Campbell (2010), teenagers take away four themes from social networking sites: "I must be entertained all the time; If you've got it, flaunt it; Success means being a consumer; Happiness is being a glamorous and sexy adult." These themes can malign teens as too superficial, yet these themes do exist and represent dramaturgical choices people make in self-expression. A focus on showing off possessions and good looks populates many profiles. Such themes are consistent with the same "look at me" sensibility associated with social network sites. Further, as Twenge and Campbell note, a new comparative narcissism is emerging as people engage in a rat race of escalating self-obsession.

Facebook images, like other online profiles, can bridge gaps between who we are and how we want others to see us. An element of wish fulfillment, of aspirational self-fulfilling prophecy, occurs when people hope that they can will the content they post to reflect reality instead of reflecting virtual reality. "Just look at this status, I really am clever." "Just look at my picture—I am really pretty." The medium of *Facebook* (and others) can offer an escapist aspirational product in providing a means for people to show who we "really are," through a series of posted likes and photos. *Facebook* is accepted as a social media form through which individuals define themselves and can peer into other people's purported lives. In an impression management sense, *Facebook* provides a venue for redefining the self and what reality is as pertaining to that person, as there is a working consensus that *Facebook* stands in for depicting "real life." Digital citizens rely upon *Facebook* and other forums to provide a reliable narrative for how "someone is," which can be distant from truth. Users can look at the screen and know for all intents and purposes that what they see is not fully accurate. Yet posters also scheme to have their profiles conform to an aspirational version of reality that they desire. A college male may upload a picture of himself with several attractive women at a party. He must "keep up with the digital Joneses." Projecting an aspirational outward image in a hope to have it be taken as true reality involves an implicit request that people take up that depicted narrative. As long as he can get friends and others to view his profile, follow along, and accept the current discourse, then *Facebook* is more than a narrative vehicle for self-presentation—it is an affirmation of a fantasized or at least highly selective self-presentation. Online media can enable a purely representational ideal to be viewed akin to a concrete thing that is made manifest for others to see and acknowledge. Consider the work people put into "selfies" to capture the best possible look. There is allegedly even a modern boom in plastic surgery procedures that is attributable to people wanting to perfect their physical image for future selfies. Social media, especially for a younger generation, are magnifying the pressure on people's appearances. People may spend hours working to take the right photo at an event or party in order to post a photo that will garner the right reception on *Instagram*. Digital media emphasize a dramaturgical imperative in urging a repetitive cycle of seeking validation through appearance and external approval of one's appearance and projected image. Consider the pressure placed on people in this new world where people must have a virtual face broadcasting the right image. People have to worry about proper impression management in person, and the advent of the Internet extends that battle to another front—the digital stage. The enhancement of insecurity through pervasive social media usage is a new influence of the digital era.

Snapchat, for example, enables people to send images, pictures, and video clips that disappear in seconds or minutes. The idea is to have nonarchivable screenshots that recipients can see that then fade away. *Snapchat* communications are vulnerable to being stored if they get screenshotted, meaning if someone takes a quick enough picture of the screen, the onscreen *Snapchat* message is archived. *Mystory* offers content, for a longer period of time, like a day, and recipients can review that content for more time than they can using *Snapchat*. *Mystory* also enables senders to give recipients a sense of what activities he or she is involved in, all documented as if the recipient was there to observe them. Observers also send them about other people to share what they did with others. *Snapchat* and *Mystory* center on impression management, as posters reveal how they want to be perceived via the messages that they communicate.

We know that people are self-interested in the activities they depict, and these media enable them to refine that ability. Hence college students send "cool" *Snapchats*, like videos of a crazy party, to sustain an image that they "must be cool and party all the time." The Internet helps people get closer to bridging the gap between whom they are and whom they want to be seen as, because we can now cut and paste aspiration into virtual being. Surveillance of peers seems a consistent trial for digital natives. Any moment in real life could be recorded on *Snapchat* or *Insta-gram* or other programs. While people rightly worry about government and corporate surveillance, peer-to-peer surveillance takes place too. So an open question is how voluntary this self-enhancement is or whether the pressure to create the most appealing online persona is constant. As in off-line life, people can feel trapped to portray the most desirable image, and variations of life lived online may just be a more exquisite prison hosted as a democratic stage, especially in an online world where nega-tive commentary often rules the interactive roost.

Internet Ranting and Impression Management

The adages "everyone's a critic" and "everyone has an opinion" are apt for describing much Internet commentary. People post comments online, and before long, rants can ensue that beget more rants. Feeling under siege from harassing rants has led some websites to cancel comment sections, and there is no doubt that rants poison many potential wells of communication. The tendency to rant may be increasingly acceptable, or at least accepted with a sense of inevitability. Where people once claimed, "If you don't have anything nice to say, don't say anything," the new ver-sion seems to be, "If you don't have something nice to write, go ahead." Online commentary seems exempt from the "not nice" ban, despite guide-lines to the contrary. Whether in cruel things that trolls write, acerbic and opinionated reactions to posts, or mean-spirited derision in an *Amazon*, *TripAdvisor*, or *Yelp* review, a new abrasive standard is settling into being. Expressing a critical response to something is understandable. Doing so in a diatribe and using corrosive prose risks making, or has already made, denigrating discourse an interactional default online.

Some companies fight this emerging new standard by eliminat-ing comments from their websites. Others like Botto Bistro, an Italian restaurant, took a different tack and fought the "everyone's a critic" sensibility head-on.[3] Botto claims that once they stopped advertising on *Yelp*, *Yelp* removed a positive review, and more negative reviews suddenly appeared, which Botto interpreted as an attempt to intimidate and retaliate against them. Rather than capitulate, the restaurant decided to become a one-star-rated restaurant on *Yelp*. Botto's strategy was to try to remove the stigmatizing power that *Yelp* has to broadcast bad reviews (although *Yelp* the company does not write the reviews). So Botto offered patrons 25% off a pizza to write one-star reviews of the restaurant. These reviewers then wrote sarcastic and tongue-in-cheek reviews (like from Nicole, "Their pizza ruined my marriage, my relationship with all my friends, I can no longer go out cause I'm too fat, I lost my job, and I think I might even have borderline PTSD at the sight of pizza now. That's my relationship with this place. It did that to me . . ."). The restaurant management decided to insult previous reviewers further in a "hall of shame," including any diners whose "stupidity" warranted mention as the "village idiot" of the week. This strategy rejects people's feelings of entitlement to review any business negatively, just because the business is in business, and people think having to value customer service must equate to tolerating abuse. However, there is a difference between offering service and being servile, such that any customer's whim is law, whether unreasonable or not. Though perhaps overkill, Botto also gave people a dose of their own humiliation medicine. As an example, one patron threatened to call the health department when he could not figure out how to use the faucet in the bathroom, which had a knob that pushed down instead of twisted. He said he would never return to the restaurant because the "staff acted like it was his fault" that he could not operate the faucet. The restaurant placed him in the "hall of shame" and urged him to let the authorities know about the faucet: "Yes, you should contact immediately the proper departments and also the White House—the president needs to be informed about this mysterious device placed in our bathroom. We are so glad you did not hurt yourself trying to make the faucet work."

The Botto Bistro strategy counterpunches the Internet's current review mania. Suddenly, everyone is welcome to your opinion, whether requested or not. Archived judgmentalness overrunning us all is a threatening situation in an impression management sense, as anticipation of being evaluated and subsequent reactivity produces more pressure to hit an idealized performance. With people now rating everything, from

---

[3] See http://www.bottobistro.com/.

doctors to professors, and posting those ratings everywhere, one can feel assessment's icy touch potentially imperiling their identities and services at every turn. Ratings may be positive, but the specter of the mean or unfair review still instills a dread and foreboding. Everyone who sees a negative review is now a potential rejecting audience. The Botto strategy is an attempt to go against an "entitled critic" sentiment that the audience now should be even more powerful in determining and putting individuals and organizations on guard.

Stigma and Cyberbullying

How people mock individuals online is also a growing concern. Cyberbullying invokes an intense targeted attack of degradation online against a specific person or persons. Infamous cases typically center on school-age students who are targeted by a specific circle of aggressive peers and/or by one particularly aggressive one.[4] Cyberbullying transcends mocking or teasing, as cyberbullying's intent is to cause real and severe harm to the target. The victim is stuck in a relentless fishbowl, where they are attacked in school and off-line at home with every intent of humiliating and shaming the individual, sometimes to the point of encouraging them to self-harm. For adolescents and high schoolers, who are experiencing a period of heightened self-consciousness and sensitivity to peer judgments, being bullied in this way can be the realization of their worst fears of being ostracized. Cyberbullying means to devastate and, in the worst cases, has resulted in suicides. Peers and strangers are encouraged to join the trolling, and that widening circle adds to the damage. Cyberbullying is prosecuted and punished legally but the litigation path is also uncertain in having thorny legal nuances blocking enforcement and punishment.

Goffman's analysis of stigma places cyberbullying into clear analytic relief. A stigma, as discussed previously, is a discrediting characteristic someone has, like a negatively assessed body feature, social habit, or connection to a disrespected group. "Normals" and people in a deviant category experience what Goffman calls "strained" interaction. People with a visible discrediting characteristic put others off by inserting a pariah identity into what people prefer to be a social oasis where the illusion of normality pervades as the pretended social status quo. Stigmas also

---

[4] There are also cases of parents posing as fake people online to bully a rival of their child.

represent a social weapon that people use against others to gather power over them. As any child (or adult for that matter) remembers, cliques often include and exclude people based on who is stigmatized and who can stigmatize (Adler & Adler, 1995). Reminders of human frailty are typically unwelcome, and people do not tend to act kindly toward those who represent an undesirable identity. For example, sometimes a lack of familiarity with the conditions ill people bear frightens observers.

Belonging to a stigmatized category adds a burden to people beyond whatever consequences they contend with, for example, as a disfigured or ill person or minority group member. That extra burden involves dealing with and attempting to manage mistreatment by others. As an example, it is not enough to suffer the ravages of an illness that puts someone in a wheelchair; that person must also add anticipating and managing social alienation and people's negative actions toward them to the burdens they bear. Nobody wants to be treated poorly. Further, stigmatized people can feel tasked with working to put friendly others at ease and to dispel any awkwardness that arises from stigma's presence in interaction. People with concealable stigmas have a different management problem. People that have been incarcerated, have a past diagnosis of mental illness, are involved in affairs, or have physical ailments that they can disguise can pass as "normal." Concealing defects or a past disreputable history involves stigmas that are not visible but potentially discreditable. As an example, think about the dramatic tension every soap opera evokes through concealing discrediting secrets. In cases where a stigma is *discreditable* but not *visibly discrediting,* a person can work to decrease how visible the stigma is. Maybe they make up a past biography to cover up for institutionalization, hide their binge eating or purging behind closed doors, or put a veneer of civility on to disguise a violent past. With discreditable stigmas, the Internet is both friend and foe. People can investigate someone's past, as evidenced in sites that offer to search anyone's arrest records at a customer's request. The Internet can also offer a supportive haven and instructional resource for living with a stigma, as examined later in the case of people that self-harm.

Stigma categories seem consistent over time in terms of the reasons why someone's identity is spoiled. Timeless cases for why someone is stigmatized include that a person weighs too much or too little, has a history of mental illness or incarceration, is handicapped, has some kind of sexual otherness, is considered unattractive or poor, or is a member of an ethnic, racial, or religious minority. Stigma categories do change over time and can lessen or increase. In the United States, being born out of wedlock now is less controversial and homosexuality is more accepted. Yet obesity is increasingly stigmatized today, where in some historical contexts, obesity was esteemed as a symbol of wealth, as having the material capacity to be overweight meant you were rich and successful. An important consideration exists between institutional and personal stigmatizing. Being stigmatized by an individual who insults you is different than when an institution discriminates against a category of people who are stigmatized. Institutions are more resourced and can represent a different scale of power in potential negative impacts. For example, a potential employer refusing to hire people based on a stigma and the criminal justice system targeting people in a stigmatized category for special social control efforts are different in having wide-ranging negative effects. Attacking or mocking an isolated individual for bearing a stigma may be devastating, but that happens to one person, while institutional actions can reach potentially across many persons in a stigmatized category.

While the content of what is stigmatizable and stigmatized may be consistent over time, the capacity to stigmatize others has undergone revolutionary change. As with other forms of online impression management, stigmatizing has entered a 24/7 space. Physical copresence of the abused and abuse is no longer a typical requirement. Practically, opportunities to escape stigmatizing also get diminished. Where abuse might once have been limited to in-person encounters in school hallways, in locker rooms, and at water coolers, insults are now viral. They can be stored for a large audience to view at their convenience. People also can now become stigma curators who can create their own museums of deviance. Surf the web for humor, and you will see sites like *People of Wal-Mart, College Humor, Funny or Die, Texts From Last Night, Tacky Weddings, Idiots on Facebook,* or *Fail* blog. These sites collect examples of humor around a theme of an embarrassing quality like people dressing poorly, saying something stupid, or failing at an activity. They may hope to entertain others for fun or for profit, eventually releasing books like the People of Wal-Mart and Texts From Last Night sites did. Other sites curate X-rated or illegal stigmas. Some curate unconventional subjects that are not illegal to consume but are likely to be considered weird interests. For example, there are sites that people curate involving legal sexual fetishes. These sexual fetishes can involve people with all sorts of bodies or people that are attracted to all kinds of objects. There is squashing, which involves men who want very heavy women to sit on them; sites for "looners" (people who are sexually attracted to balloons); and sites for people with foot fetishes and who are furries or are in love with cars or want to have sexual relations with aliens and robots.

Sites exist for people who see themselves as "otherkin," namely elves, fairies, dragons, and other supernatural creatures who presently live in human form. There are sites for people who are into cults, hunting for aliens, and any unusual subculture imaginable. Support groups and curated groups exist for deviant behaviors, such as for people who encourage romantic partners to become morbidly obese and pro-ana groups that provide "thinspiration" and for people who self-harm or engage in extreme body modifications. Sometimes individuals curate normal behaviors that are camouflaged to avoid embarrassment and a spoiled identity. Such sites overturn the covert nature of when these behaviors occur and heighten their guilty pleasure visibility, such as on sites that collect examples of popping pimples. Pornography is abundant, and people who pursue polyamory and variations within that practice can potentially find partners a few clicks away. The Internet makes deviant behavior easily visible, which defies censors and social control efforts and expands opportunities for personal freedoms. These sites also can spread misinformation and support harmful behaviors.

From the perspective of controlling information, which is an important aspect of stigma management and impression management, the now heightened visibility of deviant behavior affects the labeling process anew. People cannot hide information as well as they once might have. The concrete or ephemeral criteria that people use to define behaviors as deviant, and to characterize how deviant people act, now can be checked against information provided on the Internet. A person's secret deviance is more discoverable. Efforts to use images against subordinate groups is tougher when dissonant information is available online. Alternatively, slandering someone has never been easier since one can just post embarrassing information online with apps that work to guarantee anonymity like *Yik Yak*, a social messaging platform that invites anonymous comments in a locally prescribed area. Making negative generalizations stick when groups can fight back using counter images of their own changes the nature of what Edwin Schur (1980) referred to as *stigma contests*. In stigma contests, each group attempts to apply a stigma to an opponent while evading the stigmas being tossed back their way. The Internet has opened a new, seemingly infinite, battlefront in stigma contests.

How should people try to control these new conditions for stigmatizing others? People have always identified a strong place for social control authorities in addressing some universally derided online activities. Few would argue, for example, against social control authorities combating the spread of child pornography online. Many people are also concerned about halting cyberbullying. On the other hand, the presence of authorities is controversial when pursuing less heinous activities. Authorities now also must fear exposure of problematic actions. As an example, filming law enforcement agents and posting their activities online is ongoing. Parents, schools, and religious organizations, not to mention government agencies in various forms, all seek to create a monolithic viewpoint in audiences in constructing a view of what reality is that people should accept without challenge. Would corporate organizations mind being able to remove any negative online publicity or reviews of their services? Once posted, the web makes the permanent removal of information difficult. A court or threat or suit can make a primary poster take information down, but if that information has been put up once, then someone has the material archived and other sites will have the information. In the past, this multiple siting of information was not as available. In historical situations, perhaps information could be presented as an unimpeachable "party line," and individuals could perform images that were less susceptible to cracks or dissonant leaks emerging. The camouflaging of potentially stigmatizing information was easier historically when there were fewer places where a person could find different interpretations. Those days have changed. An organization or person could hide their warts by drawing a curtain around them without countless people who have the technical capacity to pull the curtains back allowing others to probe backstage at that individual or group. Today, finding the way backstage is easier thanks to curators, double agents, hackers, leakers, trolls, and whistleblowers that want to expose secret information.

While some may curate content that does not harm others, others turn to cyberbullying as their medium for curating, and they create collections of information intended to humiliate specific victims. Such people are specialists in stigma. They can surreptitiously film people who exhibit some behavior considered deviant and then broadcast that content, such as in the case of Tyler Clementi, the Rutgers student whose roommate filmed and publicized him having a homosexual encounter without his knowledge. The roommate's actions contributed to Clementi's tragic suicide.

Think of the escalation in humiliation involved in terms of moving from someone telling a hypothetical story of someone having homosexual sex, versus setting up a webcam, filming images of the activity, streaming that content, and writing commentary in tweets. The shaming goes viral and is more vivid. Clementi's roommate was prosecuted and punished for his actions in the criminal courts.

In recalling high school bullies, we might remember those who went out of their way to find the person they liked to insult and their work to torment those people during in-person meetings. The cutting remark was there and could stick in the mind of the bullied person for years. Now there is a whole new set of tools for the stigma specialist to put to use. Photoshop, video, links, and avenues of communication can hit a target 24/7. There is time to rehearse, research, and egg on insults. A person can find whatever social approval they might seek from insulting others in forming or joining a secret community designed to humiliate someone. In many cases of cyberbullying, a person is targeted for ongoing torrents of abuse. In the past, school could have been the primary place that was a nightmare to be. Thanks to the Internet, a new form of stigmatizing claustrophobia exists. Stigma has gone mobile, as the Internet has brought about mobile physical stigmatizing that can follow a person wherever they are connected. People can argue that a person can escape that bullying by just turning off devices and staying away from tormentors, but that end may be easier said than done when so much of someone's social connections live online.

Danah boyd (2014) argues that much of a teenager's social life occurs online. Overscheduled days of off-line activities cause teenagers to lack the time, and sometimes the places, to hang out in person. That change makes hanging out online an even more valued space and one that is harder to cut out of one's life. So people hang out online as a form of social interaction, and when bullying occurs, that bullying migrates online to envelop the person after hours wherever they go online. People can still work to get off-line or to expel others who insult them, but to leave the Internet is to forgo hanging out. Further, reporting offenders to web gatekeepers and/or de-listing or de-friending someone will not always do the trick. Tormentors are innovative and persist in finding ways to get back online under new login schemes to torment their victims. Too many workarounds exist for people who are banned, who find Achilles heels in gatekeeping protocols and then reemerge. As long as anonymity protects them, they can repopulate online under new names.

People can clamor for less anonymity online and for more safeguards against people bullying others through social media software. Yet altering the technical capacities available online is easier said than done. People do enjoy the capacity to have private conversational groups and feel that to ban or restrict them is overkill just because a secondary effect is that they also create opportunities to bully. Further, while authority figures attend to bullying, adult-and teens are already adept and sophisticated in figuring out how to exploit Internet social media platforms to thwart attempts to stop their activities. There is always another medium to use like *Yik Yak* and others. Abusers can continually flip through usernames to avoid being shunned and banned from sites as people weary of their aggression.

Specialists in tormenting others also ply their trade as lurkers who troll. Some individuals enjoy giving noxious opinions in order to see if they can get a response as a kind of fun game, hence the expression "don't feed the trolls."People value freedom of expression, and sometimes that value emerges as an open license to rant. There is an entertainment appeal in seeing people be mean. Further, there is a new availability for like-minded people who want to get together to hate a particular group or individual to find common "virtual clubhouses" for catching up and planning. Locations like *4chan* had a reputation for providing this safe port, and there are many other "underground" anonymous sites. Some sites advocate racist and/or sexist beliefs; some advocate violence; some do both.

In terms of less severe mocking between strangers, the usual avenue is that an individual posts content and denigrating commentary appears. These cases are not cyberbullying per se. A random stranger calling you stupid is different than someone telling you endlessly that everyone (who you both know) hates you. Today, people are aware that any person who posts content publicly is vulnerable to mocking, as they are now treated as a "public figure" that by the act of putting content out there "invites" being in everyone's crosshairs. Teen singer Rebecca Black is an infamous example. Black posted a video of a song called "Friday" that thousands of people watched and then mocked vehemently. While some defended her song and video, many posted insults and piled onto the humiliating, transforming one upload into a process of stigmatizing Black and her video that involved thousands of obnoxious comments. Thirteen million views spawned a torrent of venom directed at a then thirteen-year-old singer, which is an intense punishment for a singer and song whose crime is not appealing to others' musical tastes.

To be fair, many people supply encouraging, helpful, and supportive reactions to comments and videos that others post online. The Internet also offers a counterbalancing haven to off-line negativity, in providing a community for many people who seek and find helpful support online. As negative commentators exist, so do many people who want to genuinely connect to and support others. People share helpful answers to questions posted online probably more readily than they insult the poster's intelligence for asking "dumb" questions or having particular opinions. Unfortunately, with the Internet's larger potential population of viewers, trolls can find targets more easily. Negative comments coexist with positive ones; the Internet has Dr. Jekyll and Mr. Hyde commenting together. However, empowering and supportive communities do exist online as well.

Internet communication can be more impersonal and distant than face-to-face communications, yet close relationships can also form there. People can find a community online of individuals who are receptive to them and become interested mutual confidants. Mutual confidences and solidarity are a click or tap away with no one in the off-line world having to be the wiser. In such cyberrelationships, people may reveal aspects of the "real me" that they won't expose locally.

Patti Adler and Peter Adler (2008) found that "socially proscribed and severely sanctioned behavior that was once relegated largely to secrecy among isolated individuals is now at the center of cybercommunity in which all manner of support is readily available." In their research, people who "cut" or self-injure could find others online and find a community of fellow "deviants." Comraderie in a misunderstanding and hostile world is a vital comfort. People who "really get it" are able to help in ways that others cannot—if help is the aim. Similar comraderie exists for people through pro-ana websites and across sexual fetishes, yet these sites may be more about enabling the action as opposed to understanding. The problem of reaching people "like you" is now surmountable. The web also offers vital support, rationalizations, and techniques through which one can continue to pursue some activity of interest. For sociologists interested in different theories of deviance, the Internet's capacity to teach techniques of rationalization and ways to engage in deviant behavior is unprecedented.

Moral Entrepreneurs

Howard Becker (1963) described moral entrepreneurs as people acting on behalf of groups who work to construct a particular version of reality as *the reality.* Many people might see reality as an objective truth; there are facts, and whatever is a fact is the reality. That sensibility might work in cases where there is a natural law at work. If individuals slam their heads into concrete, they will be injured, because concrete is objectively a hard surface. In cases where people have beliefs about what the facts are, reality is more slippery than determining whether people need oxygen to breathe or whether someone gets hurt by smashing into concrete. Beliefs about political positions, the best path to rear children, whether ghosts exist or marijuana should be feared as a gateway drug or accepted as beneficial, make reality more up for grabs in terms of selling a particular point of view about what is real to someone. A moral entrepreneur is a person who is busy working to get someone to believe some set of beliefs as the beliefs to truly have and advocate. The person who argues that creationism is the truth belongs in that category, just as the person who campaigns for evolution does.

As an example, people might advocate for criminalizing marijuana by promoting a reality that ingesting this drug makes people mentally ill, sick, and deluded, and causes them to harm others and themselves. Law enforcement agencies and some lobbyists portrayed marijuana as a gateway drug to self-destruction, along with other arguments, like in a recent public service advertisement that held that buying marijuana funds terrorism, even though the average person does not see that lineage directly. Such narratives counter the claims of experts on the other side, who propound alternative narratives that show marijuana use as much less dangerous than alcohol consumption and that identify many economic and medical benefits of the drug. The connection to Goffman's ideas is that the dramaturgical perspective is a medium through which a particular version of reality is sold. As in the cases where individuals attempt to show that they represent established social status and culturally valued attributes to observers, moral entrepreneurs choreograph persuasive efforts to have their versions of reality become attributed as reality. A dramaturgical sensibility helps people understand that they witness strategically intended performances when moral entrepreneurs make their arguments. Today's Internet era has another double-edged sword present here. This era makes dramaturgy and moral entrepreneurship more difficult as performances can be spoiled more easily; at the same time, everyone has a pulpit and potentially a wide audience to hear them pitch their truth.

Typically, large organizations and government agencies have the upper hand in labeling activities and in creating moral contexts for judging behaviors. These groups can make persuasive demands on media out-lets, paying for advertisements, or offering "official" versions of events through hiring public relations specialists and talking heads. Historical cases include media moguls like Rupert Murdoch and William Hearst, whose media empires made sure to echo their owner's preferred framings of events. Government agencies have regulatory powers and a guaranteed capacity to expose citizens to their messaging. As an example, the content of textbooks that each state approves for their public school systems can downplay evolution or intelligent design, and public schools have (for the most part) captive audiences. Governments can fund advertisements about the dangers of marijuana while profiting from alcohol sales and participating in gambling. Government agencies can influence industry self-regulation and cultural rules about what entertainment content can be displayed on public airwaves. For example, American standards for public airwaves seem to be that any displays involving sexuality are more problematic than images of violence.

When individuals and groups portray a particular version of what is true about the world, they do so because they have a vested interest in getting people to accept that belief. When people believe something to be true about the world, the concept of self-fulfilling prophecy and other theories inform us that people will treat subjective claims as authentic claims and work to make their beliefs become "true" in the world. So if a prior belief is held to be true, people will interpret evidence and actions to confirm that belief, which can help make the world a place where that belief becomes true. Famous examples described in the scholarly literature are of runs on banks and gas stations. If people start hearing that these organizations are on the verge of running out of the resource that they store, people converge there in a panic and start withdrawing everything from that organization, which actually makes the prophecy come true. If people believe that some kids are bad kids and other kids are good kids, they may start to treat those kids in ways that sustain these attributions, and that treatment may cause conditions that make the good kids stay or become good and the other kids stay or become bad (Chambliss, 1973). Powerful moral entrepreneurs like government agencies, industry groups, religious organizations, and the wealthy enjoy more control over what constructed images of reality are made available to others and how actions and kinds of people are to be perceived. There are always individuals who stand against such monolithic images, including people who fight to expose deception and misconduct by the powerful. Other individuals might fight against established knowledge because they are con artists or cranks, and they want to get people to believe in quack cures or "sure-fire" investments that run counter to acceptable business practices or scientific knowledge. Many people are also curious and want to know more about what they do not know. Sometimes people prefer to wallpaper the world over to only highlight information that they prefer, hence the existence of filter bubbles, where the information that people want to see online is only information that they prefer and which accords with their preconceived views (Pariser, 2012). An example is when some religious families remove all nonreligious worldview culture, objects, and communications from their households.

The Internet is a powerful tool for promoting monolithic images while also being an obstacle to those portrayals. There are good reasons for totalitarian governments to ban the Internet, when Arab Springs can spread like wildfire through virally accumulated mobs, and news coverage counter to the wishes of authority figures must be stopped. There has never been a time when people could explore the other side of an argument more easily. Take a person who was frightened of expressing a deviant interest prior to the Internet. He or she may have never had the capacity to learn more information about that behavior from people nearby. In today's world, someone can locate a subculture of deviants and acquire a backstage picture, rather than accept a public script that a congregation, family, or school perpetuates. People who are labeled deviant may just want to count on similar people to understand them. To use Goffman's term, the Internet era now has more people who can be made "wise" to a deviant identity, other than just their "own," because people can educate themselves about such groups online. In doing so, will they encounter moral entrepreneurship by those deviant groups? Absolutely, but the nature of people is to present images of themselves that will foster a more positive impression by an audience. A more comprehensive understanding occurs when people can have different competing ideas in their heads instead of just one ethnocentric or tunnel-vision view of the world.

Filter Bubbles

Impression management requires some instructional information. As an example, to play a role, someone must imagine a substantive guide for that performance. People might train to learn what to do or observe someone else in the role. They might research the role in how-to books. They could draw on a movie they saw. Inputs flow in and an output performance results. As Goffman (1974) clarifies, frames and keys help signal what "is going on here."

An important contemporary change in framings is the development of filter bubbles on the Internet. A filter bubble refers to filtering information in and out selectively so that all someone chooses to be exposed to is information and perspectives that they already favor, consciously or unconsciously, which places them in a bubble. Everyone has points of view on issues that impose blinders on what they notice or ignore. We self-select on our preferences such that our terrorist is someone else's freedom fighter, and our president is heroic while that same president is someone else's definition of a disaster. We allow information in that supports our views and filter out alternatives.

What is new, and of vital importance in the Internet era, is the accelerated technical capacity to aggregate information and build more powerful filter bubbles. Using our own private tastes, we can go to a bookstore and choose a book we want to read. In making that preference, just like with TV, we know what we choose to avoid because we can see the options that we reject. *Google* and *Facebook* alternatively use previous personalized use patterns to filter content for feeds. The upshot is that users only start to see what they like—more what an algorithm thinks they like. The filter is automatic so that what you see is all prefiltered content to your preference. The resulting world created out of those preferences appears for all intents and purposes as the "objective" world "as it is." You then draw conclusions from those displays based on what you know about the world without a consistent knowledge of alternative or additional information.

Gilad Lotan (2014) writes in reference to contemporary Internet media saturation and filter bubbles:

> Not only is there much more media produced, but it is coming at us at a faster pace, from many more sources. As we construct our online profiles based on what we already know, what we're interested in, and what we're recommended, social networks are perfectly designed to reinforce our existing beliefs. Personalized spaces, optimized for engagement, prioritize content that is likely to generate more traffic; the more we click, share, like, the higher engagement tracked on the service. Content that makes us uncomfortable is filtered out.

Filter bubbles have big consequences. The first is that filter bubble feeds do not encompass all the news or knowledge or perspectives out in the world, but are subjective samples cued to your preferences. What that means is that the actor has knowledge from a filter bubble that is suited for that audience and has cultural capital that is appropriate to act within that world and to know what to do and say with better fit. That knowledge is useful if one only lived in a world that was absolutely consonant with the filter that a person chooses to install. So for example, in the 2012 U.S. presidential election, many people who just watched *Fox News* and had news feeds composed of conservative stories were shocked to their core when Mitt Romney lost the election. Everything they had read had made an election result of Romney winning as a foregone conclusion given how much anger they read about in the electorate. Yet the electorate that they considered was composed of people who thought like them, not of all voters, and they ignored the possibility that their view had limited applicability because that view was all they chose to perceive. A phenomenon of unsubstantiated generalizing occurred in which the subjective preferences in a filter bubble were taken as an objective real preference.

As another example, the conflict in Gaza (see Lotan, 2014) also produced social communications geared to what preexisting views audiences might have. A viewpoint of Israel needing to defend itself filtered into news stories that affirmed that perspective by showing clips of Hamas fighters launching missiles in civilian areas and stories about weapons found in United Nations Relief and Works Agency (UNRWA) schools. Audiences who preferred the perspective that Israel was not defending itself but acting like "war criminals" received news feeds that matched that perspective. Stories about bombing the UNRWA schools and civilian casualties constituted the coverage. In color-coded maps of blue for the pro-Israeli news coverage and green for the pro-Palestinian news coverage, the maps are almost completely either blue or green, not a mix. Some outlets may cover stories across a range of perspectives, but by and large, the predetermined view that someone has is going to create the news world that the person experiences. On a day that a UNRWA school was hit, there was no coverage of that event in some papers; while there is no coverage of missile launches and weapons being found in those schools in opposing news. The event that is not covered in the news feed does not manifest in that world.

An implication here is that an Internet that appears to be an instrument of opening people up to all kinds of alternate news and viewpoints can sometimes do the opposite. Instead, the Internet can serve to maximize preexisting subjective views of situations by technically filtering out worldview alternatives. The upshot is that audiences are more segregated and impression management becomes increasingly skilled with an audience one knows and progressively weaker with audiences one does not know. What is dangerous here is that the person *thinks* that they know more about the audiences that they do not know because their filter gives an appearance of objective portrayal that is subjective. While the Internet is thought to hold promise for more global communication, there is a danger that we just communicate a choice of what we know rather than having learned that there is more that we do not know. When we just choose what we know to like, and only like what we know, we do not know what else there is to know or like.

Glossary

Note: This glossary includes concepts originated by different scholars. I list the originator's initials at the end of each entry to identify the source of the concept. A full listing of the authors that correspond to the initials is provided at the end. Full citations for the relevant author's work are provided in the reference section. I do not provide initials in cases where I identified the author in the entry itself or when I thought the term was in enough general use so as to not need to attribute an originator. In cases where Goffman is the originator, I also list initials to identify the paper or book from which the term comes (following the requisite "EG").

Achieved Status: A social status you achieve in society based on your own doings, such as being captain of an athletic team or employee of the month.

Actual Social Identity: The actual identity that an individual has as opposed to the virtual social identity he or she presents to an audience. (EG S)

Altercasting: Performing in a way that tries to force other people to take on certain roles as a result. (W&D)

Ascribed Status: A social status in society you are born into like being a particular gender or race.

Attributive Tactics Versus Repudiative Tactics: Attributive tactics intend to express something about "you" while repudiative tactics are meant to disassociate you from a particular label. (ML)

Audience Segregation: Separating the audience for one persona from being able to observe performances that could contradict that distinct persona and spoil that image. For example, politicians will claim to be monogamous at press conferences but cheat on partners at locations hidden from the press. Audience segregation prevents embarrassment. (EG PS)

Auditions for Opportunity: The term refers to the social importance of carrying off vital scenes in impression management like job interviews and appearances before bureaucracies like the court system, in which performing well is linked to potential success and upward mobility. The ability to succeed in these auditions is enhanced by social class and other background variables of cultural capital, in combination with the person's performative agency. The term connects dramaturgical events to social mobility. (DS)

Authentication Practices: Tactics people use to create credible deceptions or to otherwise demonstrate that a performance is credible and honest, including when telling the truth in suspicious circumstances. (DS)

Backstage: A region in which people prepare a performance in anticipation of a front stage audience's judgment and/or where they can also relax a persona that they have to maintain for an audience when on the front stage. (EG PS)

Backstage Staff: People who work in the backstage to help people rehearse for performances. (H&B)

Basic Interpretive Competence: An audience must have the appropriate cultural knowledge and capacity to interpret the performances that they observe so that the performance has a chance to achieve its purpose. (DS)

Bask in Reflected Glory: To reflect in the glory of something else as a presentational strategy. Examples are when hometowns publicize celebrities who were born there, swath themselves in a winning team's colors, or parents brag about a child's achievements. (ML)

Calculated Impression: The impression that one seeks to make versus making a secondary impression, which is one left in the minds of the audience, and that may or may not be the calculated one that was sought. (ML)

Calculated Unintentionality: A term describing when calculated thought and preparation go into an affectation and effect that is meant to come across as unintended, unplanned, spontaneous, and "natural" in interactions. For example, the saying "I chased him until he caught me," or acting as if bumping into someone who you strategized how to run into was just a fortunate coincidence rather than the result of a conscious plan of action. (EG PS)

Celebrity: A person "well known for their well-knowness"; a "human entertainment." (DB)

Chainscape: The landscape created by retail chains and their themed atmospheres that form a dominating presentational context in which people shop and spend time. (DS)

Chorus: A reference group that supports the front stage narrative and performance. (H&B)

Civil Inattention: Giving a rudimentary acknowledgment of another person in public while being careful to give no invitations to interact—like in public transportation or on an elevator. Some might extend this idea to explain why people will not make any public acknowledgment of problematic behavior that they see. A similar but slightly different terminology for that action is "tactful blindness." (EG PS)

Code of the Streets: Refers to Elijah Anderson's conception of how Black men in Philadelphia develop a "streetwise" persona suited to the perceived attitudes of an audience approaching them while they are on the street. A larger dramaturgical variation on Anderson's conception describes the public face that an individual feels is appropriate on a public stage such as the street, as a result of race, religion, or another factor.

Communication out of Character: Communications that contradict a given performance. (EG PS)

Control Moves: "The intentional efforts of an informant to produce expressions that he thinks will improve his situation if they are gleaned by the observer." (EG SI)

Cooling Out the Mark: Tactics to alleviate a person's feelings after they have experienced a loss of status. (EG CM)

Copresence: Two parties being simultaneously available and aware of one another in performance.

Cut Off Reflected Failure: An attempt to distance oneself from a perceived disreputable failure. An example is when Americans clarify that they did not vote for Bush or support Obama. (ML)

Cuts: Practices of pointedly denying overtures for interaction. Cuts are rude, so people may try to do cuts by appearing to make them accidents to deny encounter overtures. "Didn't see you" or by appearing to be on a cell phone call so as to not be able to talk in person with someone. (EG BPP)

Deep Versus Surface Acting: Deep acting involves actually trying to summon up emotions to connect authentically with a part one is playing. Surface acting is going through the motions of giving a performance without actually trying to authentically feel that part. (AH)

Defensive Practices: Strategies to protect one's own claims of identity. (EG PS)

Deference: Symbolic power in potential form: Once deference is acquired, it can be deployed as the symbolic power to frame (define) actions, situations, and events in ways that induce compliance and constitute the social order.

Definition of the Situation: An understanding that a given or specific state of affairs applies to the situation that someone is in, such as being in a class or on a date or a job interview. The prevailing definition informs people how to act to sustain that given state of affairs. (EG PS, FA)

Definitional Disruptions: When events occur that contradict or shatter the definition of the situation that an actor tries to present.

Degradation Ceremonies: Shaming ceremonies that punish the status of someone with a spoiled identity. (HG)

Demeanor: The attitude and behavior a person projects toward others.

Depiction Fallacy: Taking a depiction or representation of reality as actual reality. (DS)

Director: The person who provides an interpretation for the script, rehearses the action, and provides cues at performance time. (H&B)

Discreditable: Someone who has a potentially "spoiled identity" that can be kept secret. (EG S)

Discredited: Someone who has a visible "spoiled identity" that cannot be hidden. (EG S)

Discrepant Roles: Poses a problem to the credibility of the performance because someone has access to the backstage and is also a member of the audience. (EG PS)

Display Rules: The rules for displaying emotion that are considered appropriate in a setting. "There is no crying in baseball." "Don't laugh at customers."

Dramatic Realization: How individuals infuse all sorts of subtle social activity by communicative signs to get their characters across. For example, nodding's one's head to feign attention when someone else talks to show interest even when uninterested. (EG PS)

Dramaturgical Awareness: Awareness of being judged. (B&E)

Dramaturgical Camouflage: That front stage and impression management behaviors constitute barriers to information gathering and research by observers, as they obscure true attitudes and behaviors and produce blind spots in knowledge. (DS)

Dramaturgical Circumspection: Deliberating beforehand and taking steps connected to putting on the best show. (EG PS)

Dramaturgical Discipline: Giving a disciplined performance that fits expectations such as playing parts and attending to details. (EG PS)

Dramaturgical Loyalty: Loyalty to fellow performers on a team that encourages partners to accept an obligation to perform appropriate to the mutual performance. (EG PS)

Dramaturgical Residences: When people choose to "reside" in a fictional character when they can, in addition to, or other than, their "civilian" identity. Examples include in popular culture when a person chooses to identify as a vampire or a lieutenant in Starfleet or as a Furry, while they also recognize being the more conventional mortal "Fred" or "Jane" at work. Dramaturgical residences require intense commitment to fictional identities including enacting costuming, language, and behaviors in rigid dramaturgical discipline to the conventions of the character. (DS)

Embarrassment: Negative feelings felt in the aftermath of a spoiled identity or performance.

Embarrassment Grenades: A description of efforts to use dramaturgical expectations and frame traps to try to embarrass or shame someone and gain some social leverage and power over him or her. While many focus on the acting steps people take to avoid embarrassment, there are many ways that people try to embarrass others by invoking how those others have some sort of spoiled identity in a situation. A stigma is the shaming characteristic; the "embarrassment grenade" is the delivery vehicle to harness that shaming power against someone. (DS)

Embracement: To embrace a role is to disappear completely into the virtual self that is available in the situation, to be fully seen in terms of the image, and to confirm expressively one's acceptance of it. (EG FA)

Emotional Labor: The displays of emotion expected in a particular work role. (AH)

Encounters: Face-to-face interaction sequences. They are "when persons are gathered together and sustain a joint focus of visual and cognitive attention, mutually ratifying one another as persons open to each other for talk or its substitutes." (EG E)

Expression Games: The game of trying to gain information from others while concealing information yourself. People engage in covering, uncovering, and counter-uncovering moves; in others words, they hide information, attempt to find out information about others, and try to avoid the attempts others make to learn their information. (EG SI)

Expressions Given: Any sign activity consciously intended to communicate a message to an observer. (EG PS)

Expressions Given Off: Any sign activity that is seen as unintended, nonverbal. (EG PS)

Expressive Control: Efforts to keep inconsistent feelings from disrupting the performance. (EG PS)

Extravagant Expectations: Overly heightened social expectations that influence consumption behavior. These expectations address "what the world holds," of how sparkling and vivid life can be, of being able to achieve purposes easily, and solve problems without delay. (DB)

Fabrication: When people are led by others to have a false belief about what is going on. Fabrications can be benign, like a surprise party, or exploitative, like in a con job. (EG FA)

Face: An image of self in terms of approved social attributes. The positive social value a person effectively claims for themselves by the line others assume they have taken during a particular contact. "Reputation in the eyes of others." (EG PS)

Faking in Bad Faith Versus Good Faith/Connection to Deep and Surface Acting: When a person gives a superficial performance in a role, they are faking in bad faith. When a person gives a performance in which they commit emotionally, they are faking in good faith. (R&S)

Fancy Milling: Describes "where the action is" for people in consumption, in people enjoying getting to be big shots by displaying an association with opulence and conspicuous consumption in front of others in designated places for that activity. "Adults in our society can enjoy a taste of social mobility by consuming valued products, by enjoying costly and modish entertainment, by spending time in luxurious settings, and by mingling with prestigeful persons—all the more if these occur at the same time and in the presence of many witnesses. This is the action of consumption." (EG IR)

Feeling Rules: The rules people encounter that structure how they are supposed to feel, like the perennial "boys don't cry." (AH)

Footing: The point of view and understanding that an individual participant adopts within a particular frame. How they associate themselves with a particular frame of reference. (EG FA)

Frame and Framing: Principles of organizing experience that govern the subjective meaning that people assign to social events. (EG FA)

Frame Trap: Once stuck in the wrong frame, people are trapped by the descriptive power of the wrong frame, like from a stigma or label. (EG FA)

Front Stage: A region where people present and are expected to present in front of an audience. (EG PS)

Identity Tags: "Officially recognized seals that bond an individual to his biography" (Goffman, 1969, p. 22). They connect an actor to a claimed identity or affiliation; for example, there are official tags like passports, driver's licenses, and birth certificates. Unofficial identity tags are informal, such as proper apparel, business cards, letterhead, accents, and physical markings. (EG SI)

Image: An image is a "visible public personality as opposed to a private character. The idea is that images can be shined, developed, and refined for public consumption. It is a studiously crafted personality profile of an individual, institution, corporation, product, or service." (DB)

Image Life: Sustaining the image or persona as a pristine real construct over time. (DS)

Imagination Products: Products that exist in fantasy realms that encourage us to fantasize to consume them, such as literary creations, movies, and amusement parks. (DS)

Information Preserve: The set of facts about himself or herself to which an individual expects to control access while before others. (EG RP)

Interaction Membrane: A protective filtering boundary metaphorically cutting an encounter off from the wider world, protecting its integrity and rewards. (EG E)

Keyings: Signals to participants about the nature of a particular framing that apply to signalling "real" meanings within frame and frame changes. A keying transforms meaning in an interaction that then determines what people think is really going on. For example, a keying can be that something is "make-believe." The fight is play, not a real fight. (EG FA)

Know Your Audience: A person should try to understand the affinities and assumptions of particular audiences to avoid performing the wrong thing in front of them. (DS)

Line: A perspective taken and performed in an interaction that also reflects a definition of the situation that a team sustains in public.

Meso-Level: Theories that apply microsociological data and thinking in shaping conclusions about larger level societal phenomena.

Mystification: Concealing mundane aspects of putting together a performance so that the effect seems more powerful and magical. For example, hiding a magic act behind a curtain. In Kenneth Burke, mystification refers to using language to disguise actual conditions or truth. (EG PS)

Nonfiction Performance: A term used to communicate that performance here is not of artistic and literary works. The performances here refer to real actions and intentions and are interpreted and communicated as truthful and happening in real life and real time. The use of nonfiction refers to the distinction between fictive literature and nonfiction literature, in which the former is understood as made up with imaginary characters while nonfiction is understood as referring to real people and events and to be literally "true." (DS)

Persona: The identity and behaviors that an actor puts forth that are considered appropriate to the social situation.

Personal Front: Items intimately connected to the performer and considered a part of him or her apart from items in the setting, such as clothing, sex, age, racial characteristics, size and looks, speech patterns, body, and facial expressions. (EG PS)

Playwright: Provides idea or script for performance. (H&B)

Positive Idealization: Presenting yourself as if you live up to very ideal standards—which can also conceal inconsistencies. (EG PS)

Prescriptive Versus Restrictive Norms: How people should appear versus how their performances are meant to be restricted. (ML)

Production: An organizationally developed presentation informed by resources and meant to have a calculated, typically commercial effect. Values are nested in productions just as they are nested in the dramaturgical performances that individuals give. (DS)

Programming and Trimming: Work to get someone socialized into a new identity by chipping away aspects of old identity through programs that force one into a new identity. (EG A)

Props: Physical objects that are meant to aid a performance.

Protective Practices: Strategies intended to protect the projected definition of others. (EG PS)

Rationalization of Dramaturgy: A term to describe the larger systematized organizational insistence on rigid adherence to specified dramaturgical norms. For example, total institutions insist on certain dramaturgical patterns of responses by performers. The term *rationalization of dramaturgy* refers to an imposition of rigid dramaturgical social requirements across groups and organizations. (DS)

Rationalization of Symbols: This term addresses the idea that organizations strategically implement semiotic and symbol displays to exercise control and create an "iron cage" around people. In essence, a contemporary matrix of symbolic control over people. (DS)

Regions: Any place that is bounded to some degree by barriers to perception. "Within the walls of a social establishment we find a team of performers who cooperate to present to an audience a given definition of the situation. . . . We often find a division into the back region, where the performance of a routine is prepared and front region where the performance is presented. . . . Among members of the team, we find that familiarity prevails, solidarity is likely to develop and the secrets that could give the show away are shared and kept (p. 238)." (EG PS)

Repetitive Monotony: The means through which people live together in a normal state of predictability, in overwhelmingly familiar and routine patterns of social interaction, that are routine in everyday life, work, and among family and friends. (DS)

Republic of Entertainment: A cultural criticism that the most profound impulse in the United States is now to be entertained or amused by images and celebrities rather than by ideas or higher forms of culture. The urge to be entertained is creating more and more spectacle and less thought. (NG)

Role: Refers to obligations, behaviors, duties, and feelings associated with a named status. For example, a drill sergeant performs a role that demonstrates authority.

Role Dispossession: Being forced out of a role. (H&B)

Role Distance: An "effectively" expressed pointed distance between the individual and his putative role . . . not actually denying the role but the virtual self that is implied in the role for all accepting performers (p. 108)." Shows that as a person you perform this role but you are not "the" role. You have some distance from an attribution about you based on you performing that role. For example, winking when scolding someone or doing a service job in a scattered way to show that you are "too good" for that work. A person will try to distance themselves from any stigma associated with the persona connected to that role. (EG E)

Role Embracement: Occurs when someone is attached to and identifies with a role, they have the quality or capacity to play that role, and they are engaged in the role. (EG E)

Role Segregation: Keeping people who figure in one role set out of the other— don't mix fraternity or sorority peers with how one acts in front of professors.

Scaling: Appreciating the implications associated with moving up in scale from individual dramaturgy to those actions taken by groups and organizations with more resources and power to commit to their image making. (DS)

Schemas: Sets of background knowledge that provide information about objects and ideas about the relationships between objects.

Secondary Adjustments: "Any set of habitual arrangements by which a member of an organization employs unauthorized means, or obtains unauthorized ends, or both, to get around the organization's assumptions as to what he should do and get and hence what he should be (p. 189)." Informal organizational adjustments constitute practices that achieve ends while surreptitiously evading formal organizational controls on people. (EG A)

Seduction: "Maneuvering a definition of the situation such that the subject is led to believe that the observer is to be treated as something of a teammate to whom strategic information can be voluntarily trusted (p. 37)." (EG SI)

Self-Reconstitution: Process leading to a new understanding of self.

Setting: The scenery and props arrayed in the physical space of a performance.

Sign Vehicles: Aspects of setting, manner, and appearance that people use in performances.

Sincere Versus Cynical Performances: When a person believes in the impression that he or she wants to foster versus having no belief in the performance as other than a means to an end. (EG PS)

Situational Harness: The social expectation that people must present themselves to others in a "situational harness," meaning that they must dress, speak, and otherwise enter their interactions in normatively appropriate ways. (EG BPP)

Social Situation: Any environment of mutual monitoring possibilities that lasts during the times two or more individuals find themselves in another's immediate physical presence and extends over the entire territory within which this mutual monitoring is possible.

Spoiled Identity: An identity that has been spoiled as not meeting the intended projection in front of others. (EG S)

Stage Manager: Idea that societies require regular performative management as an organizing principle of orderly life. (NE)

Staging Cues: Cues to team members about how to act during a front stage performance that are hidden from an audience. (EG PS)

Status: A named position within a network of other statuses, such as son, grandfather, woman and man, doctor, patient. Statuses involve social identities that come with specific expectations, rights, obligations, behaviors, and duties.

Stigma: A deeply discrediting characteristic that is an abomination of the body, a blemish of character, or a tribal stigma. (EG S)

Strip: Refers to a strip of interaction or a slice of ongoing activity (from the perspective of people maintaining the activity). (EG FA)

Suspension of Disbelief: Willingness to accept the authenticity of the actor and persona in a situation in order to sustain orderly relations.

Tact: Helping others save face.

Team Collusion: When members of a team refer to backstage secrets regarding the performance in a secret way without revealing that digression to an audience. For example, winking to another teammate when a member of an audience confirmed some negative appraisal of him or her that was discussed backstage but not during performance. (EG PS)

Teams: Individuals working together to express the characteristics of a social situation through giving a performance. (EG PS)

Territories of the Self: A set of fields that belong in association with a given persona and are defended. Examples include the following: (1) Personal space. (2) A stall space like a seat outside in a beach or box. A paid-for seat. (3) Use space is an area of activity in front of a person reserved for her/his use—like in front of a person at a gallery or other "stay out of the way" type positions. (4) Your turn—respecting when your turn arrives in a line or some other kind of reservation system. (5) The sheath of the person's skin and body and clothes. (6) A person's "possessional territory" which speaks to their personal effects or things in front of them, like your radio, cards, food. (7) biographical facts. (8) Conversational preserve—to reserve your involvement in conversation to ones that you can choose, including of conversational circles. (EG RP)

Theatrocracy: Idea of being systematically ruled through governing bodies using techniques of theatricality to subdue a populace. (NE)

Total Institution: A type of organization like a prison that takes over complete control of the social identity and rights of people. (EG A)

Treatment of the Absent: Basically talking behind people's backs—what people can say about or do to people who are not in the audience or present on the team. (EG PS)

Trojan or Mercenary Wholesomeness: Using wholesome and innocent-seeming displays to get people to buy things. (DS)

Underlife (Organizational): Goffman (1963) metaphorically equated a city's "underworld," such as a criminal underworld or underground-and an organization's underlife. He is referring to the unofficial, sometimes dark means through which an organization does work while not upsetting the myths about what work practices are supposed to occur. An individual's secondary adjustments, in combination with the secondary adjustments of other organizational members, make up the organizational underlife of an organization. (EG A)

Virtual Social Identity: The social identity that actors put forth to present to others in comparison to what they consider a different actual social identity. (EG S)

Working Consensus: "Together, participants contribute to a single over-all definition of the situation which involves not so much a real agreement as to what exists, but rather a real agreement as to whose claims concerning what issues will be temporarily honored. Real agreement will also exist concerning the desirability of avoiding an open conflict of definitions of the situation. I will refer to this level of agreement as a working consensus (p. 10)." (EG PS)

Author Initials:

AH = Arlie Hochschild

B&E = Brisset and Edgley

DB = Daniel Boorstin

DS = David Shulman

EG = Erving Goffman

H&B = Hare and Blumberg

HG = Harold Garfinkel

L&S = Lyman and Scott

ML = Mark Leary

NE = Nikolai Evreinov

NG = Neil Gabler

R&S = Rafaeli and Sutton

W&D = Weinstein and Deutschberger

Erving Goffman Paper and Books:

A = *Asylums*

BPP = *Behavior in Public Places*

CM = "Cooling the Mark Out"

E = *Encounters*

FA = *Frame Analysis*

IR = *Interaction Ritual*

PS = *Presentation of Self*

RP = *Relations in Public*

S = *Stigma*

SI = *Strategic Interaction*

References

Abbott, A. (1988). *The system of professions: An essay on the division of expert labor.* Chicago, IL: University of Chicago Press.

Adler, P. A., & Adler, P. (1995). Dynamics of exclusion and inclusion in preadolescent cliques. *Social Psychological Quarterly, 58,* 145–162.

Adler, P. A., & Adler, P. (2008). The cyber worlds of self-injurers: Deviant communities, relationships, and selves. *Symbolic Interaction, 31,* 33–56.

Alexander, J. (2004). Cultural pragmatics: Social performance between ritual and strategy. *Sociological Theory, 22,* 527–573.

Arnould, E., & Price, L. L. (1993). River magic: Extraordinary experience and the extended service encounter. *Journal of Consumer Research, 20,* 24–46.

Baehr, P., & Collins, R. (2005). The sociology of almost everything: Four questions to Randall Collins about interaction ritual chains. *Canadian Journal of Sociology Online.* Retrieved from http://cjsonline.ca/pdf/interactionritual.pdf

Barry, D. (2010). *I'll mature when I'm dead: Dave Barry's amazing tales of adulthood.* New York, NY: G. P. Putnam's Sons.

Barthes, R. (1957). *Mythologies.* New York, NY: Farrar, Strauss and Giroux.

Baudrillard, J. [1981] (1994). *Simulacra and simulation.* Ann Arbor: University of Michigan Press.

Beard, H., & Cerf, C. (2015). *Spinglish: The definitive dictionary of deliberately deceptive language.* New York, NY: Blue Rider Press.

Becker, H. (1963). *Outsiders: Studies in the sociology of deviance.* New York, NY: The Free Press.

Belk, R. (1988). Possessions and the extended self. *Journal of Consumer Research, 15,* 139–168.

Bellatti, A. (2013, Nov. 13). Coca-Cola's assault on tap water. Retrieved from http://civileats.com/2013/11/13/coca-colas-assault-on-tap-water/

Biehl-Missal, B. (2011). Business is show business: Management presentations as performance. *Journal of Management Studies, 48,* 619–645.

Bitner, M. J. (1992). Servicescapes: The impact of physical surroundings on customers and employees. *Journal of Marketing, 56,* 57–71.

Boje, D. M. (1989). Postlog: Bringing performance back in. *Journal of Organizational Change Management, 2,* 80–93.

Boje, D., & Rosile, G. A. (2003). Theatrics of SEAM. *Journal of Organizational Change Management, 16,* 21–32.

Boorstin, D. J. (1962). *The image: A guide to pseudo-events in America.* New York, NY: Vintage.

Boorstin, D. J. (2012). *The image: A guide to pseudo-events in America.* New York, NY: Knopf Doubleday.

Bosk, C. (1979). *Forgive and remember: Managing medical failure.* Chicago, IL: University of Chicago Press.

Bourdieu, P. (1987). The forms of capital. In J. Richardson (Ed.), *Handbook of theory and research for the sociology of education* (pp. 241–258). New York, NY: Greenwood.

Bourgois, P. (2002). *In search of respect: Selling crack in El Barrio* (2nd ed.). New York, NY: Cambridge University Press.

boyd, d. (2002). *Faceted id/entity: Managing representation in a digital world* (master's thesis). Massachusetts Institute of Technology, Cambridge, MA.

boyd, d. (2014). *It's complicated: The social lives of networked teens.* New Haven, CT: Yale University Press.

Brissett, D., & Edgley, C. (1990). *Life as theater: A dramaturgical sourcebook* (2nd ed.). New Brunswick, NJ: AldineTransaction.

Bullingham, L., & Vasconcelos, A. C. (2013). The presentation of self in the online world: Goffman and the study of online identities. *Journal of Information Science, 39,* 101–112.

Burke, K. (1945). *A grammar of motives.* Berkeley: University of California Press.

Burns, T. (1992). *Erving Goffman.* London, UK: Routledge.

Butler Breese, E. (2010). Reports from "backstage" in entertainment news. *Society, 47,* 396–410.

Chambliss, W. (1973). The saints and the roughnecks. *Society, 11,* 24–31.

Chandon, P., & Wansink, B. (2011). *Is food marketing making us fat: A multi-disciplinary review* (INSEAD Faculty & Research Working Paper). Fontainebleau, France.

Chayko, M. (2014). Techno-social life: The Internet, digital technology, and social connectedness. *Sociology Compass, 8*(7), 976–991.

Chriss, J. J. (1995). Some thoughts on recent efforts to further systematize Goffman. *Sociological Forum, 10,* 177–186.

Collins, R. (2004). *Interaction ritual chains.* Princeton, NJ: Princeton University Press.

Craven, G., & Moseley, R. (1972). Actors on a canvas stage: The dramatic conventions of professional wrestling. *Journal of Popular Culture, 6*(2), 326–336.

Dalton, M. (1959). *Men who manage.* New York, NY: Wiley.

Debord, G. (1994). *Society of the spectacle.* New York, NY: Zone Books.

Diamond, N., Sherry, J. F., Jr., Muniz, A. M., Jr., McGrath, A. M., Kozinets, R. V., & Borghini, S. (2009). American Girl and the brand Gestalt: Closing the loop on sociocultural branding research. *Journal of Marketing, 73,* 118–134.

DiMaggio, P., Hargittai, E., Neuman, W. R., & Robinson, J. P. (2001). Social implications of the Internet. *Annual Review of Sociology, 27*, 307–336.

Dion, D., & Arnould, E. (2011). Retail luxury strategy: Assembling charisma through art and magic. *Journal of Retailing, 87*, 502–520.

Donath, J. (1999). Identity and deception in the virtual community. In P. Kollock & M. Smith (Eds.), *Communities in cyberspace* (pp. 29–59). London, UK: Routledge.

Donath, J. (2007). Signals in social supernets. *Journal of Computer-Mediated Communication, 13*(1), 231–251.

Durkheim, E. [1915] (1965). *The elementary forms of the religious life* (J. W. Swain, Trans.). New York, NY: The Free Press.

Edgley, C. (Ed.). (2013). *The drama of social life: A dramaturgical handbook*. Surrey, UK: Ashgate.

Ekman, P. (1985). *Telling lies*. New York, NY: W.W. Norton.

Ellis, A. (2012). Rational emotive behavior therapy in the context of modern psychological research. Albert Ellis Institute. Retrieved from http://albertellis.org/rebt-in-the-context-of-modern-psychological-research

Ellison, N. B., & Hancock, J. T. (2013, September/October). Profile as promise: Honest and deceptive signals in online dating. *Security and Privacy Economics*, 84–88.

Ellison, N. B., Hancock, J. T., & Toma, C. L. (2011, June 27). Profile as promise: A framework for conceptualizing veracity in online dating. *New Media and Society*, 1–18.

Evreinov, N. (1927). *The theater in life*. New York, NY: Brentanos.

Ewen, S. (1988). *All consuming images: The politics of style in contemporary culture*. New York, NY: Basic Books.

Farid, H. (2009). Digital doctoring: Can we trust photographs? In B. Harrington (Ed.), *Deception: From ancient empires to Internet dating* (pp. 95–108). Stanford, CA: Stanford University Press.

Fine, G. A. (1983). *Shared fantasy: Role-playing games as social worlds*. Chicago, IL: University of Chicago Press.

Fine, G. A. (1984). Negotiated orders and occupational cultures. In R. H. Turner & J. F. Short (Eds.), *Annual review of sociology* (pp. 239–262). Palo Alto, CA: Annual Reviews.

Fine, G. A. (2012). *Tiny publics: A theory of group action and culture*. New York, NY: Russell Sage Foundation.

Fine, G. A., & Smith, G. W. (Eds.). (2000). *Erving Goffman*. Thousand Oaks, CA: SAGE.

Ford, S. (2007). *Pinning down fan involvement: An examination of multiple modes of engagement for professional wrestling fans*. Paper presented at the Convergence Culture Consortium, Cambridge, MA.

Gabler, N. (2000). *Life the movie: How entertainment conquered reality*. New York, NY: Vintage.

Gardner, W. L., & Martinko, M. J. (1988). Impression management in organizations. *Journal of Management, 14,* 321–338.

Garfinkel, H. (1956). Conditions of successful degradation ceremonies. *American Journal of Sociology, 61,* 420–424.

Gilsdorf, E. (2009). *Fantasy freaks and gaming geeks: An epic quest for reality among role players, online gamers, and other dwellers of imaginary realms.* Guilford, CT: The Lyons Press.

Gladwell, M. (2005, May 16). Brain candy: Is pop culture dumbing us down or smartening us up? *New Yorker.*

Goffman, E. (1951). Symbols of class status. *British Journal of Sociology, 2,* 294–304.

Goffman, E. (1952). On cooling the mark out: Some aspects of adaptation to failure. *Psychiatry: Journal of Interpersonal Relations, 15,* 451–462.

Goffman, E. (1959). *The presentation of self in everyday life.* Garden City, NY: Doubleday.

Goffman, E. (1961). *Encounters: Two studies in the sociology of interaction.* Indianapolis, IN: Bobbs-Merrill.

Goffman, E. (1962). *Asylums: Essays on the social situation of mental patients and other inmates.* Chicago, IL: Aldine.

Goffman, E. (1963). *Stigma: Notes on the management of spoiled identity.* Englewood Cliffs, NJ: Prentice-Hall.

Goffman, E. (1966). *Behavior in public places: Notes on the social organization of gatherings.* New York, NY: The Free Press.

Goffman, E. (1967). *Interaction ritual: Essays in face-to-face behavior.* New York, NY: Doubleday Anchor.

Goffman, E. (1969). *Strategic interaction.* Philadelphia, University of Pennsylvania Press.

Goffman, E. (1971). *Relations in public.* New York, NY: Basic Books.

Goffman, E. (1974). *Frame analysis: An essay on the organization of experience.* Cambridge, MA: Harvard University Press.

Goffman, E. (1979). *Gender advertisements.* New York, NY: Harper & Row.

Goffman, E. (1983). The interaction order. *American Sociological Review, 48,* 1–17.

Goleman, D. (1996). *Vital lies, simple truths: The psychology of self-deception.* New York, NY: Simon and Schuster.

Gottdiener, M. (2001). *The theming of America: American dreams, media fantasies and themed environments.* Boulder, CO: Westview.

Gottschalk, S. (2010). The presentation of avatars in Second Life: Self and interaction in social virtual spaces. *Symbolic Interaction, 33,* 501–525.

Grandey, A. A. (2003). When the show must go on: Surface acting and deep acting as determinants of emotional exhaustion and peer-rated service delivery. *Academy of Management Journal, 46,* 86–96.

Grayson, K., & Shulman, D. (2000). Impression management in services marketing. In T. Swartz & D. Iacobucci (Eds.), *Handbook of services marketing and management* (pp. 51–68). Thousand Oaks, CA: SAGE.

Griswold, W. (2012). *Cultures and societies in a changing world* (4th ed.). Thousand Oaks, CA: SAGE.

Grove, S. J., Fisk, R. P., & John, J. (2000). Services as theater: Guidelines and implications. In T. Swartz & D. Iacobucci (Eds.), *Handbook of services marketing and management* (pp. 21-35). Thousand Oaks, CA: SAGE.

Hallett, T. (2003). Emotional feedback and amplification in social interaction. *Sociological Quarterly, 44,* 705–726.

Hallett, T. (2010). The myth incarnate: Recoupling processes, turmoil, and inhabited institutions in an urban elementary school. *American Sociological Review, 75,* 52–74.

Hancock, B. H., & Garner, R. (2011). Towards a philosophy of containment: Reading Goffman in the 21st century. *The American Sociologist, 42,* 316–340.

Hare, A. P., & Blumberg, R. H. (1988). *Dramaturgical analysis of social interaction.* Westport, CT: Praeger.

Head, S. (2014). *Mindless: Why smarter machines are making dumber humans.* New York, NY: Basic Books.

Herman, M. (2013, October. 29). Evangelical "hell houses" still a thing this year, now with additional creepiness. *Pacific Standard.* Retrieved from http://www.psmag.com/politics-and-law/evangelical-hell-houses-still-thing-year-now-additional-creepiness-69117

Hewitt, J. P., & Shulman. D. (2011). *Self and society: A symbolic interactionist social psychology* (11th ed.). Boston, MA: Allyn and Bacon.

Hiassen, C. (1998). *Team rodent: How Disney devours the world.* New York, NY: Balantine.

Hochschild, A. R. (1979). Emotion work, feeling rules, and social structure. *American Journal of Sociology, 85,* 551–575.

Hochschild, A. R. (1983). *The managed heart: Commercialization of human feeling.* Berkeley: University of California Press.

Hogan, B. (2010). The presentation of self in the age of social media: Distinguishing performances and exhibitions. *Bulletin of Science Technology & Society, 30,* 377-386.

Holiday, R. (2012). *Trust me I'm lying: The tactics and confessions of a media manipulator.* New York, NY: Penguin Books.

Huehnergarth, N. (2014, January. 7). Water is the enemy, Gatorade mobile game tells youth. Retrieved from http://civileats.com/2014/01/07/water-is-the-enemy-gatorade-mobile-game-tells-youth/

Hughes, E. (1984). *The sociological eye.* New Brunswick, NJ: Transaction Press.

Jackall, R. (1988). *Moral mazes: The world of corporate managers.* New York, NY: Oxford University Press.

Jackall, R., & Hirotta, J. M. (2000). *Image makers: Advertising, public relations and the ethos of advocacy.* Chicago, IL: University of Chicago Press.

Jenkins, H. (2008). *Convergence culture: Where old and new media collide.* New York, NY: New York University Press.

Johnson, S. (2005, April 24). Watching TV makes you smarter. *New York Times Magazine*. Retrieved from http://www.nytimes.com/2005/04/24/magazine/watching-tv-makes-you-smarter.html?_r=0

Joost, H., & Schulman, A. (Producers & Directors). (2010). *Catfish* [Motion Picture]. United States: Universal Pictures.

King, S. (1980). *Danse macabre*. New York, NY: Everest House.

Kozinets, R. V. (2001). Utopian enterprise: Articulating the meanings of Star Trek's culture of consumption. *Journal of Consumer Research, 28,* 67–88.

Lamont, M., & Lareau, A. (1988). Cultural capital: Allusions, gaps and glissandos in recent theoretical developments. *Sociological Theory, 6,* 153–168.

Lasch, C. (1976). *Haven in a heartless world: The family besieged*. New York, NY: W.W. Norton.

Leary, M. R. (1995). *Self-presentation: Impression management and interpersonal behavior*. Oxford, UK: Oxford University Press.

Leidner, R. (1993). *Fast food, fast talk: Service work and the commercialization of human feeling*. Berkeley: University of California Press.

Lemert, C., & Branaman, A. (Eds.). (1997). *The Goffman reader*. Oxford, UK: Blackwell Publishing.

Lemert, C., & Branaman, A. (Eds.). (2007). *The Goffman reader*. Malden, MA: Blackwell.

Linderoth, J. (2012). The effort of being in a fictional world: Upkeyings and laminated frames in MMORPGs. *Symbolic Interaction, 35*(4), 474–492.

Ling, R. (2012). *Taken for grantedness: The embedding of mobile communication in society*. Cambridge, MA: MIT Press.

Lipman W. (2011). *Public opinion*. Digireads.com publishing.

Lively, K. J., & Weed, E. A. (2014). Emotion management: Sociological insight into what, how, why, and to what end? *Emotion Review, 6,* 202–207.

Lotan, G. (2014, August 4). Israel, Gaza, war and data: Social networks and the art of personalizing propaganda. Retrieved from https://medium.com/i-data/israel-gaza-war-data-a54969aeb23e)

Luhmann, N. (1982). *Trust and power*. Chichester, UK: John Wiley.

Lutz, W. (1989). *Doublespeak: From "revenue enhancement" to "terminal living": How government, business, advertisers, and others use language to deceive you*. New York, NY: Harper & Row.

Lyman, S. M., & Scott, M. B. (1975). *The drama of social reality*. New York, NY: Oxford University Press.

Lyman, S. M., & Scott, M. B. (1982). *The drama of social reality*. New York, NY: Oxford University Press.

Maines, D. R. (1982, October). In search of mesostructure: Studies in the negotiated order. *Urban Life, 11,* 267–279.

Mamet, D. (2012). *The secret knowledge: On the dismantling of American culture*. London, UK: Sentinel/Penguin.

Manning, P. (1992). *Erving Goffman and modern sociology*. Cambridge, UK: Polity Press.

Manning, P. (2000). Credibility, agency and the interaction order. *Symbolic Interaction, 23*, 281–298.

Manning, P. K. (2008a). Goffman on organizations. *Organization Studies, 29*, 677–699.

Manning, P. K. (2008b). Organizational analysis: Goffman and dramaturgy. In P. Adler, P. du Gay, G. Morgan, & M. Reed (Eds.), *Oxford handbook of sociology, social theory and organization studies: Contemporary currents* (pp. 266–298). New York, NY: Oxford University Press.

Mazer, S. (1998). *Professional wrestling: Sport and spectacle*. Jackson: University Press of Mississippi.

McLeod, J. (1987). *Aint no' making it*. Boulder, CO: Westview.

Mead, G. H. (1934). *Mind, self, and society*. Chicago, IL: University of Chicago Press.

Mears, A. (2011). *Pricing beauty: The making of a fashion model*. Berkeley: University of California Press.

Meltzer, B. N., Petras, J., & Reynolds, L. T. (1975). *Symbolic interactionism: Genesis, varieties and criticism*. London, UK: Routledge.

Meyrowitz, J. (1986). *No sense of place*. Oxford, UK: Oxford University Press.

Mills, C. W. (1959). *The sociological imagination*. Oxford, UK: Oxford University Press.

Misztal, B. (2001). Normality and trust in Goffman's theory of interaction order. *Sociological Theory, 19*, 312–324.

Moisio, R., & Arnould, E. (2005). Extending the dramaturgical framework in marketing: Drama structure, drama interaction and drama content in shopping experiences. *Journal of Consumer Behavior, 4*, 246–256.

Montemurro, B. (2008). Toward a sociology of reality television. *Sociology Compass* 2/1:84–106.

Ouellette, L., & Murray, S. (2004). Introduction. In S. Murray & L. Ouellette (Eds.), *Reality TV: Remaking television culture* (pp. 1–18). New York, NY: New York University Press.

Pariser, E. (2012). *The filter bubble. How the new personalized web is changing what we read and how we think*. New York, NY: Penguin.

Patwardhan, A., Noble S., & Nishihara, C. (2009). The use of strategic deception in relationships. *Journal of Services Marketing, 23*, 318–325.

Peirson-Smith, A. (2013). Fashioning the fantastical self: An examination of the cosplay dress-up phenomena in Southeast Asia. *Fashion Theory, 17*, 77–112.

Pine J. B., II, & Gilmore, J. H. (2011). *The experience economy*. Cambridge, MA: Harvard Business Review Press.

Postman, N. (1985). *Amusing ourselves to death*. New York, NY: Penguin.

Poulter, D., & Land, C. (2008). Preparing to work: Dramaturgy, cynicism and normative "remote" control in the socialization of graduate recruits in management consulting. *Culture and Organization, 14*, 65–78.

Rafaeli, A., & Sutton, R. I. (1987). Expression of emotion as part of the work role. *Academy of Management Review, 12*, 23–37.

Raghunathan, R., Walker Naylor, R., & Hoyer, W. D. (2006). The unhealthy = tasty intuition and its effects on taste inferences, enjoyment, and choice of food products. *Journal of Marketing, 70*(4), 170–184.

Rettie, R. (2004, October). Using Goffman's frameworks to explain presence and reality. Paper presented at the 7th Annual International Workshop on Presence Valencia, Spain.

Ritzer, G. (2005). *Enchanting a disenchanted world.* Thousand Oaks, CA: SAGE.

Ritzer, G. (2008). *The McDonalization of society.* Thousand Oaks, CA: Pine Forge Press.

Roberts, L. N. (2005). Changing faces: Professional image construction in diverse organizational settings. *The Academy of Management Review, 30,* 685–711.

Rowling, J. K. (1998). *Harry Potter and the sorcerer's stone.* New York, NY: Scholastic.

Rudder, C. (2014). *Dataclysm.* New York, NY: Crown.

Sammond, N. (Ed.). (2005). *Steel chair to the head: The pleasure and pain of professional wrestling.* Durham, NC: Duke University Press.

Scheff, T. (2006). *Goffman unbound! A new paradigm for social science.* Boulder, CO: Paradigm.

Schur, E. (1980). *The politics of deviance: Stigma contests and the uses of power.* Englewood Cliffs, NJ: Prentice Hall.

Schwalbe, M. L. (2013). Situation and structure in the making of selves. In C. Edgley (Ed.), *The drama of social life: A dramaturgical handbook.* Burlington, VT: Ashgate.

Schwalbe, M., & Shay, H. (2014). Dramaturgy and dominance. In J. D. McLeod et al. (Eds.), *Handbook of the social psychology of inequality, handbooks of sociology and social research* (pp. 155–180). New York, NY: Springer.

Scott, J. C. (1992). *Domination and the arts of resistance: Hidden transcripts.* New Haven, CT: Yale University Press.

Scott, S. (2011). *Total institutions and reinvented identities.* Basingstoke, Hampshire: Palgrave Macmillan.

Seife, C. (2014). *Virtual unreality: Just because the Internet told you, how do you know it's true.* New York, NY: Penguin.

Sherr, I. (2014, January 27). Player tally for "league of legends" surges. *Wall Street Journal.*

Sherry, J. F., Jr., Kozinets, R. V., Duhachek, A., DeBerry-Spence, B., Nuttavuthisit, L., & Storm, D. (2004). Gendered behavior in a male preserve: Role-playing at ESPN Zone Chicago. *Journal of Consumer Psychology, 14,* 151–158.

Shulman, D. (2007). *From hire to liar: The role of deception in workplace culture.* Ithaca, NY: Cornell/ILR Press.

Simon, B. (2011). *Everything but the coffee: Learning about America from Starbucks.* Berkeley: University of California Press.

Smith, R. T. (2008). Passion work: The joint production of emotional labor in professional wrestling. *Social Psychology Quarterly, 71,* 157–176.

Strauss, A. (1978). *Negotiations: Varieties, contexts, processes and social order.* San Francisco, CA: Jossey-Bass.

Strauss, A., Schatzman, L., Bucher, R., Erhrlich, D., & Sabshin, M. (1963). The hospital and its negotiated order. In E. Friedson (Ed.), *The hospital and modern society*. New York, NY: Free Press.

The Onion. (2014, January 1). Report: Today the day they find out you're a fraud. *The Onion, 50*(4). Retrieved from http://www.theonion.com/article/report-today-the-day-they-find-out-youre-a-fraud-35133

Themed Entertainment Association. (2008). *Architecture and placemaking: Architects share hard-won insights with TEA* (Report from TEA Market Sector Briefing Series).

Thoits, P. A. (1996). Managing the emotions of others. *Symbolic Interaction, 19*(2), 85–109.

Todd, P. (2014). *Extreme mean: Trolls, bullies and predators online*. Toronto, CA: Random House Canada.

Toma, C. L., & Hancock, J. T. (2010a). Looks and lies: The role of physical attractiveness in online dating self-presentation and deception. *Communication Research, 37*, 335–351.

Toma, C. L., & Hancock, J. T. (2010b). Lying for love in the modern age: Deception in online dating. In M. S. Mcglone & M. L. Knapp (Eds.), *The interplay of truth and deception: New agendas in theory and research* (pp. 149–164). New York, NY: Routledge.

Toma, C., Hancock, J., & Ellison, N. (2008). Separating fact from fiction: An examination of deceptive self-presentation in online dating profiles. *Personality and Social Psychology Bulletin, 34*, 1023–1036.

Trevino, A. J. (Ed.). (2003). *Goffman's legacy (legacies of social thought series)*. Lanham, MD: Rowman & Littlefield.

Turner, J. (2009). The sociology of emotions: Basic theoretical arguments. *Emotion Review, 1*(4), 340–354.

TV Tropes. (n.d.) National stereotypes: North America. Retrieved from http://tvtropes.org/pmwiki/pmwiki.php/NationalStereotypes/NorthAmerica

Twenge, J., & Campbell, W. K. (2010). *The narcissism epidemic*. New York, NY: Free Press.

Tychsen, A., Hitchens, M., Brolund, A., & Kavakli, M. (2006). Live action role-playing games control, communication, storytelling, and MMORPG similarities. *Games and Culture, 1*, 252–275.

Van Praet, E. (2009). Staging a team performance: A linguistic ethnographic analysis of weekly meetings at a British embassy. *Journal of Business Communication, 46*, 80–99.

Waskul, D., & Lust, M. (2004). Role-playing and playing roles: The person, player, and persona in fantasy role-playing. *Symbolic Interaction, 27*, 333–356.

Watts, D. (2012). *Everything is obvious*. New York, NY: Crown.

Weinstein, E., & Deutschberger, P. (1963). Some dimensions of altercasting. *Sociometry, 26*, 454–466.

Wherry, F. (2012). Performance circuits in the marketplace. *Politics & Society, 40*, 203–221.

Ytreberg, E. (2010). The question of calculation: Erving Goffman and the pervasive planning of communication. In M. Jacobsen (Ed.), *The contemporary Goffman* (pp. 313–332). New York, NY: Routledge.

Zerubavel, E. (1997). *Social mindscapes: An invitation to cognitive sociology*. Cambridge, MA: Harvard University Press.

Zerubavel, E., & Smith, E. (2010). Transcending cognitive individualism. *Social Psychology Quarterly, 73*, 321–325.

Zhao, S. (2005, Summer). The digital self: Through the looking glass of telecopresent others. *Symbolic Interaction, 28*(3), 387–405.

Zubernis, L., & Larsen, K. (2012). *Fandom at the crossroads*. Newcastle upon Tyne, UK: Cambridge Scholars.

Index

Note: Page references in *italics* refer to figures.